Best Streams
for Great Lakes
Steelhead

What it's all about. Marc Linsenman gently releases a bright summer steelhead from The Rapids of the St. Mary's River, Ontario.

Best Streams for Great Lakes Steelhead

A Complete Guide to the Fish, the Tactics, and the Places to Catch Them

Bob Linsenman

The Countryman Press
Woodstock, Vermont

Library of Congress Cataloging-in-Publication Data has been applied for.

ISBN 0-88150-584-6

Maps by Paul Woodward, © 2005 The Countryman Press
Book design by Faith Hague
Composition by Melinda Belter
Cover photograph © Henry F. Zeman
Color plate photographs of fly patterns by Jeff Selser, © 2005 Jeff Selser.
Interior photographs by the author unless otherwise specified.

Published by The Countryman Press, P.O. Box 748, Woodstock, Vermont 05091

Distributed by W. W. Norton & Company, Inc., 500 Fifth Avenue, New York, NY 10110

Printed in the United States of America

10 9 8 7 6 5 4 3 2 1

This book is for the Riverkeepers.

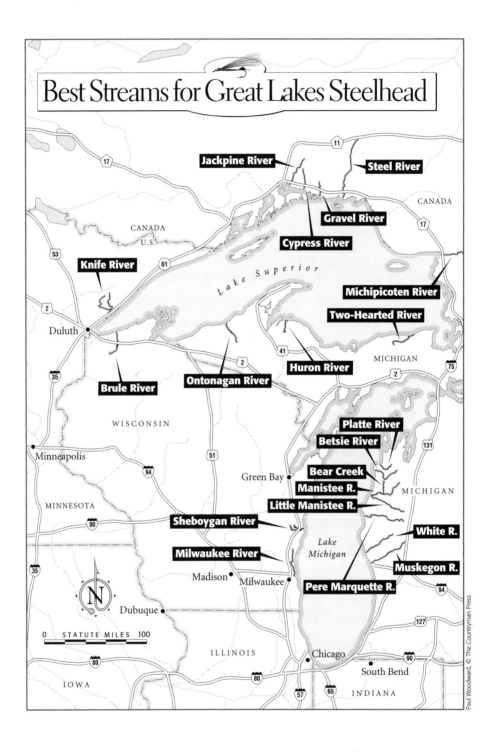

Best Streams for Great Lakes Steelhead

Jackpine River

Steel River

CANADA

Gravel River

Cypress River

CANADA
U.S.

Michipicoten River

Knife River

Lake Superior

Two-Hearted River

Duluth

Huron River

MICHIGAN

Ontonagan River

Brule River

WISCONSIN

Platte River

Betsie River

Minneapolis

Bear Creek

Green Bay

Manistee R.

MICHIGAN

Little Manistee R.

MINNESOTA

Sheboygan River

White R.

Lake
Michigan

Milwaukee River

Muskegon R.

Madison Milwaukee

Pere Marquette R.

N

Dubuque

0 STATUTE MILES 100

ILLINOIS

Chicago

South Bend

IOWA

INDIANA

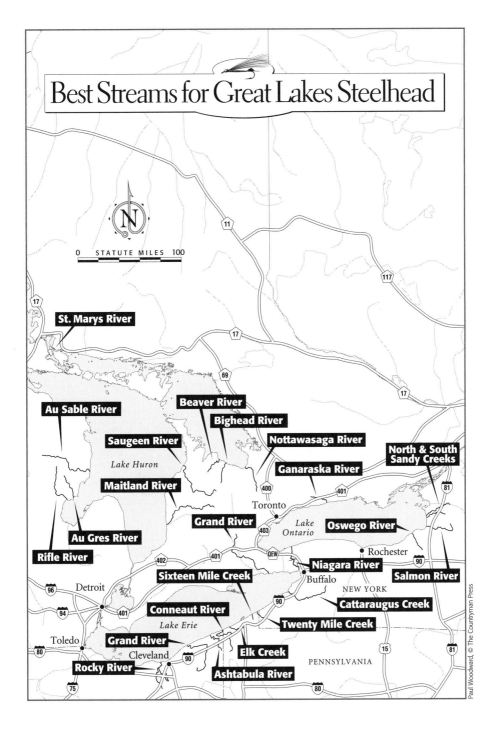

Best Streams for Great Lakes Steelhead

N

0 STATUTE MILES 100

St. Marys River

Au Sable River

Beaver River

Bighead River

Saugeen River

Nottawasaga River

Lake Huron

North & South
Sandy Creeks

Ganaraska River

Maitland River

Toronto

Au Gres River

Grand River

Lake
Ontario

Oswego River

Rifle River

Rochester

Niagara River

Sixteen Mile Creek

Detroit

Buffalo

Salmon River

NEW YORK

Conneaut River

Cattaraugus Creek

Lake Erie

Twenty Mile Creek

Grand River

Toledo

Elk Creek

PENNSYLVANIA

Cleveland

Ashtabula River

Rocky River

Contents

Acknowledgments

Authors need help every step of the way. I probably need more than most. This book would not have seen completion without selfless assistance from conservation-minded steelhead anglers and scientists in Ontario, Minnesota, Wisconsin, Indiana, Michigan, Ohio, Pennsylvania, and New York. Thanks to all and especially to Bear Andrews, Mike Bachelder, Bob Blumreich, Carlene Bischoff, Jeff Conrad, Jerry Darkes, John Dembeck, Ed Devine, Fred Dobbs, Kevin Feenstra, Dave Green, Rob Heal, Dr. Mark Kilen, Rick Kustich, Jeff Liskay, Steve Madewell, Brian Morrison, Kelly Neuman, Joe Penich, Rob Powell, Ray Schmidt, Scott E. Smith, Matt Supinski, John Valk, Fran Verdoliva, and the professionals at The Countryman Press.

Foreword

It was quarter after something on the last Saturday morning of November, when I met my friend Jerry Darkes and a fellow by the name of Bob Linsenman. We were at a little restaurant near the Grand River located in the center of Lake Erie's steelhead alley. Bob was working on a book about Great Lakes steelhead and I suspected that he simply wanted to know where I fish, how to get there, and what I fish with. I was in for a surprise.

Bob said his book was going to have some basic information on steelhead and how to catch them, but he wanted this book to be more than just your basic "how-to" manual. He wanted to identify unique elements of each of the Great Lakes and their major river and stream systems and describe any conditions that threaten their stability. "Jerry says you may have some concerns with the present and the future of steelheading in Ohio; let me know what the issues are and I will see if I can incorporate them into this book." This wasn't what I was expecting at 6:30 in the morning.

As a fisherman, I certainly have agenda items, but as a conservationist who uses fishing as a promotional and a lobbying tool, I see many related problems that go beyond the recreational pursuit of steelheading that need attention, too.

I believe that we are currently in the golden era of Great Lakes steelhead. I don't have a concern with the number and quality of fish across the lakes. The Great Lakes have amazing catch rates, and the steelhead themselves are simply beautiful. There are, however, several other problems that affect steelhead anglers today: stream access, recreational carrying capacity, and stream etiquette. There are millions of people who live, work, and play in the Great Lakes basin and, collectively, the basin is a huge tourism draw. As the awareness of the quality of this fishery continues to grow, especially in states like Ohio, or near the urban areas of any large Great Lakes city, stream access becomes more and more of an issue. Conservation agencies on all levels need to continue their commitment to purchasing stream frontage.

In some instances, public land managers need to recognize that there are areas that could benefit by using some of the same methods to control recreational user carrying capacity that many European countries established years ago. Selected reservation areas could ensure a high-quality experience in relatively urban areas and protect fragile ecosystems in more pristine settings.

Of course, with increasing numbers of anglers, the need for a consistent standard in streamside behavior is essential. To this end, the role of fishing clubs is paramount in going beyond just developing knowledge on how to catch more fish or how to tie better flies. We need to establish widespread standards of etiquette on how to behave on streams with regards to respect for landowners, other river users, the environment, and the fish.

There are also many issues that all outdoor enthusiasts need to be aware of and should be concerned with: the relationship between land use and water quality, the effects of air pollution on water quality, and biological stability, to name a few.

Lake Erie was an ecological mess in the 1960s and was a general indicator of the health of the Great Lakes. While it has partially recovered, thanks in large part to the effects of the Clean Water Act, which was passed in 1972, we cannot allow the advances we have made to be reversed or eliminated. The great environmental legislative initiatives that were passed in the 1970s, because things—lest we forget—really were that bad, are under threat of repeal. Economically and environmentally, we simply cannot slide backwards. Anyone who throws a line in the water, launches a boat, or watches a bird through a pair of binoculars has a vested interest in seeing the health of the Great Lakes maintained and protected.

In addition to the recreational activities afforded by the Great Lakes, they also contain an estimated 20 percent of the world's fresh water. Efforts to preserve open space along rivers and streams not only provide fishing access and protect habitat, they also positively affect water quality. Metropolitan areas around the Great Lakes continue to grow in land mass, but city populations are growing slowly or have remained relatively stable. This shift in land use has resulted in increased storm water runoff, excessive siltation, and accelerated alterations of stream channels. It has also has led to increased air pollution and other impacts on water quality. Unchecked suburban sprawl threatens the countryside. Maintaining the forested corridors along streams helps to keep water temperatures cool, filter runoff, stabilize bank erosion, and provide habitat for birds and other wildlife. All outdoor enthusiasts need to be concerned and active in the support of efforts to preserve and protect riparian corridors.

Biological stability is something more and more anglers are beginning to appreciate and understand. However, most people I know—even serious angling enthusiasts—have no idea of the tremendous biological productivity of the Great Lakes before overharvesting and pollution decimated fish populations during the Industrial Era of the 19th century. The recovery potential for many species is simply gone, along with the habitat that was destroyed more than a hundred years ago. It is hard for me to imagine, but I have read reports of lake sturgeon being so plentiful that they were dried and burned like wood in steamships. Likewise, during the Civil War, spawning muskellunge were so abundant that they were harvested with pitchforks to feed troops camped along the Cuyahoga River. Of course, this is the same river that caught fire in the 1960s. While it may be difficult for me to imagine these historical images, it may be equally as difficult for my children to imagine that just a few decades ago the clear, sparkling waters of Lake Erie were so loaded with nutrients that the lake was literally the color of pea soup. Clean water and a healthy ecosystem are essential for good fish populations.

Increased media attention on the effects of nonnative, invasive species has stimulated awareness of how fragile the ecology of the Great Lakes really is. It has also brought about a greater understanding of terms like native species, wild fish, and stocked fish. We must all be aware of the impact that nonnative invasive species can have and support efforts to control and prevent accidental introductions. Steelhead are in fact a nonnative species, introduced to the Great Lakes more than 120 years ago. In some areas they have thrived and become self-sustaining; in other locations, naturally spawning populations are supplemented with stockings; and in still other waters their presence is the result of continued ongoing stocking. Of course, many anglers happen to like them, and steelhead seem to be thriving in one manner or another in all the Great Lakes. In some instances, steelhead may have replaced species that are extinct; in other waters they may be displacing species that could come back. The decision to continue ongoing stocking is made by our resource management agencies, and they need an informed and active clientele to review and support their actions. We are beyond the days of denying our effects on "naturally balancing ecosystems" and are responsible for the stewardship of our resources. Our decisions have impacts and effects on these resources. We as recreational users need to be informed and educated to maintain a value system that promotes the biological stability of the Great Lakes.

This book not only makes a contribution to the promotion and understanding of steelheading, but also contributes to the efforts to perpetuate the conditions that have enabled the Great Lakes to recover to where they are today. It is a celebration of the incredible role that steelhead are playing in recruiting more people to experience the Great Lakes. Through the steelhead fishing experience, people will develop a greater value and perhaps a greater understanding of what the Great Lakes provide to us today. Read it and I am sure that you will enjoy its information, stories, and photographs. Let it motivate you to enjoy and marvel at the bounty of these wonderful freshwater seas. Perhaps then you may ask yourself, "What can I do to contribute to the continued restoration of the Great Lakes and the fish and wildlife populations that call them home?"

—Steve Madewell,
Angler/Conservationist
Deputy Director, Lake Metroparks

Part One

*In nature there are no rights;
there are only duties.*

—Emerson

Mykiss, a Magnificent Creature

An instance of significance can be a life-altering event. They are popularly referred to as *defining moments,* occasionally as *passages.* We remember them with crystal clarity. Sounds, like the throaty exhaust of a 1965 GTO, or the rhythmic beat of a popular song, take us back to a moment in time. A reference to Neil Armstrong and the lunar expedition, the smell of fresh-baked bread, or an old photograph often fire a synapse that floods the brain with nostalgic memories. My steelhead memory triggers often and easily, transporting me always to a defining moment.

In the late fall of 1965 I was a few months into my first job after graduating from college. My responsibilities required a trip to Sault Ste. Marie, Michigan, at the end of the week. On Saturday I drove to the Two-Hearted River, partly just to view it for the first time but more to see if I could catch, or at least see, a steelhead. I had read about them and heard about them enough to be intrigued. A kindly fellow at a sporting goods store in Newberry said that there were fish in the river, but more along the shoreline at the mouth. He pointed to a map and told me to take the Coast Guard Road as far as I could and to fish the surf close to the river.

"Will they eat flies?" I asked.

"Some people say they won't, but I'd try a streamer," he said.

I parked next to a shiny new Jeep and hiked to Superior in baggy waders. A middle-aged man and woman were casting into the lake. They were using spinning gear and throwing large silver spoons. Wind was light and came from the northeast. The sun was shining but it was cold. Lake Superior's shoreline is always cold. The surface was smooth with a light roll. I remember that several small flights of ducks, probably divers, scooted low over the water. Two or three times steelhead leaped with long, dark lampreys hanging from their sides.

After a quick greeting we all cast wordlessly for several minutes. My tackle was inadequate but the best I had at the time. The rod was fiberglass, 8 feet long and soft by today's standards. The fly line was a floating double-taper. I tried one of the streamers purchased at the store in Newberry, a white featherwing with gold tinsel body and red tail. As I cast and retrieved, I remember timing little hops off the bottom to raise the top of my waders above the rolling swells.

It might have been as long as 30 minutes before anything happened. The man a few yards away on my right hollered "I've got one!" The fish jumped twice within a few seconds and his line went slack. "Lost him," he said.

Invigorated by the sight of the bright silver trout, I cast more deliberately, trying for more distance and actually managed a few that might have reached 60 feet. Cast–hop–strip–hop–strip–hop. In mid-strip, a heavy weight stopped my white streamer followed by a jolt and a fast run and leap. Adrenaline nearly overpowered me. I'm lucky not to have drowned in the excitement and chaos. It was a steelhead!

I did not land it but managed to fumble through enough raw luck to get it close enough to see clearly. The woman and man grabbed their net and tried to help secure the prize, but the hook pulled out and that was that. At the time I thought the fish was 7 or 8 pounds, but now guess it was closer to 4 or 5. It certainly was the biggest trout I had ever hooked. A few days later I actually landed one. Steve Nevala and I were fishing the lower Platte River near Lake Michigan. Steve netted the sleek hen of about 6 pounds and we marveled long at its power and beauty.

Looking back after 40 years, that small slice of time at the mouth of the Two-Hearted River was one of my life's defining moments. It changed me, put a fire in my blood that still burns. Just the thought of these fish in their wild environment excites me.

Steelhead were first introduced into the Great Lakes in 1876. Dan Fitzhugh of Bay City, Michigan, made the plant of McCloud River (California) rainbows in the Au Sable River near the town of Oscoda on Lake Huron. This initial plant proved successful. Wild fish soon began to appear in the Au Sable, Rifle, AuGres, and other area streams. Word spread quickly and generated a "silver rush" of plantings in Lake Michigan, on both the Wisconsin and Michigan shores, in Lake Superior by the Province of Ontario, more in Huron by both Michigan and Ontario, in Lake Erie, and in Lake Ontario in both New York State and Ontario.

Over the years a wide array of genetic stocks have been introduced into the Great Lakes, with varying degrees of success. All the coastline states and Ontario have experimented with different strains. Some have been "wild stock" fish from selected West Coast rivers, others have been genetically engineered in hatcheries. Kamloops, Donaldson, Chambers Creek, Brule River, London, Arlees, Skamania, Normandale, McCloud, Campbell River, Klamath River, and more strains of rainbows have seasoned the soup.

We can thank a lucky star for nature's power of natural selection and evolution. The Great Lakes, from north to south and from east to west, encompass the climatic conditions found in the natural geographic range of steelhead in the Pacific Ocean and its watersheds. Steelhead thrive along Lake Superior's North Shore, where the brutal conditions actually exceed those found at the northern limits of West Coast fish in Alaska and Russia. And they do exceedingly well at the southern tip of Lake Michigan, in Lake Erie, and in Lake Ontario, where life support conditions for steelhead more closely approximate those found along the coast of central California. This giant, sweetwater cauldron we call the Great Lakes is a living, changing force of nature. Five giant, interconnected pools of adapting, evolving life ultimately control the success or failure of individual species.

After more than 130 years of competition and interbreeding among different genetic strains, nature has, for the moment, made its choice. Two closely related strains now dominate both wild and hatchery-introduced stocks throughout the Great Lakes. The Manistee strain comes from wild Lake Michigan fish that ascend the perfect spawning habitat of the Little Manistee River in Michigan. Each year the hatchery southeast of Manistee, Michigan produces millions of fertilized eggs. Both eggs and sperm are taken from that year's crop of migrating wild fish rather than from hatchery brood stock. These eggs produce millions of fry and eventually smolts that are introduced into rivers from Lake Superior to Lake Ontario. Most fisheries divisions within the states now recognize the superiority of the Manistee strain and have switched their stocking programs. Ohio is notable in this regard, with a recent change to the Manistee strain that has greatly improved survival and return along Lake Erie's southern shore. Although the base for the Manistee strain of steelhead has been influenced and altered by a variety of different stocks over the years it remains tightly linked to the original McCloud River fish introduced in 1876.

The Ganaraska strain has emerged as another very successful steelhead in the Great Lakes. It is probably a mix of Normandale and

The steelhead we catch today are the product of more than 130 years of inter-breeding and natural selection.

Chambers Creek strains introduced into Lake Ontario by Ontario and New York State, respectively. The upshot is a unique genetic profile that produces rapid growth and heavy bodies.

Like the Manistee strain, the annual production of fertilized eggs is taken from wild fish rather than from penned, hatchery stock. This maintains the wild "selectivity" of natural reproduction. The largest steelhead caught to date by sport fishing methods in the Great Lakes basin is a Ganaraska-strain fish exceeding 31 pounds caught in Lake Ontario in August 2004.

Provincial fisheries managers in Ontario use Ganaraska smolts in Lake Ontario, Lake Erie, in the streams of Georgian Bay through the Gray–Bruce Peninsula, and along the Ontario shoreline of Lake Huron proper. In addition, Wisconsin utilizes Ganaraska fish in its Lake Michigan tributaries.

Both wild progeny and hatchery-based smolts roam to a degree as they mature. Identifying fin clips show Ontario-based fish in Michigan, Michigan fish in Ontario, and roamers between Michigan, Indiana, and Wisconsin. Wisconsin and Minnesota steelhead show up in Michigan's and Ontario's Lake Superior streams. And, they interbreed. The soup has not finished cooking.

Two more steelhead strains are worthy of note. The Skamania fish is a summer-run powerhouse with incredible fighting and leaping characteristics. It is a "designer" fish in the true sense of the term. The Skamania strain was specifically engineered by biologists to spawn in the late winter or early spring and thereby increase year-round angling potential. Skamania steelhead typically enter rivers in midsummer and hold over to the following winter before spawning. This timing produces fishable riverine populations in midsummer and early fall, when shirtsleeve weather is the norm. They are more aggressive than other strains and are especially susceptible to large streamers and leech patterns in a mix of white and gaudy fluorescent colors.

Skamania steelhead are long, slender, and mean. They hit with a jolt, not the often subtle take of other steelhead. They leap and run with reckless abandon and often exhaust themselves beyond the point of possible resuscitation and survival. These fish became instantly popular after their initial introduction, and significant stocking programs were undertaken by Indiana, Michigan, Wisconsin, and New York, with varying success. Subsequently, stocking of Skamania smolts has been terminated in northern rivers by the state of Michigan. Indiana has continued its large Skamania program, and Wisconsin and New York carry on a limited production.

The Salmon River hatchery in Altmar, New York is the cradle for another successful rainbow trout strain that has evolved into a solid match for Lake Ontario, perhaps filling the unique predatory niche left open by the long absence of once-prolific Atlantic salmon stocks. Based largely on the Chambers Creek strain, Salmon River progeny not only do well in the lake but are now enjoying good success at natural reproduction in several south shore tributaries. The balance of wild, born-in-the-river fish with hatchery smolts is not yet clear, but we do know that natural reproduction is significant in several rivers and that the percentage of return for wild fish, and their subsequent contribution to the sport fishery, is moving upward.

Change is forever. The minute adjustments made by the natural forces of the lakes and their tributaries add up over time. Great Lakes steelhead continue their adaptation and evolution to a point of near perfection for their environment. Subtle changes in color, size, and shape evolve quickly.

The timing of spawning runs adjusts more slowly, but eventually settles on a perfect point for the highly specific characteristic of each natal stream. Fish behavior adapts to accommodate population density, spawning conditions, weather patterns, and food sources in both lake and riverine environments. All of this is inevitable and as it must be.

During the fall of 2004 some new information came into focus. Kelly Neuman guides steelhead fly anglers on the Au Sable extensively from late fall through late spring. He reported seeing steelhead on redds throughout October and November and catching, photographing, and releasing several hens and bucks that had been actively spawning. The Au Sable's steelhead are Manistee-strain fish that typically spawn in late spring. We have known for years that Lake Huron steelhead roam from Canada to Michigan and intermingle in streams along both coasts. It makes one wonder if a new, lake-generated strain has evolved over time from interbreeding Ganaraska and Manistee steelhead that takes advantage of favorable spawning conditions in October and November. Perhaps it is reflective of a one-year anomaly, but I think not.

While fishing Ohio streams in the fall of 2004 I noticed very subtle coloration differences in hen fish. These are Manistee-strain steelhead, and one would think they should look pretty much like their relatives in

This bright hen from Lake Erie had grown a patch of new skin near her tail.

A driftboat in the morning fog on Michigan's Au Sable River. The mighty Great Lakes tributaries deserve our loving concern and vigilant protection.

Lake Michigan and Lake Huron. For the most part, they do, but a soft, pale yellow tint showed along the lower jaw on all the females I saw. I asked my hosts, Jerry Darkes and Jeff Liskay, if that was a common band of color. Neither had noticed it before. Ohio has only recently switched to the Manistee strain. Some rapid adaptation has already occurred, perhaps to accommodate conditions in the central pool of Lake Erie, perhaps to adapt to the coloration of shale and ledgerock rivers.

On Pennsylvania rivers, I was surprised by the number of steelhead in the obvious act of spawning in November but my hosts told me that that was no longer considered a phenomenon, that they had noticed a significant increase in fall spawning over the past few years.

One of the Lake Erie fish caught was remarkable for another reason. She was bright silver, fresh from the lake, and fat. Near her tail, at the "wrist," she had a patch of new skin. Roughly circular, it was complete with spots and scales. It showed a definite edge, almost as if it had been attached as a repair job by a steelhead body shop. We speculated that this new growth might be in response to a lamprey scar or other injury, but we had seen many old scars on steelhead over the years that had simply healed without growing new skin as we noted on this obvious patch.

From 2 pounds to 20 plus, the continuing success of steelhead depends on the health of the big lakes. The lakes' health in turn is dependent on the health of tributary rivers and streams. Each tributary is unique, worthy of man's concerned, vigilant guardianship. Industrial pollution, insecticides, agricultural runoff, dams, and stormwater bearing highway sludge are continuing, clear, and ever-present dangers to our rivers in both the United States and Canada. I have long held the belief that moving water is a great gift, that rivers have incalculable value in and of themselves, far beyond their capacity to entertain and comfort us. A river is a life-supporting universe that sustains separate, wild, and equal nations we will never understand completely. The fact that one of these wild nations is the mysterious and magical *Oncorhyncus mykiss* is our great fortune and clear responsibility.

Steelhead Angling in the Great Lakes— A Brief History

It is likely a safe bet that the first person to hook a steelhead in the Great Lakes basin did so by accident and that the shocked angler did not land the fish. I picture a middle-aged man wearing a red and black woolen coat, wool pants, some kind of heavy swamp boots, a fur-lined cap, and drifting his rig through a riffle hoping for a trout, maybe a sucker. The hook and sinker tick along the bottom, then stop. He lifts his rod to set the hook and is greeted with a surge of power and speed running straight downstream away from him. The man struggles along the bank, splashing and dodging alders and cedars trying to keep up. His poor reel chatters and grinds and, as a great crimson-sided steelhead leaps below him, freezes solid. The line snaps. He sits on the bank and breathes heavily, noticing his wet pant legs and water-filled boots. The reel is ruined so he pulls his line back, hand over hand. "What was that?" he wonders aloud.

Fishermen noted the presence of super-sized rainbow trout in Lake Huron tributaries in the early 1880s. By 1890, anglers along Lake Michigan's coastline were seeing early returns of spawning fish. Lakes Superior, Erie, and Ontario showed building populations and recorded catches shortly thereafter. By 1920 large numbers of huge rainbows were showing up in the nets set for whitefish and lake trout by commercial fishermen in all five lakes, and spring season sport angling began to accelerate. Touring sportsmen with the financial means to pursue their dreams began to show up in Wisconsin, Michigan, New York, Minnesota, and Ontario. They came from Chicago, New York City, Boston, Kansas City, Toronto, and Europe. The *silver rush* was on.

The word "steelhead" became a more popular, accepted term during this time period. Pacific coast influences, perhaps from professional fisheries people, perhaps the popular works of writers such as Zane Grey in sporting journals of the era, created the initial terminology distinction. This was based largely on the notion of the time that steelhead and rainbow trout were closely related but distinct species. *Salmo gairdneri* was the scientific name of rainbow trout, while *Salmo irridensci* was widely used to classify steelhead. In 1989, scientists decided to clearly separate Atlantic and Pacific salmonids. All Atlantic stocks retained *Salmo*. Pacific salmonids became genus *Oncorhynchus* and rainbow trout, including steelhead, were noted as species *mykiss*. Anglers did not care much, if at all, beyond grumbling that *Salmo* was a lot easier to say and spell than *Oncorhynchus*.

In the early 1920s an article by Ernest Hemingway appeared in the *Toronto Star* about "The Greatest Rainbow Trout Fishing in the World." He was writing about the St. Mary's River, specifically The Rapids on the Ontario side of the river. He wrote about clear, wild water rushing from Lake Superior to fill Lake Huron, about wind, people, and trout. The trout were steelhead from Lake Huron ascending the high-gradient flow

Ernest Hemingway's *Toronto Star* article helped make The Rapids of the St. Mary's River a world-famous steelhead destination.

to feed in the rushing current and spawn in the mix of boulders and gravel. Hemingway's newspaper account of fishing for huge rainbows measured in pounds fanned the fire already glowing in the bellies of sport fishermen throughout Canada, the United States, and Europe.

The popularity of sport fishing for steelhead grew quickly. Charter captains who had targeted lake trout were not at all dismayed when their customers caught the large rainbows. River anglers enjoyed ever-increasing success on a growing number of streams throughout the system as naturally reproducing fish expanded their range and as hatchery programs in Ontario and the states expanded. Things looked rosy for steelhead into the 1940s, but this would not last.

A combination of invasive, exotic species and the long accumulation of industrial pollution caused a crash in fish populations by the early 1950s. Both sea lampreys and alewives made their way into the upper Great Lakes, with devastating impact. Sea lampreys, efficient parasitic predators, prey on both lake trout and steelhead, and they nearly destroyed the entire base population of both.

Fisheries managers scrambled for a fix, but it was not until the 1960s that any measurable success could be observed. Electronic weirs attempted to electrocute bottom-hugging lampreys as they ascended rivers to spawn while allowing steelhead to safely bypass the electrical current by swimming higher in the water column. Poisons were developed to kill the burrowing immature lampreys. These poisons are applied after the lampreys hatch from eggs and squirm into the stream's bottom to grow before descending to the host lake. Both methods are effective but not perfect. The application of poisons often decimates aquatic insect populations along with the juvenile lampreys.

Pacific salmon were planted in Michigan's Platte River in the spring of 1966 in the hope that they would target alewives and ultimately control that population. The plan worked. The initial plant of silver (coho) salmon by Michigan was quickly embraced, and subsequent stocking programs proliferated throughout the lakes and expanded to include king (Chinook) salmon. Alewives are no longer a problem in the big lakes, but lampreys require constant vigilance. More recently, invading exotic species such as gobies, ruffes, and zebra mussels have established themselves in the Great Lakes, and concerted international containment efforts are underway.

With the noted success of introduced Pacific salmon and measurable positive results in lamprey control programs, stocking of steelhead picked up, with heavy plants beginning in the 1960s. By the late 1960s sport fishing, both on the lakes and in the rivers, had significantly improved. An interesting side benefit to the salmon programs is that salmon spawn in the fall and stream anglers began to catch growing numbers of steelhead at that time of year. This increased awareness of the fall run of hungry steelhead in many rivers and jump-started the popularity of fishing specifically for steelhead in October and November.

I have not been able to find any written references to document the first steelhead caught on a fly in Great Lakes waters, but it was probably a big surprise for someone fishing for stream trout in the 1890s time frame. Dedicated fly anglers were certainly in hot pursuit around the outbreak of World War II. A vivid, boyhood memory centers on a small gathering of my father's fishing pals talking about casting large streamers for the great fish. They talked about the Little Manistee and Betsie Rivers, but centered on a forthcoming trip to the Two-Hearted. Vern Clain, a Chippewa friend of my father, was acknowledged to be the best fly angler in the group. He talked about catching the large rainbows on flies before he went off to the Pacific theater. This memory places me at about six years old, so it probably took place in 1949.

My generation took up the chase in the 1960s and 1970s. Fish populations were rebuilding, but few of us enjoyed consistent success in those early years. Fly fishing for steelhead in Great Lakes rivers was largely a hit—and often miss—proposition. It was mostly experimentation and often frustrating. Steelhead literature, such as it was, extolled the virtues of West Coast steelhead and presented the classic techniques that work well along the Pacific range. With limitations imposed by the tackle then available, and the very different nature and configuration of holding water in our regional watersheds, we were severely handicapped. It was trial and error. Bait and lure anglers scoffed and chided. It is amazing, now with the clarity of hindsight, how many people of that time honestly believed that steelhead would not eat flies. And, they told us so—repeatedly.

We muddled forward, experimenting with rods, lines, leaders, weight, and fly patterns. We froze in poor waders that were heavy, bulky, and susceptible to cold-weather cracks and seepage. The "wicking" properties of today's wonderful fleece garments were not yet available, so we perspired, then chilled. Truly waterproof and windproof wading jackets had not yet hit the market. We were a mess, but kept at it.

Watching the ease of delivery and drift enjoyed by spin fishers, we replaced fat fly lines, which were quick to build up ice in rod guides, with various types and sizes of monofilament. But the mono coiled and tangled and ultimately proved unworkable. About this time, Ray Schmidt, then a young fly-fishing guide and tackle representative, and Bruce Richards, of Scientific Anglers, put their heads together and designed the first workable "shooting" lines for the region's rivers. These were true fly lines, complete with appropriate coatings, of thin diameter that shot well, were mendable, and did not have the dreaded "memory"—the coiling and tangling properties—of monofilament. Over the years these lines have been constantly refined. They were then, and are now, the single most important item for the "chuck-and-duck" method of fly delivery to steelhead.

Through the 1970s other tackle refinements aided the quest. Graphite fly rods with sensitive tips and powerful mid- and butt sections proved to be a great boon in strike detection, tippet protection, and fighting capability. Better reels began to hit the market. They had smooth disk drags and sufficient line and backing capacity for the trophy rainbows. It was true then—and still is—that the best fly reels in the world are manufactured in the United States. Seemingly small things made a big difference. Fly anglers adapted the successful bait-angling technique of drifting

An Ohio nymphing setup. Modern developments in fly tackle have made steelheading easier and more enjoyable than ever before.

spawn under a large bobber, and smaller, castable, seeable strike indica-tors soon arrived on retail shelves. Large, unwieldy aluminum boat nets with coarse, abrasive netting and small, totally inadequate trout nets gave way to short-handled, wide-bowed nets with soft mesh crafted especially for the steelhead market. Polarized sunglasses improved dramatically in optical quality and weight. Short, well-designed, durable vests hit the market; they allowed deep wading without soaking flies and cameras.

Nothing less than a revolution in outdoor clothing has helped a great deal. Breathable, lightweight, warm, and quick-drying fleece garments are perfect for steelheading. They come in a range of weights, colors, styles, and prices that cover every conceivable weather condition from balmy to incredibly horrid. Once, while fishing the St. Mary's Rapids in Ontario, I watched a young man chase a steelhead through a stretch I thought to be a bit on the dangerous side. One second this guy was in full view, the next second he was gone—underwater. Luckily, he was young and strong and popped up looking quite sheepish. He reeled in his slack line, waded to the berm, and sat down next to me.

"Are you all right?"

"Sure, but I hated to lose that fish," he said.

He took off his vest, fleece pullover, and fleece undershirt. He un-hooked his wading belt and checked his pants. "Dry inside." It was cold and the wind was blowing and he shivered while wringing out the soaked fleece. Then he whirled each garment high and hard overhead for several seconds and laid them down on the berm while he checked his fly boxes. Both fleece shirts felt *completely* dry to my touch. He was wading (albeit more carefully) and fishing again within five minutes of being drenched.

Gore-Tex rain parkas and neoprene waders made similar, positive im-pacts in the clothing category. Gore-Tex garments kept the rain, snow, and wind out while allowing perspiration to escape through the coating. Neoprene waders made walking easier and provided superb insulation and a bit of buoyancy. These might seem to be minor improvements today, but they were very significant at the time.

Through the 1970s and 1980s, fly development accelerated. Nymph patterns became more realistic and lifelike, and available in a range of sizes that approximated the true size of the bugs at a specific time of year. Egg patterns got smaller, more life size, and came in a wider range of solid and mixed colors. Both egg and nymph flies with chemically sharpened hooks became the standard. During this period, interest in classic, Pacific Coast steelhead flies and methods began to resurface. Creative tyers

Originally developed in Scotland for Atlantic salmon, distinctive Spey patterns are increasingly popular with steelheaders on the Great Lakes tributaries.

adopted the style and concept of Pacific patterns and incorporated much of the British/Scottish Spey fly style into elegant creations that began to produce Great Lakes steelhead on a regular basis. And, it wasn't long after this when the logical, accompanying use of two-handed Spey rods began to grow.

All this occurred while fisheries managers in Ontario and the States increased stocking programs of various steelhead strains throughout the region. Fish numbers were up and climbing, lamprey control programs were working, tackle and clothing were vastly improved, and we fly anglers had accumulated knowledge based on success. This was knowledge we shared widely through slide programs, seminars, magazine articles, and books aimed squarely at the Great Lakes market. Fly anglers no longer took a backseat to bait and lure people; we often enough outfished them with our little flies. And, a swelling of regional pride emerged. We no longer accepted the barbs and darts thrown by West Coast traditionalists. Our methods are true fly-fishing techniques and our fish are the same as Pacific steelhead. We use fly rods, fly lines, leaders, and flies. Our steelhead run as fast, jump as high, and are every bit as beautiful. There are only two distinctions. Our fish are nurtured in sweetwater caverns rather then in salt, and our rivers are generally shorter with more pocket water than long, smooth glides and runs. Oh, one more thing. We have more steelhead here, and we catch more of them.

New product development and refinement of techniques and tactics continued through the 1990s and remains promising at the leading edge of the 21st century. The specifics of some new and very effective techniques will be covered in Chapter 3. New products appear annually and all you have to do to stay current is visit a local, professional fly shop.

Two aspects of our sport still need a lot of concerned attention. Fly fishing for steelhead has exploded in popularity. This is, of course, a direct result of success. Success comes from the evolution of products and techniques *and* the numbers of steelhead, both hatchery and wild, in our rivers. Millions upon millions of people live within a few hours' drive of our best steelhead waters. Our best, our most popular rivers can get crowded at various times during the year. Crowding can cause short tempers and rude behavior. Compounding this is the easily observable fact that big fish will attract some bad people and will occasionally bring out some bad traits in otherwise good people. We need to consider each other with respect and courtesy. It is not acceptable behavior to wade in close to another angler and start casting. It is not proper to wade through a run while others are fishing, nor to usurp a location while an angler has moved to fight and land a fish. It is not at all wise to trespass, to walk through someone's yard and trample the lawn and banks. The solution to all this is elegant in its simplicity. Ask first. "Will I crowd you if I fish here?" "Is it okay to pass behind you?" "May I cross your property to reach that pool on the corner?" Ask and smile. Ninety percent of the time you will get the answer you want, with a smile in return. And, it won't hurt to say "Can I help you net that fish?" Carry a small garbage bag and pick up trash. Landowners notice and are grateful. If you have caught a fish or two in a favorite run, consider moving on and offer your spot to someone else. If you see someone struggling with their casts, or with a bewildered look, offer to help. These are small things, but they will make a big impact on how much we enjoy our days on the water.

The second issue is fish kill, and there are two parts to the problem. "Creel" limits are simply too high in many areas. Steelhead are certainly a renewable resource to a point, but fish kill limits do add up quickly. They seem insignificant on a per-angler basis, and perhaps are to a biomass statistician, but the accumulation of three, two, or even one fish per angler per day can be devastating. This is simple arithmetic, not multi-variate analysis. If a stretch of river, say the Au Sable between Foote Dam and the Whirlpool access, has a thousand fish in late October and sustains a two-fish-per-day harvest for 30 anglers, the impact is severe and obvious, and the math is simple—we run out of steelhead very quickly. Who can possibly eat two, or one, steelhead per day? How many people are we trying to feed with this resource? Kill tags, like those used in big game hunting, are a better idea. A valid, yearly license comes with a kill tag that must be notched or otherwise altered to reflect the number of fish harvested in a season. Individual tags are placed on the fish. You get three or four or five, some reasonable number of fish per season. Who could possibly eat or otherwise use more than five per year? Steelhead are not perch or bluegill. They are big game and should be afforded the same respect and protection.

Part two of the kill issue centers on well-intentioned but careless handling before release. Get your camera ready beforehand. Do not keep your prize out of the water more than ten seconds. Revive the fish carefully—take all the time the steelhead needs to fully recover.

Play steelhead quickly, handle them gently, and revive them with the utmost care before release to ensure good fishing for many years to come.

Steelhead fly fishing in our wonderful Great Lakes rivers has come a long way since Mr. Fitzhugh released those fish in 1876. And it continues to get better each year. Our techniques, fly patterns, and equipment improve with each season. Respect, courtesy, and watchful concern for each other, the great fish, and our beautiful yet fragile rivers are the key elements in continuing the pleasure and passion.

Presentation Strategies and Techniques

3

The only thing that is proven to be an absolute fact about fly fishing for steelhead is "Never say 'never' and never say 'always.'" Steelhead are capricious wild creatures completely in tune with and affected by the prevailing conditions of their environment. They are efficient predators, at once shy and aggressive, bold and secretive. Their interest in eating or attacking a well-presented fly fluctuates to accommodate natural forces over which we have no control. This chapter outlines the most critical factors that impact steelhead behavior and discusses technical approaches for these problematic trophies. The best we can do is to understand how various conditions affect our quarry, and be prepared and competent enough to deliver the right type of fly at the proper depth in the most productive water. There are basic, tried and true techniques as well as newly developed tactics to consider. The techniques we employ on any given day come down to a matter of choice. Do I want to simplify all this and simply accommodate conditions, or is there a specific method, a special technique that I most enjoy?

Steelhead Behavior

They advance nervously into rivers from the protective security of big, deep water. Instinctively they know they are vulnerable in these shallow currents and they seek out the relative comfort of depth and structure. This instinct to shy away from light, to camouflage and hide from overhead predation is paramount to survival. It is part of their genetic makeup and has been fundamental to their behavior since they emerged from eggs.

Aside from humans, there are few predators capable of whacking an adult steelhead—maybe an eagle, otter, or musky. Still, true to nature's imprint, they remain fearful in thin water. A three-year-old steelhead has escaped countless attacks by otter, mink, mergansers, cormorants, kingfishers, and herons, as well as predatory fish. They are tense and anxious, and remain so throughout their stay in rivers, whether they are fall- or spring-run fish.

The good news is that there is a counterbalance to this state of high anxiety. Steelhead fresh from the Great Lakes are hungry. In preparation for the upstream odyssey, they have been feeding voraciously on smelt, alewives, immature trout and salmon, just about anything they can grab. When they settle, usually after a few hours, the urge to eat rekindles and the instinct to eat eggs and nymphs kicks in to complement their adult menu of fish. We anglers have adopted the "drifting food" stratagem almost completely when fly fishing in rivers. Almost all our fly patterns represent eggs and aquatic insects. We should be prepared to accommodate a steelhead's adult orientation to larger food forms with streamers and Spey patterns. More on this later.

Water temperature is important. Degree range, and whether the water is warming or cooling, often makes a dramatic difference in how steelhead react to artificial flies. At temperatures below 40 degrees Fahrenheit (4 degrees Celsius), steelhead are usually lethargic and disinterested. They

Brown trout fingerlings. Steelhead feed voraciously on a wide variety of natural foods, including immature trout and salmon.

will rarely move *any* distance to inspect or eat a fly. Flies have (hopefully) no odor to complement appearance. At low temperatures this seems more critical. When skilled fly anglers are dramatically outfished by bait anglers, it's a good bet that the water is very cold. Fish slowly and patiently. When the water is cold, steelhead tend to shelter in deep holes with slow current to conserve energy.

There is a dramatic change at 40 degrees F (4 degrees C) and up; the fish become much more active as their metabolism shifts toward high gear. If the fish are close to their spawning period, the urge to breed intensifies and males become especially aggressive. The ideal range of water temperature for fly fishing for steelhead is actually quite broad. The best results seem to come in the span from 42 to 60 degrees F (5.5 to 15.5 C), with 45 to 58 degrees F (7 to 14.5 degrees C) being dead-solid perfect.

Many years ago a friend and I were fishing the Pere Marquette in late April. It had been a long winter followed by a late, cold spring. On day one we each hooked a couple, maybe three fish in the stretch close to Lumberjack Trail. My notes indicate that the water temperature was 39 degrees F (4 degrees C). The morning of the second day was very warm; the air temperature was close to 60 degrees F (15.5 C) at dawn. The last vestiges of snow on the banks had disappeared by the time we began fishing, and a light southwesterly breeze pushed temperatures higher. A thin layer of high clouds reduced glare, and we began to see and hook fish almost immediately after entering the river upstream from the Green Cottage. I took a temperature reading about midmorning. The water was now 47 degrees F (8.5 degrees C), an 8-degree jump from the previous day. We knew enough to recognize a very good thing, but not enough, at the time, to know that we were being blessed with near perfect conditions. The steelhead were electrically charged. If they had had hair it would have been on fire. We hooked a dozen or more fish and landed six or so by noon. It was wild, laughing, hooting fun, but too easy. We quit shortly after noon and left to eat lunch and shoot pool.

If the water is below 40 degrees F (4 degrees C), a warming trend is very good. If the temperature is stable between 40 and 50 degrees F (4 and 10 C), prospects are excellent. A warming trend above 50 degrees F (10 C) is not quite as good. This can panic steelhead and may shut off the bite. If the water temperature is 60 degrees F (15.5 C), pray long and hard for a cooling trend. All of this varies a bit by subregion within the Great Lakes basin. Steelhead on the North Shore of Lake Superior are more attuned and active at slightly cooler temperatures, while fish along the south shores of Erie and Ontario can be comfortable in a slightly warmer range. But, keep that ideal range in mind. It is pretty consistent throughout the region.

Barometric pressure is another variable to consider. After years of wonder and confusion, I decided to buy a modest barometer for my house. It had seemed that, among other factors, a steady, relatively high pressure in the low 30.00s produced the best steelhead fishing. This was proven generally true when I began to take specific notes based on my inexpensive gauge. Rapidly falling or rising pressures, with one notable exception, seemed to slow the bite for a few hours at least. That exception took place a few years ago on the lower Au Sable in mid-April. I was guiding two young doctors on their first try for steelhead with fly gear. Throughout that day a series of mini-fronts attacked the area. The weather would alternately hit us with heavy clouds and wind-driven, very heavy snow, then clear for a few minutes and show blue sky. It seemed to change every hour. We could actually see the next squall coming on most occasions. Each time the sky darkened and the wind picked up and snow began to fall, the fish went nuts and seemed willing to eat anything and everything that hit the water. When the sky cleared, they stopped. Amazing.

We cannot do anything about weather beyond trying to understand how it might impact our efforts. Light, water level and clarity, temperature, and pressure are all important factors in determining how steelhead behave. These are critical elements in their predatory environment. The best conditions we can hope for stack up like this: overcast to heavy cloud cover, light and steady breeze from the west or southwest, stable barometer, comfortable air temperature (for us), and water temperature in the high 40s to low 50s F (8 to 10 C). We fish when we can, but if there is a forecast for that set of conditions, consider an emergency leave of absence from your job.

Tried and True—the Basics

Probably 90 percent of Great Lakes stream steelhead hooked on flies ate a nymph or an egg pattern fished near the river's bottom. The basic casts and drifts—the presentation—are the same for either type of fly. We want to get the fly drifting naturally near the bottom quickly and efficiently. Much of the best holding water in our rivers consists of relatively short, deep pockets, and our flies need to reach the upstream edge of the effective feeding zone very soon after hitting the water. It is rarely possible to accomplish this without added weight. This weight can be in the form of a sink-tip line, a weighted leader, or a weighted fly. It is best if our fly rides a few inches off the bottom rather than rolling directly through gravel, sand, or whatever. Unweighted flies that are pulled to a drift line near the bottom by weight on the leader do this best.

The most basic and most widely applied method to accomplish this is with a dense weight—split shot, pencil weight, or the like—attached to the leader some distance above the fly. Leader length varies a bit by water type, turbidity, and depth, but should generally be longer than most people think. A leader of 10 feet is about as short as I would ever suggest. More often, 12 to 15 feet is preferable. The leader is attached to a floating fly line, either a light weight-forward taper or a shooting line. Because there is added weight on the leader, a lighter fly line works well and shoots for distance better than the line designated on a rod heavy enough to handle steelhead, and a floating WF3 mends just as well as a WF7.

The Reach Cast

This cast is one of the *basic* tools for steelhead angling. It aids the rapid attainment of drag-free drift, and this is its greatest value. Most simply stated, the reach cast is achieved by shift in direction of casting arm and rod through the power stroke of the forward cast.

Visualize the standard forward cast: Pick up with power between 10 o'clock and 12 o'clock, drift to 2 o'clock, slight pause, forward power stroke from 2 o'clock to 12 o'clock, then drift. Remember to slow everything down to accommodate added weight, if it is being used. Then all you have to add to the standard forward cast to achieve the reach cast is a shift in rod and arm direction.

Assume that the current in front of you is moving from right to left. There is a deep pocket that looks promising about 25 feet in front and 8 feet downstream from your position. You want to drop your nymph slightly above the upstream edge of the pocket so that it sinks to the bottom quickly. A drag-free drift on the first cast is critical.

Because a reach cast produces an exaggerated upstream belly—like a huge mend—in the line, it shortens the effective distance of your cast: for example, 35 feet of line and leader will accommodate a fishing distance of 25 to 27 feet.

You need to throw 35 feet of line and leader to fish that pocket. On your forward power stroke, you will need to shift the direction of your rod-arm lever approximately 45 degrees upstream. Your rod has prescribed an arc to this point and pushed a loop into the line that falls on the water in an upstream curve. This upstream curve uses up about 10 feet of line and effectively aids the desired drag-free drift. The reach cast throws a large upstream mend while the line is still in the air.

The Roll Cast

Quite often in steelhead fly fishing, the leader is encumbered by one or more weighty and less-than-aerodynamic attachments. Strike indicators, slinky weights, split shot, and droppers complicate any cast and seem to affect the roll cast most negatively of all.

The theme bears repeating: All of the early part of the roll cast needs to be in slow motion. You are raising your terminal rig from depth. Your leader probably carries a strike indicator, a split shot or two, and perhaps a weighted dropper fly. You cannot raise this mess into a smooth forward roll without following this procedure:

With the line and leader under the water in front of you, take up the slack with your free hand, secure the line against the grip with your rod hand, and *slowly* raise the rod until the entire leader, with all ornaments and flies, is on *top* of the water. The fly line should form a *moving* loop that extends from the top of the rod down behind the rod and out to the fly. As the fly breaks the water's surface, continue the pull toward you by accelerating and extending the rod in the backward motion. The forward power stroke should start between 2 and 3 o'clock and be applied with smooth but exaggerated power through the 10 and 9 o'clock positions. There. You've done it without breaking the rod.

With our backs frequently against a tree-lined bank, a roll cast is quite often the only way to deliver a fly to a likely position in the river. Practice until you can deliver a 35-foot cast with accuracy 90 percent of the time. That distance will cover most of your needs, and frankly is about the effective limit for a weighted terminal rig on a 9½-foot, 7- or 8-weight rod.

The Chuck-and-Duck

This is a popular technique that employs a weighted leader rather than a heavy fly line as the propellant of a cast. In the Great Lakes region, we often fish in subfreezing temperatures. Frequently we are up to mid-thigh in 36-degree F (2-degree C) water, the air temperature is about 30 degrees F (-1 degree C), and the river is making ice—all day. The ice slowly builds on the roots and stumps at the banks, in the slow edges of deep holes, and most significantly in the guides of our fly rods. As often as not we are in a narrow slot with little or no room for a standard cast. The small hole in front of us is dark and *very* deep. If we are not shivering, either we have reached the second level of hypothermia, or we are properly clothed with layers of fleece and warmly gloved. In either case, casting is difficult. Under these extreme conditions the "chuck-and-duck" delivery was developed, and here it finds the widest base of appreciative practitioners.

A point of controversy surrounding the chuck-and-duck approach centers on the line itself. In most cases, a fine-diameter floating, shooting line—or a fly line of 2 or 3 weight—is used instead of a standard, tapered fly line of the proper weight for the rod. Since there is very little weight in the line, the weight attached to the leader carries the fly to the desired location.

The trick is to get everything moving under some sense of control so that an accurate cast can be made. With your rod in the 10 o'clock position, let the leader and about 2 feet of running line out through the tip guide. Hold about 15 feet of running line in three or four large coils in your free hand. Now raise the rod past 12 o'clock, slowly to 2 o'clock, and back from 2 o'clock, slowly, to 10 o'clock. You have now created a moving pendulum with the weight as the pulling force. Take care to keep the weight of the pendulum and its arc to the outside of your rod to minimize the potential for graphite tragedy. When the weight swings forward through 8 o'clock (remember the arc and pendulum are at the bottom of the clock face), release the line in your free hand, and the moving weight will pull the cast outward to a point near the target.

Take care not to overpower the delivery, firmly entangling your intricate rig in the trees on the far bank. When the fly and weight enter the flow, take up slack immediately to control the drift. Strike indicators are commonly used and should be positioned properly, depending on depth, on the butt section between the running line and the tippet. If you are using an indicator, lift the rod to clear enough line to raise the indicator to a visible position.

Some anglers advocate overhand delivery of this assembly, but effective control is difficult when this is attempted. Unless you like headaches, tying knots, and fumbling for more flies, work on a sidearm "chuck," both backhand and forehand.

Mending the Line

Careful mending is the best answer to twisting, conflicting currents, both those that are obvious on the surface and those less so, hidden beneath, that cause drag. A reach cast will start the drift properly, but it must be nursed through to the end.

Mending line is a simple action that should be taken on nearly every cast and drift. An upstream mend throws a curve of line upstream, or *behind* the leader. This allows the fly and leader to precede the line in its downstream drift, ideally making the fly the *first* thing a fish sees. And by preceding the fly line, the leader and fly are less likely to be influenced by drag. Conversely, a downstream mend throws a curve of fly line *ahead* of the fly and leader, which serves to pull the fly more quickly through its drift. This is rarely a good move, but is necessary on occasion to move your fly into a chosen drift line when currents conflict.

To "throw a mend" in your line, you need only move your rod in an overhand 180-degree arc. This arc can be large, throwing a large curve, a "heavy" mend, or small curve, a "mini" mend. To throw a heavy mend you need to move your rod arm at a higher angle through the 180-degree arc—the bigger the arc, the bigger the mend. A small mend is accomplished with little more than a flip of the rod tip in the form of the 180-degree arc.

A series of smaller mends, as stated earlier, is usually more effective than one or two larger efforts. Smaller mends allow continuous control of the drift and closer contact with the fly. Throwing larger mends often results in the fly actually being jerked out of its drift by the upstream energy of the line curve.

New Developments

Fishing is a dynamic sport. Professionals and addicted amateurs continually look for better, more productive, or more personally pleasing methods to connect with steelhead. During the research phase of this book I revisited many old haunts and fished new water as the guest of gracious hosts, and learned something new each step along the way. To become a consistently successful angler, it is important to fish a lot and it is best to fish with other accomplished anglers. Fresh ideas and approaches are catalysts to the learning process, the keys to growth in personal skill and success.

Call them new tactics or refinements to established methods as you will. The following three techniques, in my opinion, are significant enough to justify presentation here. Each is productive and enjoyable.

Swinging Flies, Spey Techniques

Swinging the fly to steelhead is a relatively new development in the Great Lakes area, but it is one of the oldest successful methods for presenting a fly to anadromous fish. Creative problem solvers in Scotland developed long, two-handed rods and a series of specialized casts to accommodate obstructions to backcasts along the River Spey. *Spey casting* and *Spey fishing* entered the angling lexicon as these techniques spread throughout the British Isles and Europe. Atlantic salmon, and to a lesser degree, sea trout, were the objects of desire. The long rods also facilitated precise mending of long casts, and the results were extremely positive.

Fly anglers from northern California to British Columbia were the first to try and then adapt Spey methods to North America in Pacific Coast rivers for steelhead. Success—first with traditional Pacific steelhead flies and then with new patterns—came quickly, and the method's popularity grew. Longer casts mean longer drifts through prime holding water. More effective mends result in a fly swimming properly throughout the drift.

These tools and tactics have taken a bit longer to gain acceptance in Great Lakes steelhead rivers. There was a surge of interest in the early 1990s, but this faded a bit and leveled until the turn of the century. Now, there is a revival of sorts. More regional anglers are taking to the "new" methods and equipment. For a long period it was assumed that midwestern steelhead would not eat a swinging fly—they must have a dead-drift presentation. And, we thought our fish would not eat the Pacific steelhead or Atlantic salmon patterns and their derivatives—they only eat nymphs and eggs. Of course, preceding these jewels of local wisdom, it was common knowledge that Great Lakes steelhead would not eat *any* fly—they only hit hardware, spawn bags, and live nymphs. The reason for the increased use of the longer rods and swinging techniques is simple—they work. And it is an enjoyable way to fish. It is a "new" way to present the fly with true fly-fishing equipment. It expands our base of knowledge and is a great alternative for people who have tired of standard nymphing techniques and especially the "chuck-and-duck" method.

A great deal has been written about the execution of Spey casts. Both single-Spey and double-Spey casting diagrams appear regularly in fly-fishing magazines, and several books and videos are available with detailed instructions. There is no need to replicate those fine efforts here. The basic truth is that swinging flies—Spey type, classic Pacific patterns, and streamers—is an effective tactic that catches steelhead regardless of the rod type or specific cast employed.

Picture a smooth pool or long run with a depth between 3 and 6 feet. The deeper section is at the head of the pool on your right. The current runs from right to left, and the pool shallows to about 3 feet before falling into a riffle. The pool has its deepest channel near midstream. Boulders and smaller rocks stud the bottom.

The basic approach is to cast across or slightly downstream and mend the line to achieve a drift that presents your fly broadside to the fish. Allow the fly to drift and swing through the natural arc created by the current. You may have to execute additional mends to keep the fly swimming in the proper attitude. Keep a tight line to the fly as it swings. Hits can come at any time during the drift, but most often occur as tension and current pull the fly into a swinging arc. When the cast has straightened below you, let the fly hang for a few moments before picking up and making a new cast. Steelhead often follow a fly to the termination of the swing and hit when it stops and hangs.

Make the next cast from the same position, but lengthen the distance. Two or three swings at varying distances is usually enough to cover a section of the pool or run. Step downstream 6 or 8 feet and repeat the process until you feel you have thoroughly covered the best water in the deeper channel, at the channel's edges, and the soft lies near the boulders.

Now there is another question of presentation to consider. With a floating line, the fly will typically swim within a foot of the river's surface. This is fine when water temperatures are in the ideal range for peak steelhead energy. Usually this range hovers between 45 and 58 degrees F (7 to 14.5 degrees C). It also helps if a fresh run of fish is in the river. The high metabolic rate triggered by temperature and the aggressive nature of fresh steelhead combine to generate a willingness to rise in the water column to eat a fly.

At temperatures below 42 degrees F (5.5 C) and above 60 F (15.5 C), steelhead become less active. Both cold and warm water adversely affect their metabolism and make them more lethargic and less willing to rise to or chase a swinging fly. An assortment of sinking lines in different grain weights, or sinking poly leaders like those now available from Airflo, provides flexibility in addressing issues of depth of presentation whether required by temperature or other factors.

There is a smooth, 300-yard-long run on the lower Au Sable River in Michigan that often harbors several steelhead when the water is cold or when they have been pressured away from an easily accessed area just downstream. The bottom of this run is sand. It is crisscrossed with a wild confusion of old logs left over from the lumbering era. These logs lie over each other at different depths between 3 and 8 feet. This run cannot be effectively fished with nymphing techniques. There is no possible drift available. But swinging a streamer over the tops of the logs is often productive. A 300-grain sinking line is too heavy and drags the fly into the logs. A floating line swims the fly too near the surface for this location. A 175- or 200-grain line puts the fly in the sweet zone.

Spey patterns seem to work best when allowed to swing through the drift without additional movement applied by pulsing the rod tip or stripping the line. This is true, in my experience, regardless of water depth or temperature. Baitfish imitations are another matter. Steelhead do like them on the classic swing without added action under most conditions, but when water temperatures are in that ideal range, a line jerk or pulse of the rod to impart a sporadic darting motion often brings a solid hit.

It is impossible to have too many flies. Spey patterns and streamers not only catch lots of big steelhead, but they are also handsome and different from the standard fare. From micro-Speys on small hooks to large, 6-inch baitfish imitations, these methods and patterns are reasonable justification for buying more toys. Specific patterns and color variations are covered on a river-by-river basis, in the coverage of Forage Fish Streamer Techniques later in this chapter, and in Chapter 4, Fly Patterns.

Spey Fishing with a Float

An incredibly effective drift-fishing method for steelhead has rapidly grown in popularity among bait anglers. The technique employs a long rod and a "center-pin" reel as its core components. The center-pin reel with its free-spool feature allows incredibly long, drag-free drifts. The terminal rig consists of a float (bobber) followed by leader, weight, and bait—usually spawn, occasionally live Hex nymphs, or even artificial flies. The good thing about this method is the long natural drift. This is also the bad part of the whole deal. With this method an angler can—and often attempts to—monopolize a run, seam, or pool for long distances. A drift of 200 feet is possible. On our popular and often busy steelhead rivers, this takes a lot of water out of play for other anglers, which in turn causes tension and irritation. We need to share with a smile.

Recently, guide Ray Schmidt, along with Bruce Richards of Scientific Anglers, developed a method that approximates the long, drag-free drifts of the center-pin system but allows anglers to use true fly-fishing tackle. You won't be able to run a drift as long as is possible with a center-pin reel but certainly double or triple the length achievable with our standard, nymph-drifting fly gear.

Ray calls the technique "Spey fishing with a float." Simple enough. A Spey rod, an interchangeable-tip Spey fly line, and a float (indicator) are the basic tools. The technique employs just a few simple steps. First is the Spey cast to deliver the float, weight, and fly (or flies) to the target area, let's say a long, soft current seam in the river. Once the float, leader, and flies have landed at the target, the angler slips slack line through the guides to allow enough free line on the water to execute a roll cast without pulling the float out of the target area. The roll cast is placed a foot or two upstream from the float. This creates the slack necessary to allow the weight on the leader to pull the fly to the desired fishing depth. As soon as the float tips upright, execute a reach mend to throw the fly line upstream from the float, then feed line to the float as it drifts downstream. If the float dips, or jerks sideways, set the hook. At the end of the drift, simply strip line back through the rod to the head of the Spey line and repeat the cast-and-mend process to deliver the fly back to the target area.

Because of additional weight in combination with the Spey line, casts of about 50 feet are near the maximum effective distance for this technique. But drag-free drift distances are easily twice those attainable with a traditional single-hand rod using similar methods. Line control is also superior due to the length—usually 13 to 15 feet—of the Spey rod.

This technique is very effective throughout the year and particularly so when water temperatures drop and fish move into slack water or very soft currents due to a slowdown in their metabolic rate.

The terminal rig for this technique has several key parts but is easy to set up. Attach a 6-inch piece of stiff 40-pound mono to the tip of the fly line at one end and to a small "black ant" swivel at the other end. This is followed by a 10-foot section of 40-pound mono. The float rides on this piece. This 10-foot section ends at another ant swivel. A 2-foot section of 15- to 20-pound mono follows with a small plastic bead, a short length of hollowcore weight, another plastic bead, and ends at another swivel. This is followed by 18 inches of tippet and fly number one, which is then connected to 30 inches of tippet and fly number two.

The Sinking-Leader Technique

John Valk of Grindstone Angling in Waterdown, Ontario has perfected a technique both for nymphing and swinging Spey and streamer flies that eliminates the need to attach bulky lead or nontoxic alloy sinkers to the leader yet allows fly anglers to present their offerings at proper depths. Casting a rig that includes split shot is a problem for some people and distasteful to others.

When using nymph and/or egg patterns, John uses a floating fly line looped to one of the new "sinking leaders" available from Rio and Airflo. These are true weighted leaders available in lengths from 5 to 14 feet, with densities that produce sink rates from intermediate to super fast (about 9 inches per second). Attach a length of tippet to the sinking leader and a fly to the tippet. John varies the tippet length between 3 and 5 feet and recommends a tippet strength between 6 and 8 pounds.

The basic cast is upstream, or quartering upstream, from the angler's position. Adjust the upstream angle and length of cast to accommodate depth and current speed. As current pulls the fly deeper into the run or pool, strip back excess slack, lift the rod slightly, and follow the line downstream with a slow rod path. Too little tension might cause a hang-up on the bottom, while too much tension will raise the fly out of the fishing zone. At the end of the swing, lock the rod in a position pointing directly downstream. This allows the fly to swing up from the bottom. Most takes will come between the middle and the end of the drift. John usually lets the fly hang directly downstream for a few seconds before lifting and making a new cast. Hits often come when the fly is hanging straight below the angler.

At certain times during both the fall and spring runs, river temperatures reach and hold at the optimum zone for steelhead. When this happens they often become extremely aggressive. When steelhead reach this peak of activity they can be caught on swinging flies that drift just under the surface of the water. The hits are explosive and visible, resulting in raw excitement and high drama. Under these water conditions John switches to a sinking leader with an intermediate rating, usually a sink rate of 2.5 to 3 inches per second. He switches from nymph and egg patterns to large leeches, streamers, and Spey flies tied on heavy hooks up to 3/0 in size. Use the same cast-and-drift method as described for nymphing. Be prepared. The take will occur just an inch or two below the surface. It will be heavy and fierce.

The sinking-leader technique also works extremely well when used with the traditional steelhead swing. Fast runs to a depth of 6 to 7 feet can be adequately covered with a 10- to 12-foot, superfast leader with a sink rate in the 9-inches-per-second range. For faster and deeper water John tailors the sink rate with Custom Cut Tips, a new product Airflo introduced in 2003. These come in 20-foot lengths and range from 200 to 470 grains in weight and sink rates up to 11.5 inches per second. John cuts them in varying lengths to accommodate almost any situation.

Make the cast straight across or slightly upstream and follow with appropriate upstream mends to maintain a straight line drift and swing. Follow the line and fly on its downstream path with the tip of your fly rod. Pick up and cast again if the swing comes to a stop in shallow water, but if the swing terminates and your fly is still in a run of moderate depth, hold the position for a while. Some steelhead will follow but not hit until the fly is stationary in the downstream position. John calls this the "fishing zone" and has had takes after holding the fly in this position for up to two minutes. He estimates that around 35 percent of the hits take place in the fishing zone.

It is important to fish the water thoroughly and patiently. Lengthen successive casts from a position until you reach your maximum distance for accuracy and comfort, then step downstream a few feet and repeat the process. Continue working downstream, spending more time in optimum water with up to three or four casts in a targeted area.

The sinking leader technique for nymphing and the traditional steelhead swing is easy, fun to use, and very effective. This is John's first choice whether he is guiding clients or fishing for personal enjoyment.

Forage Fish Streamer Technique

A river with an abundance of food and cover spread over many miles is a dream come true for steelhead anglers. Several rivers within the Great Lakes basin are blessed with these attributes. Canadian rivers like the Maitland, Saugeen, Nottawasaga, and Grand—as well as the Salmon in New York and the Manistee and Muskegon in Michigan—are prime examples of the near perfect combination for steelhead.

Kevin Feenstra is a young, energetic, and talented guide on the Muskegon River in west central Michigan. Kevin happily applies all fly-fishing methods and tactics appropriate to his river but particularly enjoys swinging streamers for steelhead.

The Muskegon supports a wide base of forage fish throughout the year, such as chubs, dace, shiners, sculpins, and immature suckers as well as tens of thousands of immature trout, steelhead, and salmon. Steelhead are opportunistic and aggressively feed on this bounty. Another important feature of the Muskegon is that it is full of large rocks and boulders that often make nymph-fishing techniques difficult at best. This feature is common throughout long stretches on many of our most productive steelhead rivers.

Kevin believes that steelhead acclimate quickly to the riverine environment after leaving the big lakes and begin to behave—at least in

Big water with abundant forage fish, such as Michigan's Muskegon River, is perfect for Kevin Feenstra's forage fish streamer technique.

part—like stream trout, feeding on what is abundant and, when the water is cold, on what is easy. Some fish prefer nymphs, some prefer eggs, and some prefer a fish diet.

The combination of abundant forage fish and boulders produces an ideal set of conditions for fly anglers who enjoy swinging streamers. It is important to note the word "swinging." It is integral to Kevin's forage fish streamer technique. The type or style of streamer fly is also critical to his remarkable success. I long held the notion that pulsing or jerking a streamer sporadically through a retrieve would be best for steelhead because that tactic is so clearly superior to a straight swing when used for stream trout. The truth is that the simple swing works better on steelhead in most cases. And I came to believe that moderately sized, realistic streamer patterns were best for *mykiss* based on my personal results. I was wrong on that point as well.

Kevin's base tools and casts are standard fare. He uses a medium-fast-action rod, a 300-grain sink-tip, and a short, heavy leader. He casts across or slightly downstream and allows the fly to swing at depth. He makes a small mend or two to activate, to "twitch" the fly, and follows the swing through to its end with the fly hanging directly downstream. He holds the fly motionless in this hanging position for several seconds. Close to

50 percent of the strikes come at this point. Lengthen your casts to the comfortable limit, then move downstream a few feet and repeat the process. When fishing big water, like the Muskegon, from a boat, Kevin will reposition his client by moving his boat as much as 20 feet downstream. Whether fishing from a boat or wading, move progressively downstream until the run or pool has been thoroughly covered.

For this type of fishing the right fly patterns are critical, and that is the most significant element in this approach. Kevin's unique streamer pattern style is becoming recognized nationwide as having the best combination of attributes for steelhead. He advocates big, impressionistic patterns with mottled, natural colors and breathing, pulsing materials. I do mean big. Many of his streamers designed for spring-run fish are 4 inches in length. He throws even bigger flies at fall-run steelhead. In October and November, he prefers flies from 5 to 7 inches long tied on 6XL and 8XL hooks.

Regardless of the time of year, these flies present the right profile for the season's most commonly available baitfish. They are tied with various combinations of marabou, mottled hen, emu, spikey dubbing, and Australian possum. The net effect is interesting. When dry they look a little bit like a gobbled mess the cat tore apart. When wet, they pulse and breathe life with the slightest current variation. They have the proper profile, color, and bulk to incite a hungry steelhead to riot.

Steelhead Flies for Great Lakes Rivers

Fly pattern evolution seems to be almost a force of nature. It is our tendency as anglers to wonder. *Why did that work? Why didn't that work? What if?* We ponder, scheme, experiment, and adapt how best to practice our guile and deception. There are few basic truths in a fly-fishing life, but it seems that evolution and proliferation of fly patterns are two of them. That is a good thing. It is fun to look at, touch, even to just think about fly patterns. Some of them are simple and basic, old and proven. Some are elegant works of art, almost too beautiful to put in the water. Impressionistic, realistic, large, tiny, dull, and vibrant variously describe the flies we cast to steelhead.

It has been a long time since I first cast a fly with great excitement and hope into a steelhead river. In those muddling, fumbling days we used very large yarn flies to imitate gobs of eggs drifting in the current and a few nymph patterns—usually stoneflies and Hex—tied on gigantic hooks. We figured we needed big flies to attract big fish and large hooks to hold them should we get very lucky. Sometimes these flies worked; more often, they did not. *Why? What if?*

We know a lot more about *mykiss* today. We know rivers and their changing conditions affect steelhead behavior. We appreciate differences between clear and turbid water, in temperatures, in freestone and spring-fed rivers, between relatively sterile spate rivers and fertile streams with a gentle flow. We understand that steelhead are highly adapted specialists, that their behavior on any given day is influenced by the condition of their habitat.

Our goal is to deceive, to entice steelhead to eat an illusion. Bits of feathers, fur, wire, tinsel, and a dizzying array of synthetic materials are the basic components that, when blended properly, create a specific deception. When one of these works do we leave it alone and think *good enough?* Of course not. We attempt to make it better. This urge to refine is irresistible. The net result is that today we have hundreds of seductive, viable, fish-catching steelhead flies from which to choose. Tomorrow, there will be many more.

Fly pattern development in the Great Lakes basin has been a combination of pure invention targeted to the precise nature of a given watershed, and the adaptation of existing flies designed for distinct hydraulic geographics. Fly patterns developed for Lake Superior's North Shore are a bit different than those designed for the more fertile flows entering Lake Michigan, and these vary from popular flies used along the Lake Erie and Lake Ontario coastlines. Some patterns developed for swinging fly/Spey techniques in Great Lakes rivers are carefully engineered derivatives of successful Pacific coast and British/European pattern types. Still others used with Spey techniques are uniquely ours, created as a remedy for a special need on a specific river. Many of these flies are streamers that mimic the details of baitfish.

Stonefly nymphs, in a variety of sizes, are an important part of the steelheader's arsenal.

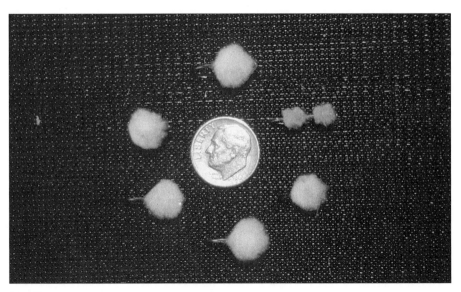

Egg flies.

The range in size of flies is truly amazing. Some, usually Spey, tube, and streamer patterns, are quite large. Some approach several inches in length and are tied on hooks ranging from No. 4 to 2/0. Tube fly patterns are relatively new to Great Lakes fly anglers. They are dressed on tubes rather than hook shanks. The tubes have the advantage of presenting a lengthy, realistic profile without the disadvantage of a long hook shank that is subject to bending and twisting by the pressure applied by a fighting steelhead. At the other end of the spectrum, miniscule nymphs tied to represent immature stages of aquatic insects catch large steelhead even when tied on No. 16 and 18 hooks. And egg patterns in the size of a natural, single egg, roughly 5mm in diameter, have repeatedly proven to be among the most effective in our arsenal.

The flies chosen for this book represent a mix of old and new, with a heavy emphasis on new. They have been created or adapted by some of the finest tyers in the country, true thinkers, artists, and anglers. These flies all produce best in the waters for which they were designed, but all also work well throughout the basin.

Following is a brief biographical note on each contributor in alphabetical order.

Jeff (Bear) Andrews

Bear is a commercial tyer and avid, accomplished steelhead fly angler. His innovative nymph patterns are in wide use throughout the Great Lakes and available in most professional fly shops. He has generously given his time to raise money for coldwater resources through "Tyathon" exhibits. You can order flies from Bear at: 517-627-7606. He lives in Grand Ledge, Michigan.

Bob Blumreich

Bob's special, display Spey flies are in high demand by avid collectors of angling art. He also sells commercial flies and an instructional video on tying Spey patterns. Bob can be reached through his website, www .silverdoctor.net, or by phone at 608-637-3417. Bob lives in Viroqua, Wisconsin and guides for steelhead and trout throughout Wisconsin.

Jeff Conrad

Jeff is a professional musician who once played trumpet with the Ray Charles Band. He is an avid fly angler and creative fly tyer with a special dedication to Lake Erie steelhead. Jeff lives in Indianapolis, Indiana.

Jerry Darkes

As a fly-fishing tackle sales representative, Jerry travels throughout the Great Lakes states. He also guides steelhead anglers in Steelhead Alley, especially along the Ohio coast of Lake Erie. He lives in Strongsville, Ohio.

Ed Devine

Ed grew up with a fly rod. He was born and raised in Pennsylvania and has lived and fished in England, and on the east coast of the United States. He is a golf course designer and manager by profession and a fly angler and tyer by avocation. He lives in Indianapolis.

Kevin Feenstra

Slithering, breathing streamers and lifelike, undulating nymphs are Kevin's specialties. His patterns are designed first for the Muskegon River but have proven immensely successful throughout the region. Kevin is a commercial tyer and fly-fishing guide on the Muskegon. He can be reached at 231-652-3528.

Rob Heal

Rob is a young, energetic fly angler and accomplished steelhead guide on Ontario's best rivers. He can be reached through Grindstone Angling at 705-649-3313.

Rick Kustich

Rick's first book, *Fly Fishing the Great Lake Tributaries,* appeared in 1992. In 1999 he and his brother, Jerry, produced *Fly Fishing for Great Lakes Steelhead.* Both are excellent, informative works. Rick is widely recognized as an angler, teacher, and writer. He lives in Grand Island, New York.

Joe Penich

This man is one of the most creative and gifted fly tyers in North America. His residence is in Hamilton, Ontario, but he *lives* on the steelhead runs of the Niagara and Grand Rivers. Joe's flies are available through Grindstone Angling at 705-649-3313.

Ray Schmidt

Schmidt Outfitters is the shrine of Michigan steelhead fly anglers and Ray built it on a reputation of hard work, excellent service, and integrity. Ray is one of the region's true steelhead pioneers. His flies are rugged and consistently productive. Ray also owns a fly distribution company that specializes in patterns for the Great Lakes. You can buy Ray's patterns directly through Schmidt Outfitters at 1-888-221-9056.

Scott Earl Smith

Scott is a police officer in Thunder Bay, Ontario. He is a widely published author on fly fishing in general and on steelhead in Canada in particular. He is also an accomplished fly designer, angler, photographer, and public speaker. In addition to steelhead, Scott has a burning passion for the massive brook trout of the Nipigon River.

Matt Supinski

Matt is well known throughout the country as a speaker and writer on fly fishing for steelhead. His column and articles appear regularly in magazines, and his books, *River Journal—Pere Marquette River* and *Steelhead Dreams,* are bestsellers. Matt's guide services on the Muskegon River and elsewhere are in high demand.

John Valk

As a guide, tyer, and fly shop owner, John has few peers. He guides on several Ontario steelhead rivers from his shop, Grindstone Angling in Waterdown, Ontario. His flies and creative fishing techniques reflect the preferences of Ontario's magnificent wild fish.

Fly Recipes

Streamers and Leeches

Baby Lamprey (John Valk)

Hook:	Daiichi 2050, No. 6 to 2
Thread:	Black 70 denier
Body:	Grey mohair or leech yarn
Rib:	Fine copper wire
Wing:	Grey crosscut rabbit strip 2.5 times hook length
Head:	Black cone

Skinny Leech (John Valk)

Hook:	Daiichi 2050, No. 6 to 2
Thread:	Black 70 denier
Body:	Red or black mohair or leech yarn
Rib:	Fine copper wire
Wing:	Black or olive crosscut rabbit strip, 2.5 times hook length
Collar:	Red or orange chicabou soft hackle

Steelhead Leech (Rob Heal)

Hook:	Daiichi 2151, No. 4 to 2
Thread:	Black 6/0
Body:	Trilobal dubbing
Rib:	UNI French wire
Wing:	Rabbit strip with two strands of Mylar tinsel
Collar:	Crosscut rabbit strip (with hide removed) in a dubbing loop

Conrad's Sculpin (Jeff Conrad)

Front hook:	Mustad 3366, No. 2 for large fly, No. 4 for smaller fly
Rear hook:	Mustad 3366, No.6 for large fly, No.8 for smaller fly
Thread:	Color to match fly color, 3/0
Tail:	Stiff schlappen feather tips, 2 inches long, three on each side; marabou hackle, wound thick.

Body:	Five size E glass beads over connecting mono, four to six strands of Flashabou tied at bend of front hook, thick marabou hackle
Head:	Barbell eyes, spun deer hair clipped flat on bottom

Joe's Niagara Smelt (Joe Penich)

Hook:	Kamasan B 200, No. 4 to 8
Thread:	UNI-Nylon 70 denier, white
Body:	Flat silver tinsel
Underwing:	White Polar fibre extended past hook
Midwing:	Six to eight strands of pearl Flashabou
Wing:	Gray and white Polar fibre even with underwing
Topping:	Four to six strands of blue Flashabou and 4-6 strands of peacock herl
Eyes:	Streamside silver 3D eyes
Comment:	Allow head cement to dry completely before coating with five-minute epoxy to secure eyes.

Joe's Niagara Shiner (Joe Penich)

Hook:	Partridge Carrie Stevens 10X CS15, 2-8
Thread:	UNI-Nylon 70 denier, white
Body:	Metal tape folded over hook and trimmed to belly shape, covered with small silver Mylar tubing.
Throat:	White marabou
Underwing:	Six to ten strands of pearl Flashabou
Wing:	Gray and white Polar Fibre
Topping:	Four to six strands of peacock herl
Eyes:	Streamside silver 3-D eyes
Comment:	Allow head cement to dry completely before coating with five-minute epoxy to secure eyes.

Steely Crayfish (Joe Penich)

Hook:	Mustad 79580 No. 4 to 8, or TMC 300, No. 2 to 6
Underbody:	Medium lead wire (or substitute) tied parallel to hook shank
Claws:	Olive grizzly hen neck
Shellcase:	Olive scud back

Eyes:	Black mono
Legs:	Olive-dyed pine squirrel
Body and head:	Hareline Ice Dub, olive
Rib:	Twisted copper wire
Hackle:	Olive grizzly hen, folded
Head:	Medium gold cone

SNR Sculpin (Joe Penich)

Hook:	Partridge CS/10/101, No. 3/0 to 5 or Daiichi 2051, No. 1.5 to 5
Thread:	UNI-Nylon 70 denier white UNI-Cord white
Underbody:	Lead wire (or substitute) tied parallel to hook shank
Body:	Hareline STS trilobal dubbing, Hareline Ice Dub, color to match wing
Rib:	Medium copper wire
Wing:	Saltwater rabbit strip cut into a taper
Collar:	Fox fur strip, color to match wing
Gills:	Marabou
Head:	Pine squirrel zonker strip

Baby Brown Trout (and White Minnow) (Joe Penich)

Hook:	Daiichi 2059, No. 2/0 to 7
Thread:	UNI-Nylon 70 denier white
Body:	Gold STS trilobal salmon and steelhead dubbing
Rib:	Copper wire
Wing:	Ginger rabbit strip trimmed to a tapered point
Collar:	Ginger rabbit strip
Gills:	Mottled brown hen saddle hackle
Head:	Glo Bug yarn, egg color
Eyes:	Streamside 3-D eyes, gold
Comment:	Once the fly is complete, use brown marker to color the top of the head, and red and brown marker to add spots on the wing for parr markings. The White Minnow is tied the same way, but everything is tied in white. The eyes are silver 3-D eyes.

Flash Smolt (Kevin Feenstra)

Rear hook:	4XL straight-eye streamer hook, No. 10
Rear hook body and tail:	A tuft of tan grizzly marabou with a body of olive or yellow Polar Chenille.
Attachment:	20-pound monofilament
Cover-up:	A clump of Australian possum hiding the junction between the hooks
Front hook:	No. 6 Daiichi Boss or other egg hook
Eyes:	Black mono
Shellback:	Pearly or silver Krystal Flash
Front body:	Olive Polar Chenille and a little orange Ice Chenille at front
Hackle:	Large mallard flank feather, palmered
Comments:	This is a relatively new fly. The mallard flank makes it deadly whether fished on the swing or bounced along the bottom. Wrapping a mallard flank, blue-eared pheasant, or marabou around the front of a nymph can often make the fly much more versatile. This is especially true when it comes to Hex nymph patterns and smolt patterns.

Classic Emulator with flash (Kevin Feenstra)

Hook:	6 to 8XL streamer hook (Mike Martinek hook from Gaelic Supreme is a good choice, also TMC 300 and Daiichi 2220)
Tail:	Copper Flashabou and tan grizzly marabou
Body:	Emu feather wound tightly forward
Hackle:	Schlappen, usually brown or olive
Pectoral fins:	A clump of mallard flank feather fibers tied on either side of fly
Head:	Clump of Australian possum fur or ram's wool
Comments:	Day in and day out, this is an effective fly for lake-run browns, steelhead, and stream trout.

Psycho Sculpin (Kevin Feenstra)

Rear hook:	Tiemco 9394, No. 8 or 10
Rear hook body:	Green dubbing

Rear hook tail and wing:	Australian possum tail (best) or body fur
Attachment:	20-pound Maxima
Cover-up:	Australian possum clump
Front hook:	No. 4 egg fly hook
Eyes:	Pink plastic eyes from craft store
Fins:	Olive rubber legs
Body:	Thick clump of Australian possum
Comment:	Great fly to swing in small rivers.

Plastic Sculpin (Kevin Feenstra)

Hook:	6 to 8XL streamer
Tail:	A few strands of marabou, and a few strands of Sili Legs
Body:	Emu feather, wound forward, interspersed with Sili Legs as a wing
Collar:	Sili Legs, a mallard flank, and Sunburst Flashabou
Head:	Australian possum or ram's wool
Comment:	This ridiculous-looking fly has a lot of action and is at its best in slow pools and on the edges.

Sparkle Head Leech/Minnow (Jerry Darkes)

Hook:	Daiichi 1710, No. 4 to 8
Tail:	Small bunch of rabbit fur
Body:	Crosscut rabbit strip with bit of hanked Lite Brite at front
Head:	A few turns of Estaz. Natural grizzly and white rabbit are a great match for a variety of baitfish.

Grand River Bleeding Minnow (Jerry Darkes)

Hook:	Daiichi 1710, No. 4 to 8
Tail:	Pearl Krystal Flash
Body:	Wrapped pearl Krystal Flash
Wing:	Chartreuse marabou with white marabou over top, mix in a few strands of pearl Krystal Flash
Throat:	Red marabou or hackle fibers
Eyes:	Small nickel barbell eyes or bead chain

Steelhead Woolly Bugger (Ray Schmidt)

Hook:	Tiemco 3761 or equivalent, No. 6
Thread:	3/0 black waxed monocord
Tail:	Black marabou with peacock Krystal Flash or black, olive/black, or olive
Rib:	Krystal Flash
Body:	Peacock herl
Hackle:	Furnace saddle hackle or black, olive, or olive/black

Steelhead Woolly Bugger, Purple (Ray Schmidt)

Hook:	Tiemco 3761 or equivalent, No. 6
Thread:	Black
Tail:	Purple marabou with purple/pearl Flashabou
Body:	Medium variegated tinsel chenille, purple/pearl
Hackle:	Purple saddle

White Egg-Sucking Leech (Bob Linsenman)

Hook:	Tiemco 3761, No. 6
Thread:	UNI-Thread 3/0 white
Tail:	White marabou with 3-4 strands of pearl Krystal Flash
Body:	White chenille
Hackle:	White saddle
Legs:	White Sili Legs
Egg:	Root beer Estaz
Comment:	Very good in late fall and winter and throughout Lake Erie tributaries.

Sock-It-To-Me Sac Fry (Matt Supinski)

Hook:	Daiichi 452, No. 8
Body:	Pearl braid
Underwing:	Combination of pearl Krystal Flash with white, pink, and orange Ice Dub or Angel Hair.
Wing:	Gadwall duck feather
Sac:	Orange McFly foam
Eyes:	Prismatic eyes

Stoned Practitioner (Matt Supinski)

Hook:	Daiichi 1750, No. 6
Tail:	Sand grizzly marabou tips with three of four strands of copper Flashabou
Rib:	Copper Flashabou
Body:	Spirit River speckled copper/black chenille
Hackle:	Brown or rust saddle hackle
Wing:	Two layers of filoplume segments
Comment:	This fly incorporates elements of action and profiles of stoneflies, sculpins, and gobies.

Nymphs

Copper Prince (Jeff Conrad)

Hook:	Mustad 9671, No. 8 to 16
Tail:	Goose biots
Body:	Medium copper wire
Wingcase:	Wide Flashabou
Thorax:	Peacock herl
Wings:	Goose biots
Legs:	Soft hen hackle
Head:	Tungsten bead

Variegated Brassie (Jeff Conrad)

Hook:	Egg hook or heavy scud hook
Tail:	Two short strands of Krystal Flash
Body:	Two contrasting colors of wire
Head:	Peacock herl

Beadhead Flashback Hare's Ear (Jeff Conrad)

Hook:	Mustad 9671, No. 10 to 16
Tail:	Opossum guard hairs, tied short
Body:	Spiky hare's ear dubbing
Wingcase:	Wide Flashabou
Thorax:	Spiky hare's ear dubbing
Head:	Tungsten bead

Joe's Canadian Stone (Joe Penich)

Hook:	Daiichi 1270, No. 4 to 12
Underbody:	Medium lead wire tied parallel to hook shank
Tail:	Black goose biots
Body:	Hareline STS trilobal dubbing, black
Rib:	Copper wire
Wingcase:	Scudback, black
Thorax:	Hareline STS trilobal, black
Legs:	Black hen neck hackle, folded
Eyes:	Black mono
Antennae:	Black goose biots
Comment:	This fly can also be tied in gold and white. Just substitute the dubbing and goose biots with gold and white.

Tri-Color Mayfly (Bob Linsenman)

Hook:	TMC 200 R, Mustad 9672, or equivalent, No. 6 to 14
Tail:	Hungarian partridge fibers
Body:	Spiky Hare's Rar dubbing – natural, olive, or black
Rib:	Pearl Krystal Flash, doubled and twisted
Wingcase:	Swiss straw, color to match, with two or three strands of pearl Krystal Flash, pulled over top of Swiss straw from back of wingcase to hook eye.
Thorax:	Pearl Chenille or Estaz, root beer color for natural hare's ear-color nymph, chartreuse for olive nymph, black for black nymph.
Legs:	Hungarian partridge
Head:	Tiny amount of dubbing
Comment:	This fly has been the author's most productive all-purpose steelhead nymph for the past few years.

Nympho (Scott Earl Smith)

Hook:	TMC 200R or equivalent, No. 8 to 10
Thread:	UNI-Thread 6/0 orange
Tail:	Golden pheasant crest
Rib:	Oval gold tinsel

Body:	Chartreuse steelhead and salmon dubbing
Wingcase:	Six strands of peacock herl
Thorax:	Orange steelhead and salmon dubbing picked out to resemble legs.

Spring Stone (Scott Earl Smith)

Hook:	Tiemco 5263, No. 4 to 10
Thread:	UNI-Thread 6/0 black
Tail:	Red fox squirrel tail
Rib:	Gold oval tinsel
Body:	Black chenille
Wingcase:	Red fox squirrel tail
Thorax:	Black chenille
Legs:	Brown neck hackle, palmered
Antennae:	Red fox squirrel tail
Comments:	Simple to tie and extremely effective utility fly throughout the Great Lakes basin.

Better Than Spawn (BTS) (Kevin Feenstra)

Rear hook:	4XL straight-eye streamer hook, No. 10.
Rear hook tail and body:	White or tan grizzly marabou, tie in as a tail and wound forward.
Attachment:	20-pound monofilament tied as a loop between the two hooks, crimped or glued to secure. A small tuft of Australian possum fur is placed over the joint to make the body look fluid.
Front hook:	No 6 Daiichi Boss steelhead hook or other equivalent egg hook.
Eyes:	Black monofilament
Body:	Pink Ice Dub
Back and fins:	Light purple or pearl Krystal Flash, pulled over the body and split to either side as legs.
Comments:	Many Great Lakes rivers are full of Chinook salmon fry in the spring. Steelhead love to eat them, and this BTS imitation is deadly. Kevin also uses a similar Hex imitation that he calls a Better Than Hex (BTH). In that fly, the rear hook tail and body are tied with gold grizzly marabou, and the front body is tied with pale yellow dubbing.

Kevin's Possum Hex (Kevin Feenstra)

Rear hook:	4XL straight-eye streamer hook, No. 10
Rear hook body and tail:	Dirty yellow Antron dubbing, interspersed with three clumps of Australian possum.
Attachment:	20-pound monofilament
Cover-up:	A clump of Australian possum hiding the junction between the hooks
Front hook:	No. 6 Daiichi Boss or other egg hook
Eyes:	Black mono
Legs:	Partridge hackle
Body:	Dirty yellow dubbing
Shellback:	Brown Antron
Comments:	The *Hexagenia* mayfly is a common nymph in many silty rivers of the Midwest. Because they are very active swimming nymphs, they are great candidates for articulation. Deadly when fished as a nymph, but more effective as a swing fly on smaller rivers.

Elk Creek Caddis (Jerry Darkes)

Hook:	Daiichi 1120, No. 10 to 16
Body:	Spirit River Brite Blend Caddis Cream. Add collar of peacock herl or darker dubbing.
Head:	Bead matched to hook size.

EZ Stone (Jerry Darkes)

Hook:	Daiichi 1530, No. 8 to 14
Tail:	Goose biots
Body:	Stonefly blend spun in a dubbing loop
Legs:	Mini centipede or tarantula legs, dark brown
Head:	Bead matched to size of hook and color of fly

Schmidt's Hex Nymph (Ray Schmidt)

Hook:	Tiemco 200R or equivalent
Thread:	3/0 light orange
Eyes:	Small black mono eyes
Tail:	Pheasant tail central fibers

Shellback:	Pheasant tail central fibers
Rib:	Fine copper wire
Body:	Life Cycle Dubbing (golden stone color)
Wingcase:	Pheasant tail central fibers (treated with Flex-Seal or Flexament)
Thorax:	Two-thirds of a turn of peach Estaz
Legs:	Partridge or hen saddle (sparse)

Schmidt's Krystal Stone (Ray Schmidt)

Hook:	Tiemco 3761 or equivalent, No. 6 and 8
Thread:	3/0 waxed monocord, dark brown
Tail:	Goose biots, dark brown
Rib:	Small red wire
Body:	2/3 Awesome Possum (Dr. Brown), 1/3 Hareline Dubbin Steelhead/Salmon (claret), 0.035 lead strips (or substitute) tied on hook shank for flat body.
Wingcase:	Krystal Flash
Thorax:	Same as body
Legs:	Hen saddle

Schmidt's Black Krystal Stone (Ray Schmidt)

Thread:	3/0 waxed monocord, black
Tail:	Goose biots, black
Wingcase:	Peacock Krystal Flash
Rib:	Small green wire
Body:	Front 2/3 Awesome Possum, black, 1/3 Flashabou dubbing, pearl. All else is the same as the brown.

Schmidt's Hot Butt Antron Hex (Ray Schmidt)

Hook:	Tiemco 200R (or equivalent), No. 6
Thread:	3/0 monocord
Tail:	Half the yarn size of Glo Bug yarn in chartreuse or steelhead orange
Shellback:	Dark brown Antron yarn
Hackle:	Light brown or variegated #2 Metz saddle hackle

Body:	Rear 2/3 medium variegated chenille (ginger/white), forward 1/3 peach Estaz
Eyes:	Plastic bead chain

Antron Estaz Bug (Ray Schmidt)

Hook:	Tiemco 3761 or equivalent, No. 6
Thread:	3/0 waxed monocord to match body color
Eyes:	3mm black plastic bead chain
Tail:	Antron yarn, dark brown for stone and hex; white for shrimp
Hackle:	Furnace saddle hackle for stone; ginger for hex; light ginger for shrimp (white)
Body:	Medium chenille, black/coffee variegated for stone; ginger/white for Hex; white sparkle for shrimp
Throat:	Two turns of peach Estaz
Shellback:	Same as tail

Schmidt's Caddis Larva (Ray Schmidt)

Hook:	Tiemco 2457 or equivalent, No. 8
Thread:	3/0 waxed monocord, black
Rib:	Gold or copper Krystal Flash
Body:	Microchenille colors to simulate larva—caddis green, chartreuse, olive, etc.
Thorax:	Peacock herl

PCP Flash Nymph (pheasant, copper, peacock) (Ray Schmidt)

Hook:	Tiemco 2457 or equivalent, No. 8 and 10
Thread:	3/0 waxed monocord, dark brown
Tail:	Ringneck pheasant tail central fibers
Rib:	Fine copper wire
Body:	Ringneck pheasant tail central fibers
Thorax:	Peacock herl
Wingcase:	Ringneck pheasant tail central fibers, with saltwater Flashabou on top

Eddie's Special Hex (Ed Devine)

Hook:	Daiichi 1530 or equivalent, No. 10 to 14
Thread:	UNI-Thread 6/0, olive or tan
Tail and shellback:	Grizzly marabou, sand or natural
Body:	Gold sparkle yarn, sparsely wrapped
Rib:	Two gray ostrich herls, spun and palmered
Eyes:	Bead chain for larger sizes, mono or damsel eyes for smaller sizes
Comment:	Extremely easy to tie and very productive on Ohio and Pennsylvania streams.

Bear's Peacock Fuzzbuster (Bear Andrews)

Hook:	Daiichi 1530, No. 6 to 10
Thread:	8/0 UNI-Thread, brown
Tail:	Fluff from a hen grizzly, dyed brown (same feather will provide the legs)
Back and wingcase:	Pheasant tail treated with Flex-Seal or Dave's Flexament
Ribbing:	Clear monofilament or fine gold or copper wire
Body:	Peacock herl
Hackle:	Dyed brown hen saddle collared all the way through the thorax
Eyes:	Extra-small mono eyes, black

Bear's Pheasant Tail Half & Half (Bear Andrews)

Hook:	Dai-Riki 135, No. 6 to 8
Thread:	UNI-Thread in brown size 8/0
Tail and body:	Pheasant tail fibers
Ribbing:	Fine gold or copper wire or clear mono
Hackle:	Pheasant rump collared
Head:	Pheasant aftershaft feather, collared

Bear's Crossdresser Hex (Bear Andrews)

Hook:	TMC 105, No. 4
Thread:	8/0 gray UNI-Thread

Tail:	Natural grizzly marabou. First feather tied in at the bend, followed by a grizzly marabou dyed tan or sand and collared in front of first feather. In addition, a small, very sparse amount of gold Angel Hair is tied in on both sides of the tail.
Wingcase:	Pheasant tail treated with Flex-Seal or Dave's Flexament
Dubbing:	Sulphur Spirit River Squirrel Blend or any dirty yellow dubbing
Hackle:	French partridge, collared.
Eyes:	Extra-small black mono eyes

Bear's Headbanger Hex (Bear Andrews)

Hook:	Daiichi 1730, No. 4 to 8, or for shorter version use a Daiichi 1530, No. 4 to 8
Thread:	UNI-Thread, tan, size 8/0
Tail:	Micro Bug Yarn in color of choice
Ribbing:	Fine wire or clear mono thread
Wingcase and back:	Pheasant tail treated with Flex-Seal or Dave's Flexament
Gills:	Pheasant aftershaft feather
Dubbing:	Spirit River Squirrel Blend in sulphur color
Hackle:	Dyed grizzly hen saddle, brown, palmered through the thorax
Eyes:	Extra-small black mono eyes

Bear's Crossdresser Fry (Bear Andrews)

Hook:	TMC 105, No. 4
Thread:	8/0 UNI-Thread, white, size
Tail:	Grizzly marabou, first feather tied in at bend, second collared around it. Then tie in a very sparse amount of pearl green Angel Hair on both sides of the tail.
Back:	Several strands of peacock herl
Dubbing:	2/3 polar ice Firestar dubbing and 1/3 fire red Firestar dubbing
Hackle:	Teal flank, collared
Eyes:	Small black bead chain or small black mono eyes

Hex Wiggle (Matt Supinksi)

Rear hook:	Daiichi 220, No. 8
Thread:	Tan 6/0
Tail:	Sand grizzly marabou tips
Body:	Rest of grizzly marabou, palmered and clipped
Connector:	3X mono to allow enough flex to wiggle
Front hook:	Daiichi 510, No. 8
Body:	Sand grizzly marabou
Wingcase:	Brown vinyl cut in V shape
Eyes:	Black mono
Head:	Tan ostrich herl

Wiggle Flashback Stone (Matt Supinski)

Rear hook:	Fine-wire nymph hook
Thread:	Black 6/0
Tail:	Black goose biots
Body:	Ultra black Larva Lace
Front hook:	Daiichi 120 #12
Body:	Peacock Ice Dub
Wingcase:	Pearl Flashabou
Legs:	Black goose biots

Spey Flies

Rabbit Strip Spey (Jerry Darkes)

Hook:	Daiichi Alec Jackson Spey, No. 5 or 7
Tail:	Short piece of rabbit strip
Body:	Gudebrod holographic metallic braid ribbed with wire of similar color.
Wing:	Rabbit strip not tied down in back, length to blend in with tail.
Collar:	Wrapped schlappen feather with guinea in front

Valk's Micro Spey (John Valk)

Hook:	Kamasan B220 black or up-eye salmon, No. 6 to 10
Thread:	Black or olive
Tag:	Gold or silver flat tinsel
Rib:	Gold or silver flat tinsel
Body:	UNI-Stretch body floss
Wing:	Two to three layers of spooled Antron
Collar:	Two to three turns of grizzly hen hackle

Valk's Orange Micro Spey

Body:	Orange
Wing:	Orange

Valk's Green Micro Spey

Body:	Green
Wing:	Chartreuse

Schmidt's Articulated Marabou Spey (Ray Schmidt)

Trailer hook:	TMC 105 or equivalent, No. 8
Trailer hook body:	Palmered marabou to match main hook body color
Main body hook:	Diiachi 2151 or equivalent, No. 2
Connector:	20- or 25-pound Maxima leader, with three 4mm plastic beads, red.
Main body:	Lash trailer on the main body and secure with glue
Flare bump:	Red Estaz, three wraps
Body:	Marabou plume palmered up shank to hook eye; four sprigs Flashabou to contrast body color, but at least two red, then palmered Chinese rooster hackle, spade style.

Schmidt's Great Lakes Marabou Spey (Ray Schmidt)

Hook:	Tiemco 7999 or equivalent, No. 2 or 4
Thread:	Hot orange 3/0 or single-strand floss

Body:	Marabou tied in tip first, palmered to eye
Flash:	Five or six pieces of Flashabou
Collar:	Contrasting color of marabou or schlappen

Dinner Mint Muddler (Bob Blumreich)

Hook:	No. 4 to 3/0
Body:	Dark green diamond braid
Wing:	Black goat and black Krystal Flash
Head:	Black deer hair clipped to shape

Halloween Spey (Bob Blumreich)

Hook:	No. 4 to 3/0
Tag:	Fine embossed gold
Tail:	Golden pheasant crest dyed hot orange
Butt:	Hot orange ostrich herl
Body:	Black seal fur
Rib:	Medium oval gold tinsel
Counter-rib:	Fine gold wire
Hackle:	Black marabou
Throat:	Mallard dyed hot orange
Wing:	Hot orange goose

Wild Buckaroo (Joe Penich)

Hook:	Daiichi 2051, No. 3, 5, and 7
Tail:	Pink marabou tips
Body:	Chartreuse silk
Rib:	Flat silver tinsel
Collar:	Black schlappen
Wing:	Yellow goose shoulder

Niagara Morning (Joe Penich)

Hook:	Daiichi 2051, No. 3, 5, and 7
Tag:	Gold oval tinsel and gold silk
Fan:	Golden pheasant crest

Butt:	Peacock herl
Body:	Gold silk
Rib:	Flat silver tinsel
Collar:	Pheasant body feather
Underwing:	Peacock quill
Top wing:	Yellow goose shoulder

Baby Grand (Joe Penich)

Hook:	Daiichi 2051, No. 3, 5, and 7
Tag:	Silver oval tinsel and red silk
Fan:	Golden pheasant crest
Butt:	Black ostrich herl
Rib:	Flat silver tinsel
Collar:	Purple schlappen
Wing:	Black goose shoulder

Purple October (Rick Kustich)

Hook:	Daiichi Alec Jackson heavy-wire Spey hook, No. 3
Thread:	UNI-Thread, purple, 8/0
Tag:	Silver tinsel
Body:	Purple Haze SLF Salmon & Steelhead
Rib:	Silver tinsel
Body hackle:	Purple heron substitute
Front hackle:	Long purple schlappen
Collar:	Jumbo orange guinea
Wing:	Purple arctic fox

White Bunny Spey Tube Fly (Rick Kustich)

Thread:	UNI-Thread, red, 8/0
Body:	Purple Haze SLF Salmon & Steelhead
Wing:	White rabbit strip tied down at rear with a tail of ½ inch or more extending past the end of the tube.
Hackle:	Long white schlappen
Collar:	Jumbo natural guinea

Bad Hair Day Tube Fly (Rick Kustich)

Thread:	UNI-Thread, orange 8/0
Body:	Fall brown SLF Salmon & Steelhead using dubbing loop and picked out full
Hackle:	Two long brown marabou feathers wrapped one after the other
Collar:	Jumbo orange guinea

Hot Bead-Sucking Leech (Rick Kustich)

Hook:	Daiichi Xpoint X472, No. 2
Thread:	UNI-Thread, black 8/0
Bead:	Large orange Hot Bead
Tail:	Black marabou
Body:	Small or medium black chenille
Hackle:	Black saddle tied in at the tip palmered through the body with a few extra turns at the head
Dubbing:	A few turns of black dubbing behind the bead

Waking Dry Flies (John Valk and Joe Penich)

Hook:	Up-eye dry fly salmon hook
Tail:	Calftail or bucktail
Body:	Deer hair clipped to shape
Hackle:	Palmered through deer hair and heavily through wings
Comment:	Color of tail, wings, and hackle to match or compliment body color.

Eggs

Micro-Egg (Bob Linsenman)

Hook:	Tiemco 3761 or Daiichi 1560, No. 8 to 10
Thread:	UNI-Thread 6/0, white or red
Body:	At rear of hook, two turns of fluorescent orange chenille; at front of hook, two turns of chartreuse chenille
Optional:	Doubled pearl Krystal Flash wrapped over hook between "eggs"
Comment:	Try to keep the eggs about 4 to 5mm in diameter.

Single Egg Fly

Hook:	Tiemco 105 or equivalent, No. 4, 6, and 8
Thread:	3/0 waxed monocord to match yarn
Egg:	Glo Bug yarn
Dot:	Micro Glo Bug yarn

Nuke Egg

Hook:	Tiemco 105 or equivalent, No. 6 to 10
Thread:	3/0 UNI-Thread
Egg:	Glo Bug yarn
Collar:	Contrasting color of Glo Bug yarn

Crystal Meth (Jeff Conrad)

Hook:	Heavy egg hook
Thread:	3/0 white, chartreuse, or pink
Tail:	Two short strands of holographic silver tinsel
Cluster body:	Sparkle braid – orange, yellow, chartreuse, etc.
Comment:	Double sparkle braid and tie in a succession of small loops to represent individual eggs in a cluster.

Sucker Spawn

Hook:	Heavy egg hook
Thread:	3/0 white
Cluster body:	Thin strand or "rope" of egg yarn, color of choice
Comment:	Double yarn and tie in a succession of small eggs

Part Two

Adventure is not outside a man;
it is within.

—David Grayson

Lake Superior

The word *superior* is defined as ". . . higher in station, excellence, and importance; of a higher grade, quality, quantity, or amount." Lake Superior is the northernmost of the Great Lakes. It is the largest body of fresh water in the world. Superior is more than 350 miles long, covering 31,280 square miles of surface area. The lake sits at an elevation of 602 feet above sea level and its greatest depth plummets to 1,290 feet. Within 40 miles of its northern shore near Nipigon, Ontario, rivers flow northward to Hudson Bay and the Arctic Ocean. Superior stays cold enough throughout the year to create its own weather patterns. The storms of November, made famous by Gordon Lightfoot's *The Wreck of the Edmund Fitzgerald,* have contributed to a frightening toll of shipwrecks and deaths. This is big, cold water cradled by wild, untamed land. Along its coast there are more wolves than coyotes, more moose than deer, and in some areas more bears than people.

Native fish species like lake trout, smelt, whitefish, anadromous—or "coaster"—brook trout, and herring are now in company with introduced populations of Chinook (king) and coho (silver) salmon, brown trout, Atlantic salmon, and steelhead. Steelhead have adapted well to the rigors of life in Superior's icy waters and to the obstacles to propagation in its rugged tributaries. This big lake is less fertile in terms of food production than the lower lakes. Its fish tend to be lean, streamlined, and hungry. Steelhead of a particular year class will weigh, on average, a bit less than a fish from Lake Michigan or Lake Ontario. They do, however, grow large enough to be classified as true trophies of the species. There are plenty of 10-pound-class steelhead available, and a few reach the middle teens, but I have never heard of one caught that was close to 20 pounds. They more than compensate for their lack of weight with fighting spirit. Pound for pound they are the champs of the Great Lakes. In my experience, Lake Superior steelhead fight as hard as fish weighing up to one-third more from the lower lakes. That is high praise, because steelhead throughout the basin fight with great vigor and tenacity.

Superior's North Shore—from Duluth, Minnesota to Sault Ste. Marie, Ontario—is sparsely populated. Only a few centers of civilization offer the goods and services we expect to be readily available elsewhere. There are only four true cities—Duluth, Thunder Bay, WaWa, and Sault Ste. Marie—along the way, and they are separated by many miles. There are numerous towns and villages, of course, but do not count on seeing a convenience store or gas station every few minutes.

North Shore tributaries are almost exclusively spate rivers, which are dependent on precipitation for their flow volume. September and early October rains swell their currents and trigger upstream movement by salmon and steelhead. A combination of snowmelt and spring rains raises

Scott Earl Smith holds a "coaster," a prized bonus for steelhead anglers on Lake Superior's North Shore.

flows to yearly highs and bring the highest concentrations of steelhead into the rivers. This usually occurs in April but can extend into May. Because weather patterns along Superior's coastline are often local in nature, it is often the case that a river will be too high or colored to fish, but another stream a few miles away will be in perfect condition.

In addition to the streams with individual profiles in this chapter, there are several others along this coast that are worth exploring. This is particularly true if volatile weather is at hand or in the forecast.

Driving north by northeast from Duluth along MN 61, look at the Baptism River at Illogen City just south of the village of Little Marais. This is a lovely, wild spate stream with a decent run of spring steelhead to complement the river's native brook trout. There is a very nice streamside campground a few miles upstream near the village of Finland. About 20 miles farther northeast, the Temperance River flows through a scenic gorge to its mouth at Temperance River State Park. Fishing is often quite good near the mouth of the Temperance. Depending on the time of year, lake trout, steelhead, brook trout, and an occasional brown trout are available here. The Devil Track River enters Lake Superior at Croftville just north of Grand Marais. It twists and turns from Devil Track Lake in a southeasterly flow for several miles through rugged country. Steelhead runs in this stream have fluctuated widely the past several years, but it is well worth exploring for a few hours during the spring when water levels start to drop and clear.

The Canadian border is at Grand Portage, and Thunder Bay is a short drive to the north. The McIntyre River runs directly through the city of Thunder Bay. It is a surprisingly good spring steelhead stream for a short window of time near the end of April. It is a small river with nice runs and riffles, very good pocket water, chutes, and a few slower pools. The "Mac" flows alongside a golf course near the Thunder Bay Police Department's headquarters. I fished this stretch a few years ago with off-duty officers Scott Smith and Bruce Miller. We caught several steelhead on egg and nymph patterns in just a few hours.

The McKenzie River is only about 20 miles farther north along Trans-Canada Highway 17. This river has a decent fall run and a good spring run that lasts into May. You can see the river's mouth and Lake Superior from the highway bridge and the view of the river with its falls, rapids, and chutes is spectacular.

A bit farther north toward the villages of Red Rock and Nipigon, the Black Sturgeon River enters Lake Superior at Black Bay. I have not fished the Black Sturgeon, but Scott Smith rates it highly for large steelhead during the fall. The spring run also features larger than average steelhead for Superior's North Shore, but the river often runs high and cloudy at this time of year, making fly fishing difficult at best and sometimes dangerous.

From WaWa south to Sault Ste. Marie, several fine steelhead rivers are easily reached from Highway 17. The Old Woman River is a short drive south from WaWa and the Michipicoten River at the edge of Lake Superior Provincial Park. It has a good spring run of steelhead and excellent "flats" fishing opportunities at it mouth. A few miles farther to the south the world-famous Agawa pictographs are within a short walk from the highway. These pictographs are painted on a rock wall on Lake Superior, and some are believed to be more than 500 years old. There are 117 pictographs at Agawa Rock. Some depict records of vision quests, some document Ojibwa religious matters, and some acknowledge the assistance of spirits in Ojibwa victories over Iroquois raiders. My favorite panel features Michipeshu (half lynx, half lizard) and the snakes. Take a few minutes to visit this site.

Farther south, the Pancake River is a favorite of local steelhead fly anglers. It is a small, intimate stream but supports a sizable run of fish during late April and May. Continuing south toward Sault Ste. Marie, the large Batchawana, Chippewa, and Goulais Rivers also host strong spring steelhead runs as well as fall migrations of Pacific salmon.

Lake Superior's South Shore is less rugged and remote, but still wild enough for most tastes. Most of the rivers are freestone in nature but many receive the added benefit of spring water, which levels flows and moderates temperature extremes. They are typically less volatile and richer in aquatic insect life than North Shore streams.

Traveling eastward from Superior, Wisconsin on US 2, you'll find countless creeks pushing north to Lake Superior; most of them host steelhead. Near the intersection of US 2 with WI 53, the Amnicon River crosses US 2 and flows north through Amnicon Falls State Park. This small river gets a healthy spring run and a reasonable number of fall steelhead, along with fall-spawning brown trout and Pacific salmon. Several county roads between the park and Lake Superior provide bridge access.

The Poplar River is another small stream with good runs of fish in both spring and fall. The best water is north (downstream) from the village of Poplar, with some very nice holding water between Moonshine Road and WI 13.

The lower Iron River between Orienta Falls and WI 13 attracts some large steelhead as well as huge brown trout in September and October, and the lower White River east of Ashland has large steelhead but is a bit problematic to approach and fish.

The Montreal River forms the boundary between Wisconsin and Michigan. Towns and roads are in short supply in this area. Many rivers hold steelhead, but the available river flow is extremely short. Some rivers have only a few yards of run between a waterfall and Lake Superior. Two examples of this circumstance are the Black and Presque Isle Rivers near Porcupine Mountains Wilderness State Park. These are big enough rivers to excite any angler. They have excellent stream trout and smallmouth bass fishing, but only very short stretches of water are available to steelhead. Scenic waterfalls are the upstream barriers to migration. Still, the mouths of these two rivers often produce superb fly fishing for steelhead, brown trout, salmon, and coaster brook trout.

East of the town of Ontonagon, Lake Shore Road runs along and crosses the Firesteel River. This stream has a fair-sized spring run. Several streams on both sides of the Keeweenaw Peninsula host sizable fall and spring runs of steelhead, but many of these are nursery streams for coasters. The State of Michigan is applying great effort at restoring these beautiful, rare fish, so these creeks and rivers are best left unmolested.

North and east of Munising, Pictured Rocks National Lakeshore dominates tourist interest, but the Hurricane River with its strong runs of steelhead and its beautiful lakeside campground is worth a lengthy side trip. Kingston Lake Road follows tight to the pounding surf of Lake Superior and winds to the river's mouth and campsites. A bit farther east, the Blind Sucker River below Blind Sucker Flooding presents similar opportunities, good steelhead runs, scenic campgrounds, and spectacular lake views.

Brule River

There are countless creeks flowing northward through the boreal forests and small, hardscrabble farms of northern Wisconsin to Lake Superior. Nearly all of them, at various times of the year, have steelhead nosing and tasting their currents. The Amnicon, Brule, Poplar, Miller, Iron, White, Raspberry, and more support both fall and spring runs of steelhead. Of these, the Brule is the premier steelhead river.

The proper name of this beautiful river is Bois Brule, now called simply the Brule. Its headwaters are near the village of Solon Springs and its journey northward is through a mix of cedar and balsam lowlands, abandoned or marginal agricultural plots, hardwood ridges and hills, and deep pine and spruce forests. For the most part, it is a near wilderness ecological system. There is no heavy industry, and very few people live in its drainage area. Wildlife is abundant. Deer, otter, mink, eagles, ospreys, ruffed grouse, foxes, coyotes, bears, and the odd wolf and moose ramble the Brule's watershed.

BRULE RIVER

Location: Brule, Wisconsin, US 2, east of Superior, Wisconsin and Duluth, Minnesota.

Airport: Thirty minutes from Duluth three hours from Minneapolis–St. Paul or Milwaukee.

Lodging: Major chains in Duluth and Superior; River House Hotel and Restaurant in Brule, call 715-372-4815.

Fly Shops and Guides: Superior Fly Angler at www.superiorflyangler .com or 715-395-9520.

John Edstrom, 763-493-5800.

Lester River Fly Shop, 218-727-1789.

Anglers All Outfitters, 715-682-5754.

I first fished the Brule in 1971. I had no real idea of where to start beyond a "tip" indicating I should look for steelhead near the bridge on WI 13 just a few miles from Lake Superior. There was a tight curve and deep, log-strewn hole just a few yards downstream and it seemed like a good place to start fishing. After three or four casts resulting in snags and lost flies I moved to the pool's tail-out and had a strike almost immediately. It was a small, chrome male, locally called a "jack," of about 18 inches. He jerked and thrashed and jumped, as I recall. It was a fine introduction indeed. There were no more fish that day, but the Brule had captivated me for life.

Steelhead angling in the Brule starts in September and runs through early December. It picks up again in late March and will fade in May. It is a bit of an anomaly for Great Lakes rivers, but steelhead numbers seem to be considerably higher—and the fishing better—in the fall than in the spring. Salmon make their spawning runs in the fall, and there is a large migration of spawning brown trout from Lake Superior during this period. Steelhead join in the upstream rush and gorge on eggs, baitfish, and nymphs dislodged from the gravel by ardent salmon and brown trout. All these species can and do move upstream for many miles, but the best angling is typically downstream from US 2 at the village of Brule. From there to the mouth, the river's banks run through the Brule River State Forest and access is quite good. However, there are privately owned parcels (though some of these have clearly marked "fishermen's paths") and you should look for posted areas.

From US 2 in Brule, take County Road H north and you will find abundant and easy river access along the side roads heading west. There are a few spots with "launch" areas, but be forewarned that this is a canoe-sized stream not at all suited to driftboats. Its tight turns, overhanging trees, snag-filled corners, and rapids can be dangerous, especially during the brutal cold of winter and even in early spring. Look for the campground between Kauppi Road and Lepannen Road. This is a beautiful, productive part of the river. The run below Koski's Ledges is also productive. Koski's Ledges is a long, rock-filled run with a severe hydraulic drop resulting in a problematic rapids. Steelhead stack up immediately above and below. There used to be public access through private property off Koski Road, but abuses forced the landowner to close this area. Upstream (south) from Koski's Ledges, try both up- and downstream from CR FF.

At WI 13, turn west to the bridge area described earlier. I have always preferred the water downstream from this access. A small road on the east side of the bridge runs north to Wayside Park and below this spot you will find several fine runs and holes that consistently hold steelhead.

Fishing a productive pool on the Brule River.

A bit west of the bridge, Cleveland Road heads north and there is access and excellent fishing to the east at both River View and Harvey Roads. The Brule River Sportsmen's Club has published an extremely helpful angler's map of the river from US 2 to the mouth at Lake Superior. It is available at area tackle shops.

This is a medium-size river by Midwestern standards. It ranges from about 40 to 70 feet in width with depths from a few inches to several feet. For the most part it is not difficult to wade. The bottom is a mix of sand, gravel, rocks, and boulders. There are areas with deep silt and a few with slippery clay. Because the current can be quite strong in spots and because the weather can be extremely cold, caution and felt-soled waders are critical. Many of the more productive runs and holes are bordered by a mix of trees and shrubs on both banks, and the casting avenue is often very confined.

The most commonly used technique on the Brule is the chuck-and-duck, with running lines, long leaders, and sufficient weight to sink flies quickly to the proper depth in short, tight pockets and holding lies. Right-angle nymphing under an indicator is also popular and effective. And, most recently, anglers have rediscovered that Brule steelhead will slam a streamer with enthusiasm. A side benefit to this technique, when employed during the fall, is the potential to hook a trophy brown trout. These big spawners from Lake Superior often exceed 10 pounds, and they love streamers.

There are no special tackle requirements for the Brule. Your favorite gear will work just fine. If I were starting anew, I would buy a rod of 9½ feet for a 7-weight line and a good disk-drag reel with a capacity of 100 yards of backing. Two spools, one loaded with a floating nymph line and one with a sink-tip, allow a quick change from nymph/egg presentations to swinging and stripping streamers.

Effective flies for the Brule are very similar to those used throughout the region. The same egg flies work here, but I suggest carrying some tied with bright reflective material such as Estaz or Crystal Chenille for those days when the water is stained. Standard nymphs tied on stout hooks produce best in darker shades. Hex nymphs and black stonefly patterns have worked well for me. Several years ago I decided, for some lost reason, to add white rubber legs to a standard pattern, the Spring Wiggler (aka the Clark Lynn Nymph). This simple fly has fooled many Brule steelhead over the years.

On average, Lake Superior's steelhead run smaller and leaner than those in the lower lakes. Brule River fish are no exception. The average weight is probably about 5 pounds, but they do get larger and a 10-pound fish is not a rarity. What these creatures lack in size they make up for in wild determination. Brule steelhead are uncommonly strong for their size. What feels like an 8- or 9-pound Lake Michigan or Lake Huron steelhead is often a fish of just 5 or 6 pounds.

My most recent trip to the Brule was in the fall of 2003. I was accompanied by my son Marc, his good friend Aaron, and two Labrador retrievers, Bruno and Kukla. We were hosted and guided by my nephew, Rob Powell. Rob lives in the village of Poplar about 10 minutes from the Brule and he knows it well. We fished the water downstream from WI 13 along Cleveland Road. Specifically, we covered water in the vicinity of the access points at River View and Harvey Roads.

The "boys" (men in their 30s, but boys to me) spread out and fished hard with egg and nymph patterns. They worked riffle water, deep runs, smooth glides, and a few slow-moving, deep, and dark holes. A couple of smaller fish were landed and there were a few strikes without connections. The fishing was slow. I busied myself along the bankside fishermen's paths by fussing with camera and notebooks, looking for scenic photographic angles, and resisting their calls to "Come on and fish this run." To tell the truth, I did not want to fish. I wanted to watch, contemplate, and enjoy the play on its untamed stage, a younger generation of angler-conservationists wading a splendorous river, casting small flies to wild steelhead.

Ontonagon River

If a wilderness setting with little angling pressure is a key factor in how you rate a day on the water, the Ontonagon River in the northwest corner of Michigan's Upper Peninsula should be high on your list. It is truly wild if not completely remote. The Ontonagon supports both fall and spring steelhead from its Lake Superior mouth at the town of Ontonagon, a few miles east of Porcupine Mountains Wilderness State Park, to the upstream barriers of its three main branches.

Most of the best water throughout these separate, long tributaries is found in country as wild today as it was during the northern frontier period more than 100 years ago. And, the mainstream, below the convergence of the East, Middle, and West Branches south of the village of Rockland near MI 45, is hinterland, untamed bush country with limited access in the form of two-track fire roads and trails.

Among the main tourist attractions in this part of Michigan are the abundant, scenic waterfalls. Some are truly spectacular and photogenic;

The Ontonagon River country is nearly as wild and pristine today as it was a century ago.

others are more like a series of steps in a ladderlike rapids. Some are barriers to fish movement while others are passable under most water level conditions. On a cloudy, wet spring day in the late 1970s I decided to look at Irish Rapids Falls on the mainstream a couple of miles from Rockland. My plan was to fish below the falls, thinking that steelhead would congregate and hold there. The water was high and off-color, stained beyond its normal tannic condition by runoff. I must have looked befuddled or at best confused. A voice startled me. "They can't get through this area. All the steelhead are downstream. Besides, they don't eat flies," the man said as I turned. I thanked him for the advice and we talked briefly. In the course of this conversation we both stood facing the river, and three or four steelhead moved easily upstream. Surely he had seen them. I thought briefly about making a comment but decided against it.

The best steelhead fishing is along the Middle Branch and East Branch upstream from the confluence near MI 45, south of Rockland, to Agate Falls at MI 28 (Middle Branch) and near the town of Kenton (East Branch). The Jumbo River enters the East Branch after crossing MI 28 just a couple of miles west of Kenton. This smallish tributary also supports steelhead up to a spot east of Golden Glow Road, where a lovely waterfall forms the upstream barrier.

Although both branches flow through the wilds of the Ottawa National Forest, there are pockets and stretches of private property. Some of these riparian zones are remote hunting camps, more are weekend or summer vacation cottages, and a few are year-round homes. It is sometimes frustrating to find posted property in the middle of the wilderness, but it is a fact of life in the 21st century.

Crowding has never been an issue for me anywhere on the Ontonagon, even during the peak spring run. On one or two occasions I have had to share an area perhaps 100 yards in length with another angler, but this has been a rare occurrence. More typically you will find long stretches of productive water without another person in sight. A few years ago I decided to spend a morning on the water at Sparrow Rapids on the East Branch off Forest US Forest Service Highway 1100 a few miles west of Kenton. This is an easy access point with a long run of lovely pocket water. Steelhead move through Sparrow Rapids in a series of short moves and rest in obvious depressions carved in the rock ledges. There were two pickup trucks in the small parking area, and it seemed the best pocket water would not be available. Surprisingly, the trucks' occupants were not anglers. A middle-aged couple enjoyed a picnic lunch while photographing the rapids and a younger couple strolled, hand-in-hand, deep in whispered conversation, along the rock-strewn shore before leaving. I caught three fish that morning. The first was a lovely brook trout of about 10 inches in length and the third was a larger hen steelhead. I fished about two hours and moved downstream some distance without seeing another angler.

In my opinion, the best steelhead water on the East Branch is from FS 1180 upstream to a bit above Sparrow Rapids on the main flow and in

---

ONTONAGON RIVER

———◉———

Location: Near Ontonagon, Rockland, Bond Falls, Paulding, and Kenton, Michigan.

Airports: Green Bay, Wisconsin, three hours; Sault Ste. Marie, Michigan, three hours; Duluth, Minnesota, three hours; Marquette, Michigan, two hours.

Lodging: Smaller, local tourist motels throughout area.

Fly shops and Guides: Boney Falls Outfitters, www.boneyfallsoutfitters.com or 906-428-4344; John Ramsay (Black River John) at 906-932-4038.

the smaller water of the Jumbo River. This stretch is a never-ending series of tight curves with deep holes and pools, and with alternating slow runs and faster riffles. Access is limited, rugged, and challenging. A four-wheel-drive vehicle is mandatory. Good tires, a full tank of gas, a compass, and a cell phone are all important.

The Middle Branch has a good run of spring fish from mid-April to mid-May. The best water (again, in my opinion) is from the area of Three Rapids Falls to the barrier at Agate Falls at MI 28. A glance at the map shows both gravel and two-track, fire trail access on both sides of the river. Some of these end in private property areas and a few of the remote fire trails are quite rough, but you'll see good numbers of spring-run fish throughout this stretch. On the west side of the river, unimproved trails off Metos Road, Paynesville Road, and the series of roads from Black-smith to Two Mile come close to the water. On the east side, trails running west from N. Agate Road and Gardner Road come within hiking distance. I got lost in this area several years ago and had to spend a cold, miserable night in the woods. Foolishly, I had hiked in without a compass, water, or food. It was a lesson learned the hard way.

The Ontonagon has healthy mayfly, caddis, and stonefly populations along with abundant forage fish and juvenile trout—both immature steelhead and wild brookies. Steelhead eat nymphs as readily as egg patterns, and I have caught a few on small streamers. The river has a definite tannic hue throughout its course, and flies with a bit of flash seem to produce best. Egg flies should be about the size of a little fingernail. Chartreuse and bright orange colors have worked best for me. Black stonefly nymphs on No. 6 hooks, Hare's Ears, green caddis larvae, and Sparrow Nymphs on No. 8 hooks all produce fish. Egg-Sucking Leeches, sculpin imitations, and white Zonkers with silver Mylar bodies bring strikes when the water temperature moderates near 42 degrees F.

For the most part these are great, wild fish without clipped fins or other telltale evidence of a hatchery environment. They are typical Lake Superior steelhead with lean, sleek bodies and an average weight of about 5 pounds. The heaviest Ontonagon steelhead I've seen was a male released by another angler. It would have pushed the 10-pound mark.

A 6-weight rod is heavy enough for the Ontonagon's steelhead. Your favorite trout rod will probably suffice, but a rod of 9½ or even 10 feet in length is better for mending line and will give better leverage while fighting these very strong and acrobatic creatures.

As mentioned earlier, this river can cloud quickly after a rainfall and during the spring snowmelt. When this happens you will have two choices: wait in frustration or explore. Seek out the upper reaches within the water open to fishing (be sure to check the trout regulations carefully), where the water is often clear. There will be native brookies in these areas, as well as steelhead, and the fishing is often excellent. Take your camera to Agate Falls, the falls on the Jumbo River, to Sparrow Rapids, and to the lovely and serene campground on the shore of beautiful Lower Dam Pond. Watch for deer, moose, and otters and listen for the songs of magnificent gray wolves at dusk.

Huron River

The headwaters of the Huron River gurgle and seep from springs deep in the untamed wilderness of northern Baraga County near Mount Arvon, Michigan's highest point of land at 1979 feet. This is the Huron Mountain range of the Copper Country State Forest east of the village of L'Anse on L'Anse Bay and north and west of Marquette. There is no easy way in—most of the roads are gravel or dirt and they are rough. For me, this adds an aura of rugged, frontier charm to the experience of steelheading the Huron. I must add that the roads and trails, particularly those that approach from the south and east, are in the worst shape during the fall and spring; many are impassable during the winter months.

The best route to access the Huron's steelhead water is from the west at L'Anse. Skanee Road runs north from town through the L'Anse Indian Reservation, then east near the base of the Abbaye Peninsula and Huron Bay to the intersection of Portice and Eric Roads. Take Eric Road east to Big Eric's Campground near the confluence of Big Eric's Brook, Black Creek, and the East Branch of the Huron. There is a beautiful stairstep falls, really more of a steep rapids, at the campground. The most productive steelhead water is from this point downstream. If you like wilderness exploration seasoned with high anxiety, try approaching the Huron from the east or south. A cell phone and a full tank of gasoline and good maps are important for this adventure. Do not even consider it if your vehicle is not equipped with four-wheel-drive.

The Huron is a swift stream with a relatively steep hydraulic gradient. It is granite-based with large boulders, ledgerock, gravel, and sand as the dominant bottom features. Pockets of silt appear at the edges of some of the slower pools and deep holes. The Huron runs clear, much more so than the majority of the rivers along Michigan's Lake Superior coastline. The typical "tea-stain" tannic influence is rarely noticeable at depths of less than 2 feet.

Clear, shallow water makes wild steelhead nervous and uncomfortable. They are used to having lots of water over their backs in the big lakes. Under clear skies they will seek out shaded pockets, deep pools, and holes for security. This is especially true on the Huron during low water flows.

The best stretch of steelhead water on the river is from a big curve at the end of Ward Road, north on Portice Road from the campground, to a series of tight bend holes at the old fire trail that runs eastward from Huron Road farther downstream. This stretch features lively pocket water, slower runs, and the deep cover of bend pools and holes so attractive to steelhead. It is only a short distance from the mouth at Lake Superior, and fish can reach this comfortable holding water very quickly. They are often mint bright and eager in this section.

Due to the steep gradient, heavy rainfall or rapid snowmelt can quickly swell the flow and scour the Huron, pushing many fish downstream, some as far as the mouth. This is a small river; under ideal an-

John Ramsay swings a Muddler through a nice pool on the Huron River.

gling conditions it runs about 40 feet wide and ranges in depth from a few inches to 3 or 4 feet, but this can change rapidly. If you are hit by a significant precipitation event, try fishing the surf at the river's mouth at the end of Huron Road.

Huron River steelhead seem to like swinging Spey flies and streamers as much, or more, than drifting eggs and nymphs. And classic Pacific Coast steelhead patterns produce well on this river. Friend and area guide John Ramsay likes the traditional Skunk pattern and a simple orange-over-white bucktail streamer. The Muddler Minnow tied on a stout steelhead hook is another favorite for the Huron.

John feels that the *kerplunk* of split shot hitting the water spooks steelhead when the water is low. He

HURON RIVER

———⬤———

Location: Huron River Mountain Range Between L'Anse and Marquette.

Airport: One and one-half hours from Marquette.

Lodging: Campground at the river, or chain and local motels in L'Anse and Marquette.

Fly shops and Guides: See Ontonogan River.

suggests sink-tip fly lines to swim streamers and wets at the proper depth, and beadhead patterns to sink nymphs. Standard egg fly patterns in a variety of colors and a few basic nymphs—like the Hare's Ear, black stonefly, and Pheasant Tail—will cover your needs for the Huron River.

An 8-pounder is a big fish for the Huron River; 5 pounds is about average, with many slightly smaller. A rod of 9 or 9½ feet for a 6-weight line has plenty of power for these steelhead. I think a rod with powerful butt and fast action is best because it will cast streamers efficiently and, with a quick spool and reel change, will do a reasonable job with nymphing techniques. Bring an extra rod to the Huron in case the river blows out and you want to fish at the mouth. This should be a heavier stick that can deliver a big fly 60 or 70 feet into a wind. Four- to 5-inch Deceivers and Clousers in olive and white, green and white, and blue and white will work if stripped quickly.

When you fish the lower Huron, particularly at the mouth, be aware that you may catch a rare jewel, a coaster brook trout. Michigan's Department of Natural Resources is working hard to restore coaster populations along the state's Lake Superior coastline. The main work is along the Keweenaw Peninsula to the west, but these fish tend to roam and have been caught as far west as Porcupine Mountains State Park, and to the east at the Pictured Rocks area. Please release any brook trout with extreme care. It might well be the brook trout of a lifetime, and you will want a photograph. Take that picture quickly and gently ease your prize back into the water. These rare fish have incalculable value to the lake's ecosystem and to future generations.

Accommodations and conveniences are nonexistent in close proximity to the Huron. If you enjoy camping, Big Eric's is right on the river at a beautiful location complete with the evening song of rushing water. There are no fly shops anywhere nearby. Bring every item of gear you think you might need, then pack some extras.

Two-Hearted River

The proper, official name is Two-Hearted River, but Ernest Hemingway's famous short story created the popular, international notion that this river is the *Big* Two-Hearted. Hemingway fished for brook trout, and the Fox River, a few miles to the west, was his actual haunt. He used the Two-Hearted in the story because the name was more powerful, and he wanted to shelter his favorite brook trout water.

It is a beautiful, wild river and still popular as a productive brook trout stream. Most tourists and anglers visit the stream and surrounding region during the summer. They mostly want to see and touch the magic water of Hemingway's classic and, perhaps, catch a wild brook trout. The weather is fine during summer's long days, and folks can listen to wolves howl at the northern lights over Lake Superior.

Steelhead season is a little different. Both spring and fall have a snap, a sharper edge to life. The weather can be invigorating yet comfortable then change in an hour to a chilling threat. Steelhead angling pressure on the Two-Hearted is light by Great Lakes standards. A few access points—bridges with parking areas, for example—get a few cars and anglers on weekends, but the majority of the river is traffic-free. In the worst case, a short walk up- or downstream from the access point presents pressure-free water. There is no elbow-to-elbow "combat fishing" on the Two-Hearted.

In addition to weather patterns at this latitude and proximity to Lake Superior, there is another factor, a perception, that seems to affect steelhead angling pressure. This is bear country. Michigan bears are black and timid (for the most part) and present little threat to humans with an IQ above room temperature. Still, I am continually amazed by the reluctance and grave concern expressed by many urbanized humans to fish in any proximity to bears. The bears are not a problem, but bear hunters do work the area heavily. They use dogs in the fall and hunt over bait piles in the spring. The dogs can be noisy. Big deal.

Steelhead gather at the mouth and begin to enter the river in August, when Pacific salmon and lake-dwelling brown trout begin their spawning migrations. The fall run gathers momentum in September and October and peaks around mid-November. After December 1, the weather is usually too rough and the water too cold for decent fly fishing. The spring run builds from mid-March through April and early May. The best fishing is usually from the last two weeks in April through, roughly, May 15.

Steelhead use all of the main river and portions of its major tributaries. Dawson Creek and the North, West, South, and East Branches of the Two-Hearted receive fair numbers of steelhead, especially during the spring run, but tight confines with dense foliage and innumerable snags and logjams make fly fishing problematic in the extreme.

> ## TWO-HEARTED RIVER
>
> ———●———
>
> **Location:** Newberry north on MI 37 from MI 123 to Lake Superior.
>
> **Airport:** One and one-half hours from Sault Ste. Marie, two hours from Marquette, two hours from Traverse City, 90 minutes from Petoskey.
>
> **Lodging:** Smaller chains in Newberry, local tourist motels, campgrounds on the river.
>
> **Fly shops and Guides:** No local fly shops.

The best steelhead water is from the access off CR 418, near the confluence of the North Branch and South Branch, to the mouth. Moving downstream toward Lake Superior, you will find productive runs and pools near the High Bridge Campground, at the Two-Hearted River Campground, the Red and Green Bridge, and along the Coast Guard Road that parallels Lake Superior's shoreline to the mouth. Throughout this stretch the Two-Hearted twists and turns tightly; its bottom structure is a mix of pure sand, silt, rocks, and gravel. The water is clean, nearly pure, and rich in insect life, forage fish, and brook trout. The banks are rarely open, usually clogged with overhanging spruce, balsam, and cedar trees. The river's width can run to 60 feet and more, but roll casting and chuck-and-duck presentations are often a necessity. The water carries the tannic stain common to many Lake Superior tributaries. Under poor light conditions, this stain can cause one to misjudge depth. Be especially cautious at sharp bends where light-colored sand, rocks, or gravel blend to darker silt or mud.

There are two areas on the Two-Hearted that I favor above all others due to a mix of their wild natures and past successes. The first is small water, the run along CR 418 upstream from High Bridge to a point a few hundred yards above the confluence of the North Branch and the West Branch. This is a tangled, north country jungle and the casting is neither pure nor easy, but the fish are there in good numbers and they receive little pressure.

A few years ago I drove upstream along CR 418, crossed a very rickety wooden bridge, and parked at a small clear space off the narrow road. I fished upstream from the old bridge through tangles that would give a squirrel claustrophobia. I remember catching two fair-sized steelhead in about 30 minutes before the tangles and snags took too many flies. My next move was downstream from the bridge where the river channel seemed a bit wider and the banks looked more open for casting. I spent more time in that section and managed to land a fine, representative hen of 5 pounds and a gorgeous brook trout that crowded 14 inches.

My second favorite spot is really a run of the river rather than a specific location. The river flows along the south side of Coast Guard Road from the Red and Green Bridge Campground to a point near the mouth below the confluence with the East Branch. This is an intriguing part of the river that shelters good numbers of both fall and spring steelhead. There are straight riffles, smooth glides, quiet tail-outs, and deep, corner holes with crisscrossed trees and stumps for cover.

In my opinion the best part of this section is from the East Branch junction to a point a couple of hundred yards above the lake. For whatever unfathomable reason, both fall and spring steelhead, both ascending and fallback fish, seem to stage in the deeper pools and bend holes in this area. Most important, they are receptive to flies. The bright, ascending fish seem partial to white streamers, Woolly Buggers, and Mysis shrimp patterns. The drop-back (descending) fish will eat nearly anything. And there is always the chance for a trophy brook trout as a bonus.

Two-Hearted River steelhead average close to 6 pounds and a few reach or exceed 10 pounds. A 6-weight rod is plenty strong enough if you have experience fighting strong fish, but a 7-weight is better when it is necessary (often) to muscle a steelhead away from snags.

Carry an assortment of egg patterns ranging from bright and large— chartreuse, bright pink, bright orange, and a half inch in diameter—to small and pale. Simple nymphs on stout hooks are very good. Do not tie or buy intricate or expensive flies for this river. You will lose too many in the logs. I like black stonefly, Sparrow, Hare's Ear, and Wiggler patterns. A white Mysis shrimp nymph is a good alternative close to the lake.

The best holding water often presents only a short drift opportunity. You need to get the fly down quickly and repeatedly. For this reason additional weight is required. Lead-free split shot will do the job. Place the shot on a short dropper about 18 inches above the fly.

The Two-Hearted flows through boreal forestland, wild and untamed. The few times I've fished it without carrying a camera have been occasions of regret. Expect to see mink, foxes, deer, eagles, ruffed grouse, perhaps a coyote or moose. And there are wildflowers and lichens, gnarled cedar trunks painted with moss, and sweeping curves and dancing riffle water made simultaneously beguiling and eerie by fog and mist.

The town of Newberry is just a few miles south of the river, so you won't have to overnight in the wilderness unless you want to. If the weather is decent, try camping at the mouth of the river. Watch the star-filled sky for comets, and listen to the pounding surf of the largest lake on the planet.

Knife River

The steelhead fishery, both offshore and in-stream, of the Knife River has had its ups and downs through the years. It is a medium-size stream when compared to other rivers along Minnesota's Lake Superior coastline, but it contains more than half of the available spawning gravel of all these rivers. Steelhead can ascend the Knife and move for miles without encountering a waterfall barrier. Historically, the Knife has had, by far, the best fly fishing for steelhead in Minnesota waters. It is just a few minutes' drive from Duluth and Superior and less than three hours from Minneapolis–St. Paul. When the "run is on" the Knife typically receives a fair amount of angling pressure.

For several years I lived in the Twin Cities and many spring steelhead trips were decided by a flip of a coin. Heads meant we went to the Knife, tails sent us to the Brule in Wisconsin. Steelhead fever, an especially wicked form of spring fever, can come early in Minnesota. Any modest warming trend tends to warp the mind to the point where logic fails and one forgets to calculate the significant differences in temperature and wind between Minneapolis and the Duluth area.

Picture this. It is early April and relatively balmy in the Twin Cities at about 45 degrees. The forecast calls for two more days of similar weather.

Two similarly infected friends and I decide we can't take it anymore; we must drive to the Knife. We leave at 4 AM and reach the Knife near the mouth in three hours. It's really cold and the wind is blowing as we don waders, jackets, gloves, and ski masks. Shelf ice, driven by offshore winds, is packed in tiers along the beach for as far as we can see. In some places it is several feet high.

KNIFE RIVER

Location: Knife River, MN 61, northeast from Duluth.

Airport: Twenty minutes from Duluth, three hours from Minneapolis–St. Paul.

Lodging: Major chains in Duluth and Superior, Wisconsin.

Fly shops and Guides: Lester River Fly Shop, 218-727-1789; Superior Fly Angler, (715) 395-9520; John Edstrom, 763-493-5800.

At this point, we are committed. Driven by the fever and supercharged with quarts of coffee, we decide to fish the pounding surf for awhile before heading upstream. We clamber over the ice slipping and sliding to the more sure footing of the big lake. One of my friends caught a decent fish of about 20 inches after just a few casts. It ate a large smelt pattern. Adrenaline flowed, but not for long. As I recall, we were breaking ice out of our fly rod guides about every second cast. The wind was from the south, directly into our faces. That wind was no doubt warmer in Minneapolis. Here it picked up speed across the lake and slammed us with a severe chill. Someone suggested we fish upriver. There was no dissent.

We moved upstream a short distance from the mouth, just far enough to find some shelter from the freezing wind but close enough to Superior, we hoped, to hold a few early arriving steelhead. Luck was with us. We each managed to hook a couple of fish and land one. Mine was the smallest, a feisty little male of about 18 inches. The biggest steelhead that day was a hen of about 24 inches. She was a silver rocket that jumped several times despite the frigid water temperature. As she swam away we were all shivering. "I can't take any more of this fun. Let's quit and get something to eat," I said. Again, there was no dissent. Heading back to Duluth we passed a bank's flashing sign that said the temperature was 29 degrees and the wind was gusting to 30 mph. Three hours later, back in Minneapolis, the temperature was 47. Even in late summer when the air temperature is 90 in the Twin Cities it can be below 60 in Duluth. That is something to consider.

The Knife River steelhead run dipped in numbers of returning fish during the 1990s. The reasons are not completely clear. There has been a huge increase in trolling throughout the western end of the lake. These boats are not necessarily targeting steelhead, but certainly the incidental catch has increased significantly. Another factor may be an adjustment in the forage base at this end of the lake with a decrease in smelt and a corresponding increase in herring. Additionally, the Kamloops strain of rainbow trout has been stocked heavily for years in the area. The Kamloops is a fine fish, but not well adapted to the rigors of spawning in wild, spate river conditions. Although Kamloops provide a successful fishery near the mouth of the Knife, there is a dark concern that they may be interbreeding with native, wild steelhead and producing a less active and healthy fish. The Kamloops and their hybrid offspring are not likely to be able to reach the prime spawning habitat of the upper river and its small tributaries.

Steelhead runs in the Knife are now on the upswing thanks to the concerted efforts of angling groups in cooperation with Minnesota's Department of Natural Resources. Several steps have been taken to restore steelhead populations in this beautiful river to their previous levels, with positive results. A fish-counting weir has been installed to monitor the size of the run along with a smolt trap to measure spawning success and smolt survival. Some upstream gravel reaches have been closed to angling to protect steelhead when they are spawning and especially vulnerable. Special, protective regulations are now in force. All wild fish must be released and fin-clipped, hatchery steelhead must be released if they are less than 28 inches in length. The Knife, like most North Shore Superior tributaries, is a spate river, highly susceptible to wild fluctuations in flow. Drought and warm weather have an adverse effect on natural reproduction and survival but the past few years have shown an improvement in these factors. The runs are definitely rebuilding with an emphasis on the natural reproduction of wild steelhead. The numbers of repeat spawners are growing each year and this bodes well for the future.

The Knife has good aquatic insect diversity among mayfly, caddis, and stonefly species. Hare's Ears, Pheasant Tails, dark stonefly patterns, and a few olive or green caddis cover the basic requirements. And I have always liked olive-bodied Sparrow nymphs and Egg-Sucking Leeches when fishing the Knife. Simple Glo Bug egg patterns have produced fish for me. The egg should be about a half inch in diameter and have a dot of contrasting color for best results. Oregon cheese with a bright orange dot, chartreuse with a pink dot, pink with a chartreuse dot, and orange with a yellow dot are good choices. I have not fished streamers or Spey patterns within the river proper but suspect they would work quite well. My guess is that patterns tied to represent smelt or herring would work best in the lower river, while sculpin and juvenile trout patterns would be best farther upstream.

Knife River steelhead average about 5 pounds but some reach 10 pounds and more. These brutes can be an exciting handful in fast water. A 7-weight rod is a good choice.

If the river is "blown out" from spring runoff or heavy rain, try fishing the surf at the mouth with a sink-tip line and large smelt patterns or olive and white Deceivers. Another option is to drive northeast on MN 61 and try near the mouths of several smaller streams that cross the highway.

Jackpine River

The drive between Thunder Bay and Sault Ste. Marie, Ontario along the Trans-Canada Highway is one of North America's most spectacular scenic routes. The highway cuts through forested hills, slides along the high edges of Superior's lakeside cliffs, and winds past natural and man-made cuts through ancient rock dripping with springs and rivulets. Waterfalls, both tiny and large, plunge ever downward to Superior. Road signs in French and English caution the driver to beware of both falling rock and moose along the roadside.

The road is a convenience for humans cut through a wild world far removed from civilization. The Trans-Canada Highway provides a vital link between the villages, towns, and cities of northern Ontario. It is the only way to get from here to there without booking passage on the railroad or an airline.

The view to the south is the most stunning. As the road follows the land contours, a magnificent panorama of Lake Superior comes into view repeatedly. The water is clear, showing rock over sand beaches then darkening to a deep, brilliant blue. Islands stud the seascape and crashing waves topped with foam slam the beaches. If it were not for the distinctive trees—conifers rather than palms—you might think you were gazing at the crystalline flats of the Bahamas. More reminders come when you stop the car to stretch and take a photo. The wind has a bite, and tracks along the roadside indicate moose and timber wolf.

Out there to the south, in the churning blue of Lake Superior, steelhead thrive. They are a special breed within a special breed. First introduced to Superior in the late 1880s, *mykiss* populations have evolved over the years to a point that each separate drainage now hosts wild popula-

PHOTO BY SCOTT EARL SMITH

A prime male steelhead from the Jackpine River.

tions genetically perfected to individual rivers. There is no stocking program here—no fertilized eggs, no fry, no smolts. Natural reproduction, true survival of the fittest, dictates which fish ascends a specific river. Each stream is unique.

The town of Nipigon sits at the top of the lake, its northernmost point, on the Trans-Canada Highway, about 70 miles from Thunder Bay. The Jackpine is a short drive east of Nipigon. The river crosses under the highway in a hard, fast riffle. The river looks difficult to wade and to fish. It is not a venue for the faint of heart or the infirm. Depending on water height and volume, the Jackpine varies greatly in width and depth. It is, like almost all streams on the North Shore, a true spate river with flows dictated by snowmelt and rain. It is mostly rocky with pockets and glides that attract fish to rest in calmer water.

The first time I fished the Jackpine we trudged carefully upstream from the highway to a large sweeping bend at the base of a high and barren rocky slope. My friend and guide, Scott Smith, said, "We'll fish this pool for awhile." I looked around and did not see anything I would normally classify as a pool. All I saw was fast current, heavy riffle water dropping fast through the fall of land and buffeting against the boulder-strewn, dark gray hillside.

"This is a *pool?*"

"Yes. On the Jackpine, this is a pool," he answered.

That hillside is now gone, torn away and smashed by a torrential flood a few years ago. Because of the relatively precipitous drop in altitude through a narrow cut, the Jackpine is a volatile waterway. Heavy rains combined with spring's snow runoff push heavy volumes of water through a tight funnel. The resulting hydraulic chaos changes the river and adjusts and moves its "pool," riffle, run, glide configuration yearly. Under extreme conditions, massive events like the collapse of that high hill and the rapid removal of roads and bridges, can and do take place.

> ## JACKPINE RIVER
>
> ———————●———————
>
> **Location:** Nipigon, Ontario, Hwy 17, one hour northeast from Thunder Bay.
>
> **Airport:** One hour from Thunder Bay.
>
> **Lodging:** Major chains in Thunder Bay; Pinecrest Motel in Nipigon, 807-887-2813.
>
> **Fly shops and Guides:** River's Edge Fly Shop, Thunder Bay, www.riversedgeflyshop.com or 807-983-2484.

Each steelhead season on the Jackpine is a new adventure involving exploratory hikes. Some people use mountain bikes to reach favorite stretches or to look for new spots, but this can be dangerous and there are no paramedics in close attendance. Consider this. You are only a few kilometers from Lake Superior, a few more from the town of Nipigon, but you are also only a very few miles from the height of land that separates the continental divide where rivers flow north to Hudson Bay and the Arctic Ocean. There are a lot more bears, wolves, moose, and eagles here than people. On balance, that's a good thing.

Steelhead in the Jackpine are perfect creatures that adapted over the last 100-plus years to its raw, demanding characteristics. These steelhead are lean and hard and have great strength and speed. Their average size is larger now than in the recent past. This is a direct benefit of kill limits reduced to one fish per day. This reduced creel limit has pushed "meat hunters" to other water, and survival of spawning fish has blossomed. Now, fish are being recorded and aged by scale samples that are on their fourth or fifth spawning migration. Jackpine River steelhead in the 30-inch range are now being caught—and released—regularly. They are typically near 10 pounds in weight. Combine a truly wild fish of this size with rapid current and you can imagine uncontrollable mayhem mixed with an overdose of adrenaline. It is special, to say the least.

Long-held traditions die hard, but they do fade over time. Up until most recent years fly anglers used egg flies, usually large and bright, almost exclusively. Scott Smith, along with Bill Boote and Bruce Miller (all

Fishing a Spey rod on the Jackpine.

officers of the Thunder Bay, Ontario Police Department) began fishing nymph patterns long before most other North Shore anglers. Scott developed some very productive nymphs specifically for the Jackpine and other area streams. Scott's Nympho and Spring Stone patterns are effective throughout the basin but especially so in the Jackpine. Include Hare's Ears, Pheasant Tails, and a few caddis larvae in green and cream in your nymph box. The best egg flies for this river are those with some light-gathering flash. The Cactus Fly pattern in orange and white, orange and yellow, and pink and white is one of the best. If the water is low and clear, try double Micro-Eggs in orange or orange and chartreuse.

Best timing for the Jackpine is after the spring runoff has peaked and water levels begin to drop. This usually takes place in mid-April. Fly fishing for steelhead peaks at this point and continues to be very good through about mid-May. There is a fall run of steelhead but the numbers of fish are significantly lower. Water levels are typically at their lowest at this time of year and a spate of rain is usually required to swell the river and motivate fish to move upstream During the fall period a wide variety of gamefish ascend the Jackpine. Lake trout, silver and pink salmon, coaster brook trout, and steelhead make the run. You might catch any or all of these on a day in September. Be especially diligent in checking the regulations, as they dictate open and closed sections and specific rules for coaster brookies.

Coaster brook trout are treasured jewels in Ontario's North Shore crown; they are carefully guarded. The Lake Superior shoreline in the general area of Nipigon is the last redoubt with the only remaining self-propagating population of this most beautiful and guileless gamefish. Any violation of the fishing regulations affecting coaster brook trout can be extremely expensive.

This rugged river presents a unique set of challenges to the fly angler that are different from those faced in more civilized parts of the Great Lakes. The Jackpine is not close to Chicago, Detroit, or Toronto. It demands a healthy body and open mind. It is always wild and a little scary. I am 62 years old now. My knees creak and my ankles hurt in cold weather. I am slower and weaker than I used to be and have to stop more often to rest on uphill jaunts. But I will fish the Jackpine again. I simply must. I will drive to Sault Ste. Marie, then westward on the Trans-Canada to Nipigon. There I'll meet Scott and maybe Bill and Bruce. We'll hike and cast to fish that are 40 generations removed from any hatchery influence, big wild fish in a raw, wild land. Nothing could be more exciting.

Cypress River

This is one of the prettiest steelhead streams in the region, maybe in all of North America. The first view of the Cypress comes at the bridge on the Trans-Canada Highway a few miles east of the Jackpine River, about 40 minutes' drive from the town of Nipigon. As it passes under the bridge, the tannic color shows dark at mid-flow and clears to a weak tea shade at the edges. Lake Superior is only a few hundred yards farther downstream.

The Cypress is a mountain-fall, spate river that features a welcoming pool, run, riffle combination studded with ideal pocket water. It is a small stream, wild and inspiring yet delicate and highly susceptible to the whims of capricious nature. The spring runoff can scour and shift pools, deep bend holes, and favored runs from year to year. Occasionally, the annual spring snowmelt combines with enough early rainfall to produce dramatic, river-altering events such as quickly removing the bridge and a good-sized section of the highway, gathering and slamming trees together in a massive, river-blocking timber dam, or simply removing a favorite pool. This stream is as dynamic as it is lovely.

Although steelhead are available in the relatively short run between the highway bridge and the mouth at Lake Superior, the best fly fishing by far is found between the highway and a natural barrier, a stunning waterfall about 3 miles upstream. In this section the Cypress flows through a channel largely bottomed with a mix of coarse sand, gravel, and rocks. It twists and turns and forms deep, sheltering holes and pools where steelhead rest. The river also presents long straight riffles and runs over gravel, rocks, and boulders. Steelhead pause and hold in these areas as well. They tuck into quiet hydraulic zones in the pockets near boulders to both rest and feed.

I first saw the Cypress in the early 1990s. Steve Nevala and I made the drive from Michigan and pulled into Gurney-by-the Sea, at the mouth of the Cypress on Lake Superior, where we met our guide and host, Scott Smith, for the first time. We were a little tired after the long drive and were inclined to rest a bit, stretch our legs, and relax. Scott, however, was anxious to get going. Shortly after we had shaken hands and unloaded our car he pulled his waders on and grabbed his fly rod.

"Let's go, men. We have a fresh run of fish in the upper river. We can catch some before it gets dark," he said. Steve and I exchanged weary glances then smiled, pulled on our waders, and grabbed our gear.

We made an upstream hike. Upstream means uphill. We followed Scott along a winding forest trail that paralleled the river on the east bank. We hiked through low swales dominated by moss-covered logs, spring seeps, balsam, cedar, and tamarack. We flushed a ruffed grouse and saw several different sets of bear tracks. Realizing we were a little tired from the drive and obviously years older, Scott stopped to allow us to rest at the midpoint of a steep climb.

CYPRESS RIVER

See Jackpine River.

"How much farther, Scott?" I asked.

"We're almost there. We'll be about three kilometers above the highway when we start fishing. There's a fine run that dumps into a great pool there and you two can sample two different kinds of water, then we'll hike a bit farther upstream to the barrier and fish the pool at the base of the falls."

We hiked onward a few hundred yards and came to the top of a very high, open hill cut by a power line. A steep path ran downhill to our left, and we followed Scott into a rugged valley dense with trees and undergrowth. Suddenly the river was at our feet. It flowed from right to left through a straight, lively riffle and slowed and deepened into a beautiful, wide, and dark pool.

Scott helped us select flies and examined our leaders. He directed Steve to the riffle and told me to fish the head of the pool where the current fell off a ledge and spread into the pool. He had tied an egg fly to my leader as a dropper with a Spring Stonefly nymph as the point fly. Steve was similarly equipped. Low, bankside willows made backcasts a little tricky, and my excitement didn't help. I put the first two or three into the bushes. Scott was helping me untangle a mess when we heard Steve yelp. "Fish on!"

Steve came hustling down the bank, rod high and severely bent. His steelhead stopped in the pool for a moment, then made several frenetic dashes and leaped. By the angle of Steve's rod I had guessed he was into a fish of about 8 pounds, but this steelhead, a bright male, was actually close to 5 pounds. It would not give up and it required careful, patient resuscitation before it was fully recovered and charged out of Steve's grip.

That was the first of many on that initial trip to the Cypress. These steelhead ran from about 4 to 6 pounds on average. All were slender, bright silver, and diamond hard. They fought with amazing strength, determination, and speed. All were pure, wild fish, perfectly positioned genetically for the survival of their progeny in the Cypress River.

I have subsequently made several return visits to this jewel of a stream. I have fished the Cypress from the waterfall that drops off a precipitous clifflike ridge all the way to the mouth at the big lake in both fall and spring seasons. Steelhead seem to congregate and hold best in two different water types. The more productive (for me) of these two are the pools, both large and small, found at curves and bends in the river. The second water type to look for is a riffle or run of moderate depth dotted with large rocks and boulders that break or cushion the current. This provides excellent, classic pocket-water nymphing opportunities. Extra weight is required to sink the fly (or flies) to depth very quickly because the soft pockets, the quiet-water fishing zones, are usually short in length.

Probably the best approach for a day on the Cypress is to plan a *full* day and hike upstream to the falls, then fish back downstream to the highway on the lake. It is indeed a full day's outing, and you will be tired when you reach its end. But, you will likely be very pleased.

In recent years, both the size of the run and the average size of individual fish have grown significantly. More and bigger steelhead—that's good news. The main contributing factor to this recent upsurge is probably the recent implementation of a one-fish-per-day limit. Anglers who are interested in slabs of dead fish simply go elsewhere. This reduces overall angling pressure and the anglers who do come are more inclined to release their trophies unharmed. Some real brutes, up to 10 pounds

PHOTO BY SCOTT EARL SMITH

The falls on the Cypress River.

and even larger, are now being caught in the Cypress. A Lake Superior steelhead of this size is equivalent, both in trophy status and raw fighting power, to a fish in the mid-teens from one of the lower lakes. There is no doubt in my mind that a steelhead from Superior's North Shore tributaries gives the wildest and most exciting battle of any gamefish in North America. In my experience no other comes close. The closest approximation is the frenzy of baby tarpon in shallow water. That is saying a lot, and I still think these steelhead are better.

The best timing for the Cypress River is the same as for other tributaries close by. The spring run peaks between April 15 and May 15, and a few drop-back fish can be taken as late as early June in most years. The fall run is not as large in terms of numbers of fish but it is complemented by pink and silver salmon, lake trout, and beautiful coaster brookies. Pink salmon runs are heaviest in odd-numbered years. They seem to be everywhere, but are most noticeable at the tail-outs of pools. Any cast with any fly to almost any decent spot on the Cypress from late August through September can produce a surprise. Your prize may be a 6-pound laker, a 2-pound pink, a 7-pound silver, a 5-pound steelhead, or a 5-pound brook trout. Be aware that the Cypress is a nursery stream of great importance to all these species and is particularly critical for these last surviving remnants of coasters. Be precise in your knowledge of the regulations. If you catch a coaster, take one photo and release it quickly and unharmed, or be prepared to spend two days in the electric chair!

You won't need a heavy rod for the Cypress—a 7-weight is plenty, but you will want a really good reel with a smooth drag. I suggest carrying an extra spool or two. It's nice to have a shooting line setup to fish the short pocket water effectively with added weight and nymph or egg patterns. A sink-tip line is a nice change of pace and helps to swing streamers through deep pools. The rocks can be slippery and the current quite strong in a few places where you will want to cross the stream. Be sure your waders have felt soles. In the spring, when flows are highest, I have found a wading staff to be very comforting. Bring water, something to eat, and a camera with a good lens and professional-quality color film. The river and its tight valley are breathtakingly beautiful, and you might see a secretive wild critter. A few Septembers ago I walked downstream around a blind corner to fish a pool's tail-out. When I passed some bushes that obstructed my view I saw an adult bald eagle standing on the gravel ripping a salmon carcass. We watched each other for several minutes before the bird tired of me and lifted skyward. We were about 15 feet apart. Did I have a camera? Of course not.

The most consistently productive nymph pattern for the Cypress is probably Scott's Spring Stone. In addition to dark stoneflies, carry a few Hare's Ears, Scott's Nympho pattern, and some Sparrow nymphs. The Cactus Fly is one of the best egg patterns for this river. Be sure to carry several different color combinations. Various other egg flies also produce steelhead. Bring a few Nuke egg patterns and some Micro-Eggs for low and clear water conditions. Small to medium-size streamers also work well on the Cypress. I have caught steelhead and coasters on a variety of sculpin patterns, but the traditional old-style Muddler, as first tied by Don Gapen, is probably the best. Woolly Buggers in black and brown, and Egg-Sucking Leeches with either an orange or chartreuse egg are very good.

The Cypress is a living gem, as wild as its steelhead and rare like its coasters. Tread lightly and leave no trace.

Gravel River

This is another lovely, productive stream on Ontario's Lake Superior coastline. It is only a short drive east, toward Terrace Bay, from the Cypress River. Like the Cypress and Jackpine, the Gravel receives a significant spring run of steelhead and good numbers of silver and pink salmon, coaster brook trout, and steelhead during the fall.

Steelhead in the Gravel are hardened by the same forge as those that run the nearby rivers. They are pure and wild thanks to the diligent care of angler groups and the measurable, positive impact of reduced creel limits. They feed voraciously on smelt and other prey in Superior, cruising the depths of Thunder Bay, Black Bay, Nipigon Bay, around the rugged shoreline of massive St. Ignace Island, and along the coastal ridge lines from Rossport to Terrace Bay. This coastline is variously rugged and precipitous as well as gentle and smooth. Everywhere it teems with life conditioned to a harsh environment.

Steelhead, coasters, Pacific salmon, and lake trout will often hunt very close to shore in this area. Fly fishing the big water can be productive from April through the summer months and well into October. It is a form of flats fishing, more often practiced in the Florida Keys or Bahamas. The gamefish on these coldwater flats seem to gather in small packs of three to five of a species. They cruise slowly along natural depressions in depths from 2 to 4 feet and are usually visible despite their natural camouflage. I have observed small groups of lake trout followed at a short distance by a pod of steelhead, small packs of steelhead shadowed by one or two coasters, and larger groups of either pink or silver salmon (the silvers are very hard to distinguish from steelhead on the flats, so I'm not really sure on this one) tailed by steelhead and/or brook trout.

This is a fascinating way to fish for steelhead. Their numbers along the coast in the near vicinity of the Gravel and other area streams swell in early April, late May, and late August through September. The early April fish are staging for their spawning run. The late May fish are usually drop-backs and are extremely hungry. Late August through September steelhead are staging, dropping back, and intermingling with large numbers of coasters, lakers, and salmon intent on spawning. It is a potpourri, a chaotic mix of hungry salmonids eager to eat.

Fly pattern selection for fishing the flats is extremely simple. Use large baitfish imitations. I have had good success with Clousers in red and white, olive and white, and blue and white. Deceivers in the same colors are very good. The flies should be long, at least 4 inches.

More often than not a breeze will find you on these flats. A heavy rod will help punch out casts to a respectable distance. The fish you hook will want to run a long way to deep water and safety. A sink-tip line is best. Because you'll be fishing at relatively shallow depths, the line should have a moderate sink rate. You won't need one of the deep express, "cannon ball"-type lines.

Move slowly and watch closely for moving shadows at the edge of your distance vision. This is usually about 50 to 60 feet when wading waist-deep. Carry large loops of fly line ready to shoot. Speed and accuracy are important—just as when casting to moving bonefish. Throw your fly so it lands several feet ahead of the lead target fish, and strip. The result is usually instantaneous and dramatic.

One more thing to remember is that the big lake always produces low, rolling swells on even the calmest day, when the surface looks like glass from any distance. When you are hip- to waist-deep, the swells can push ice water into your waders. Even on a hot August day, Lake Superior's water temperature is in the 40s F (4–10 degrees C). Remember that. Practice a little *hop* that, when timed to an approaching swell, will raise the top of your waders a couple of inches. This works for awhile, but after an extended period your elbows will be soaked and freezing anyway, so it's best to retreat to, at most, a hip-deep wading depth.

The spring run of steelhead in the Gravel is larger than the fall run. Steelhead will nose into the current in early April, but the fishing improves greatly as the weather warms and spate conditions increase flows.

Nicollette Smith with her first steelhead, taken on the Jackpine River.

Matt Supinski caught this magnificent 18-pound winter steelhead from the Muskegon River, in December.

Morning fog on Michigan's Au Sable River.

Rick Kustich with a beautiful steelhead from
New York's Cattaraugus Creek.

A gorgeous fall day on New York's Salmon River, one of the state's most prolific—and popular—steelhead streams.

Fishing a placid pool on the Lower Saugeen River.

Kelly Galloup wth another nice steelhead from Michigan's renowned Pere Marquette River.

The author fishing the mouth of the Jackpine River, Nipigon Bay, Lake Superior.

The run usually peaks around April 25, and fishing remains good through late May in most years. The Gravel, more so than the Jackpine and Cypress, quickly clouds and become too dirty to fish after a heavy rain. Its upstream reach has several areas with large clay banks and in-stream clay deposits. These flush color into the flow and make the water too turbid for steelhead to see the fly.

The Gravel's drainage area is larger than that of either the Cypress or the Jackpine, and the fall of land is a bit less steep over a longer distance. The amount of water available to spawning steelhead between the mouth at Lake Superior and the migration barrier near the power line upstream from the Trans-Canada Highway is a significant reach. It has a wide variety of pools, riffles, and chutes with tight, twisting turns and deep holes. The bottom is a mix of boulders, rocks, sand, gravel, and spots of clay. I have noticed more woody debris clogged in the deep bend holes on this river than on others in the area. Perhaps this is due to the slightly less severe hydraulic gradient. The deep pools and sunken, tangled logs provide deep cover with overhead protection and shade for resting steelhead.

The same tackle and techniques suggested for the Jackpine and Cypress work well on the Gravel. Be prepared to switch techniques, perhaps changing spools on your reel, to accommodate different water types. Additional weight will be required for short, deep pockets in straight riffles and chutes. Carry an assortment in different sizes ranging from BB size upward. Use nontoxic, dense alloys rather than lead.

You can use the same basic egg, nymph, and streamer patterns here as on the Cypress and Jackpine. If the water is cloudy but still clear enough to fish, take a few extra nymphs in black with some built-in flash material, such as Krystal Flash, that reflects light. These patterns are easier to see in turbid water.

The numbers of steelhead that use the Gravel are not quite as high as those that ascend the Jackpine, but the fish seem to be, on average, a bit larger. You can get away with 8-pound-test tippet if the river is a little dirty, but 6-pound-test is better when the water is clear.

GRAVEL RIVER

Location: Rossport, Terrace Bay, Trans-Canada Highway.

Airport: See Jackpine River.

Lodging: Terrace Bay: Imperial Motel, 807-825-3226; Red Dog Inn, 807-825-3286.

Fly shops and Guides: See Jackpine River.

This spring steelhead from the Gravel River is smaller than average.

The Gravel is a very pretty river with large steelhead in the spring and a mix of possibilities in the fall. The short reach between the highway and the lake is a microcosm of the larger reach up to the barrier. It has twists and turns, deep holes, pocket water, and strong riffles. Being in tight proximity to Superior it holds steelhead, both fresh and drop-back fish, most of the time. This is a great place to start, or if you have just a short period of time to sample the river.

Steel River

The Steel River crosses the Trans-Canada Highway near the village of Terrace Bay, Ontario roughly an hour's drive east of Nipigon. The view from the highway shows a wide, straight run flecked with agitated current as the water pushes through pockets and over rocks and boulders. This is the lowest downstream run before the river hits Superior. It belies the true nature of the Steel's steelhead water, which is largely made up of alternating pool-and-riffle combinations. This is bigger water than the Jackpine, Cypress, and Gravel. It has wider, deeper flows and many broad, attractive pools that present shallow, easily wadable edges, mid-reaches of moderate depths, and deep, dark corners bordered by undercut banks and timber debris.

The stretch of river available to steelhead is quite long. The upstream barrier, a falls below Santoy Lake, is about 10 miles above Lake Superior. This is a rare but welcome river feature along the rugged fall of land that hugs the coast between Thunder Bay and Marathon, Ontario. The Steel's flow varies, of course, with precipitation events and becomes dangerous when snowmelt combines with heavy spring rain. But because the upstream drainage has areas with in-river clay deposits as well as some clay banks, the river clouds and becomes unfishable when this occurs. If you can't see your feet in ankle-deep water, you shouldn't fish the Steel. If the water looks like it might be deep, assume it is. If the current feels too strong, it is.

The Steel is one of the most renowned steelhead rivers in Ontario. It has excellent runs of large, wild fish both early and late in the spring and a substantial fall run of steelhead that overwinter in the river and spawn early in April. Good fly fishing can often come as early as ice-out in early April. This will last until snowmelt and/or rain makes the Steel too turbid to fly-fish effectively. As the water drops and clears in May, fly fishing again becomes a productive game. The Steel often fishes extremely well into June.

The fall run of fish begins as a trickle in August, when rains push the volume of this spate river up to a point that accommodates building excitement in silver, pink, and king salmon, lake trout, and coasters. Steelhead join these fall-spawning fish on their upstream migration and feed heavily on their drifting eggs. Fall steelhead in the Steel can be caught well into October. You will most often find them tucked in behind spawning salmon. If you spot spawning salmon, fish egg patterns downstream from their redds. If there is a stretch of deeper pocket water, or a dark riffle below the gravel, it's a fair bet that opportunistic steelhead are waiting there. In addition to the runs of Pacific salmon and coasters, there are also a few roaming Atlantic salmon in the system. These are strays and not high in numbers, but their presence during the fall months has been validated.

I first fished the Steel more than a decade ago. Steve Nevala and I were on our way to meet Scott Smith and fish the Cypress. We were early despite stopping several times to take photographs of plunging waterfalls and the awesome lakescapes of Superior's bays and inlets. With a few hours to kill, we decided to try the run directly below the highway bridge. It was early May and the water was high and a little off-color but fishable. We found a path on the east side of the river and hiked downstream about 200 yards to a spot that was safe to wade and presented a deep, slower cut next to a fast midstream run. Just below us, a soft bend to the left created a deep pool. It looked like a good place to begin. Steve moved downstream to fish the pool and I started at the upstream seam where the cut and hard run separated. After a few casts I decided to change flies; the soft cut looked too good to not hold a fish or two. While adding a black stonefly below my egg pattern, I heard Steve's "Fish on!" and turned to see my friend scurrying downstream with bending rod held high. He reappeared just moments later, and his defeated shoulder shrug told the story.

I made several casts that I thought had produced good, drag-free drifts without a take and decided to cast closer to the faster current. The flies plopped down right at the edge of the seam, and the split shot took them to depth quickly. About midway through the second or third drift the fly line's tip jerked sharply upstream and I raised my rod tip. This was met with violent reaction in the form of rapid back-to-back surges, quickly followed by a surface roll that preceded a fast downstream run. I remember trying to follow the steelhead but being stopped dead by a log obstruction that ran halfway into the river and beyond the point that looked safe to wade. The fish ran past Steve in shallow water no more than 3 feet from his boots and pulled loose in the pool.

"How big was that fish? It felt like a good one," I said.

"About five pounds. I had a pretty good view as he went by. You ever think of trying to slow him down?" Steve answered.

We hooked another fish or two each in the following hour but could not seem to muster enough skill or luck to touch one. My watch said it was time to leave, to find the Cypress and meet Scott, but we each made several of the famous "One more cast. Just one more . . ." before hiking back to our car.

More recently I had the opportunity to fish the Steel during its fall run. It was early September and I joined a group of Lansing, Michigan fly anglers in search of coasters and wild fall steelhead. The trip was organized and led by Miles Chance. His Okemos, Michigan fly shop, M. Chance Fly Fishing Specialties, had made arrangements for both Scott Smith and Bill Boote to guide our fishing on the range of rivers from Nipigon to Terrace Bay.

> ## STEEL RIVER
>
> ───────●───────
>
> **Location:** Between Nipigon and Rossport on the Trans-Canada Highway, 90 minutes from Thunder Bay.
>
> **Airport:** See Jackpine River.
>
> **Lodging:** See Grand River.
>
> **Fly shops and Guides:** See Jackpine River.

We fished the Jackpine, Cypress, Gravel, McKenzie, and Steel rivers. We hiked and explored. We fished the flats of Lake Superior and caught hefty lakers and brook trout on large Clousers and Deceivers. We caught pink and silver salmon on Woolly Buggers and nymphs, large coasters in the streams on an array of streamers, and steelhead on nymphs and eggs. It was a fantastic, joyous trip but the most memorable moments—for me—came on the Steel.

Each day we split up and fished different water by rotating who went with which guide on various rivers. On this day, Miles and I were teamed with Bill Boote for an expedition to a stretch of the Steel about midway between the Trans-Canada Highway and the waterfall barrier at Santoy Lake.

"We'll have to hike a ways," Bill said as he parked his four-wheel-drive at the end of a rugged two-track fire trail.

We followed a faint, winding trail that roughly paralleled the river along its west bank. The path ran up a high ridge, through low and dense aspen thickets, across bogs and granite outcroppings. It was sometimes too thick to clearly see a companion just a few yards ahead. We stayed close. Below and to the right, the Steel churned through dark corner holes, wide sunlit riffles, and heavy, boulder-strewn pocket water. It all looked fantastic. I thought I could *smell* steelhead.

"Why don't we fish along here?" I asked at one pause in our hike.

"It's better just a wee bit upstream. Let's keep going," Bill said.

We trudged a *wee bit* farther and came to an abrupt halt at the edge of a rock cliff stained nearly black by seeping springs. Moss and lichens, heavy brush, slippery boulders, a straight uphill climb to the left, and a straight 30-foot drop to a deep, black hole in a tight corner of the Steel on our immediate right completed the view. I looked at Miles. Miles looked at Bill.

"Follow me." Bill said.

"Follow you where? Do you know how to fly?" Miles asked.

"C'mon," he answered.

Bill reached out and took hold of an ancient, thin cotton rope and tugged. The rope was coated with a greenish mold and looked to be several years old. It was about chest high and ran from where we stood across the face of the mini-cliff to the trunk of a cedar tree on the other side of the chasm. Bill tugged again on the rope and pronounced it "good." He leaned out over the drop-off and edged along at an angle, sidestepping on a flat ledge no more than 8 inches wide. I looked at Miles. Miles looked at me and shrugged. Bill made it to the other side and beckoned.

"You next," Miles said. Bill probably weights about 180 pounds with all his gear on. I weigh a bit over 200 in waders and vest. Miles is a big man, about 6 feet, 5 inches tall and close to 270 pounds. Miles is no dummy. He was testing the breaking strength of this ragged, worn tippet in graduating steps. We both made the crossing with no serious side effects beyond blood pressure and heart rate. It was actually pretty easy.

A short distance farther along we came to an opening in the brush and a wide gravel bar that had been scoured clean sometime earlier by high water. The river ran from left to right and split around a dry gravel hump before rejoining currents and sliding into a large pool. Fresh bear tracks crossed our gravel beach and disappeared into the water. It was perfect.

Miles caught one steelhead and lost another. I caught a small brook trout, two or three pink salmon, and hooked a steelhead that pulled loose when I applied too much rod pressure too quickly after a spectacular jump. Yes, we had to tippy-toe across the "canyon of the Steel" on our way out, but it was much less daunting after our time in paradise. That evening over dinner we talked more about our death-defying, cliff-hanging heroic scaling of the *canyon* wall than about the fish we caught.

Steelhead run bigger here than in most rivers along the North Shore. In the fall you have a good chance for a laker in the 10-pound range, portly Pacific salmon, and the catch of a lifetime, a coaster brook trout of 5 pounds or more. Use enough rod—a 7- or 8-weight is a good choice. A four-piece travel rod is much easier to carry through the dense thickets that are nearly continuous along both streambanks. Felt-soled waders are a must. If I had known of the ledge crossing beforehand, I would have worn studded soles.

The basic North Shore fly assortment is good for the Steel. Carry an assortment of egg flies with built-in flash as well as some in paler hues without the sparkle. Dark stonefly nymphs, a few Hare's Ears, and some Nympho flies on No. 8, 10, and 12 hooks will cover these needs. If you visit the Steel during the early fall, be sure to carry an extra spool with a sink-tip line and several streamers, including Muddlers, Woolly Buggers, Zonkers, and Scott Smith's great pattern, the Butt-Monkey. Big coasters, lake trout, and steelhead love these larger mouthfuls.

Fishing the Steel River is an unforgettable experience complete with big, wild salmonids in an untamed primal setting. It is, in the purest sense of the term, a walk on the wild side with just a hint of danger.

Michipicoten River

WaWa, Ontario is just a few miles north of the United States–Canada border at Sault Ste. Marie along Trans-Canada Highway 17. The short journey is picturesque, with lakescape vistas of bays, waterfalls, and surging tributaries to Lake Superior. Several steelhead rivers cross under the highway between "the Soo" and WaWa. Government Creek, Pancake River, Montreal River, Agawa River, Bad Head River, and Old Woman River cross beneath the highway before you reach the Michipicoten near the southern edge of WaWa. At Old Woman Bay you can see the name-sake of the bay, the unmistakable features of an old woman's face carved by time, water, and wind into the rocks on a cliff across the water. Ojibway legend tells of the half-lynx, half-lizard monster, Michipeshu, that haunts this bay. The natives left peace offerings of tobacco around the bay to keep the monster happy.

The Michipicoten River crosses Trans-Canada Highway 17 just a short distance from Lake Superior. This is a big, wide river with a quick current throughout the stretch available to migrating steelhead. The best and most easily accessible run of river is from the upstream barrier at the old Scott Falls hydroelectric dam. A well-maintained gravel road runs from Highway 17 a few short miles to a parking area near the dam. The river is bordered here by a tumbled disarray of giant rocks and boulders that runs for quite a distance downstream. Some patience and care are required to navigate safely to the water's edge.

The river is wide and fast here. The current runs over rocks, boulders, gravel, and cobble and bounces through a series of riffles and chutes before curving slightly and slowing to a pool-riffle-pool configuration. Fish hold in the fast water stretches and are almost always found in the deep pockets behind larger rocks, where they can rest in softer water and ambush prey without fighting the main current. You will find more steelhead in the pools and at the edges of current seams where a slower flow buffers the river's force. Downstream a bit from the dam, a narrow gravel island splits the river momentarily. At the downstream edge of the island the flow rejoins and forms a productive pool. Steelhead stage throughout this pool, but most seem to want to hang in the upper end at about the middle of the river. You will find similar tendencies as you work downstream. Fish the heads of the pools very thoroughly before stepping down to cover the rest of the water.

I must caution for a careful approach to the Michipicoten River. Although the steelhead water is close to the town of WaWa, it is wild and unforgiving of foolish risks and retains a remote, untamed character. There may or may not be anyone around to hear a call for assistance. Fish here in the company of a friend. This same scary, wild profile is at least part of what many of us want in a steelhead river. It is awe-inspiring and beautiful and will make you think you are in the deep hinterlands of British Columbia.

A wide mix of steelhead year classes use the Michipicoten during the fall and spring. They range in size is from about 16 to 27 inches on average. This represents fish that have spent from less than a year to three years in lake Superior. A high percentage of the smaller fish in the 16- to 20-inch range are precocious males. This group is very aggressive and seems willing to eat most fairly presented flies.

Steelhead of the Michipicoten are all wild fish born either in the main river or one of its small, nursery-stream tributaries. Also wild are the resident, nonmigratory rainbows, which are available throughout the summer. Some of these top the 5-pound mark. These fish live a precarious life full of dangers and obstacles. They are vigorous, yet fragile. Please use great care in their quick release.

This is a freestone spate river, but its storm runoff is somewhat miti-gated by the hydroelectric facility dam. Less scouring takes place than on other rivers in the area, and one of the benefits of this is that insect and forage fish densities remain stable and at a high level. Various mayfly and caddis species populate the stream, but stoneflies are the in-sects of most interest to steelhead fly anglers. Sculpins are the dominant forage fish in the river, but because the flow to Superior is relatively short, steelhead maintain a high in-terest in smelt and herring.

Impressionistic nymph patterns are better than realistic ties on this river. Those flies tied with rough, spiky fur bodies and bold silhouettes seem to catch more fish than stonefly or mayfly nymphs that are more exact copies of natural bugs.

> ## MICHIPICOTEN RIVER
>
> **Location:** WaWa, Ontario, Trans-Canada Highway 17, 90 minutes north from Sault Ste. Marie airport, Sault Ste. Marie, Ontario, and Sault Ste. Marie, Michigan.
>
> **Lodging:** Smaller chains and local motels in WaWa; small tourist motels between WaWa and Agawa Bay.
>
> **Fly shops and Guides:** No local fly shop serves this area. Check with Karl Vogel (705-649-3313) and John Giuliani (705-942-5473 or 705-253-9017) for guiding and current information on river conditions.

Fluttering, breathing materials such as aftershaft (filoplume) feathers used for tails and gills add lifelike movement. Nymph patterns for this river should be big and dark. Black and mottled brown are the best colors. No. 6 and 8 hooks are about right on most days.

The water has a tannic stain even during periods of low flow. Egg pat-terns should carry some light-gathering and reflecting material. Char-treuse, orange, and yellow are good color combinations.

One of the best patterns for this river is a simple, lightly weighted Muddler Minnow tied with a scruffy, flat head. Tie this pattern with a slim profile in mottled gray and brown on No. 4 to 8 hooks. Other sculpin patterns also produce fish. The Zoo Cougar in yellow or olive, Feenstra's Plastic Sculpin, and Conrad's Sculpin in olive or dark brown are all good choices. Spey flies are best in dark colors. Purple or black with a red hackle collar would be my first choice. Long, slithery leech and baby lamprey patterns in black or dark gray will catch steelhead here.

Black Woolly Buggers and Egg-Sucking Leeches complete a workable group of fly patterns for the main river on most days. Occasionally, the steelhead seem to want a white streamer. This seems to occur most often when a fresh run of fish has entered the river in late fall or early spring. Perhaps they still carry the big-water imprint and are looking for smelt, herring, or juvenile trout. If dark nymphs and streamers fail, try a white Zonker or one of Joe Penich's White Minnow or Niagara Shiner patterns.

Standard nymphing techniques catch these fish regularly, but an interesting deviation from the norm seems even more effective. Cast well upstream from the intended target. When the drifting line swings even with your position, throw a large upstream mend and follow this with a series of small mends while feeding slack line out through the rod guides. As your line begins to swing below your position, take up the slack so you are drifting and swinging on a tight, straight connection. Steelhead will hit streamers and nymphs at any point in this drift but most often they take the fly as it begins to drag and sweep, or when it straightens below your position. When they hit in this later stage of the drift, they hit very hard.

A long rod is a big help on this river. A length of 10 feet for a 7- or 8-weight line is a good choice. Bring a floating line and a sink-tip to match conditions.

If the Michipicoten is running high and dirty or is too rough-and-tumble for your taste, try the bay at the mouth of Old Woman River just a few miles south on Highway 17. This is a productive flats area with cruising lake trout, salmon, and steelhead close to shore on most days. Use a rod with enough backbone to punch out casts of 70 to 80 feet. A moderate sink-tip line, a leader testing 8 pounds at the tippet, and a smelt pattern or Deceiver in olive and white is the right combination for starters. Look for cruising fish, drop the fly a few feet ahead of their path of movement, and strip hard.

Wildlife is abundant in this area. There is a fair chance to see a moose or bear close enough to make a good photograph. Carry a camera with a zoom lens.

Lake Michigan

6

The most "user friendly" of the upper lakes, Michigan's surface area—covering more than 22,400 square miles—is third in rank behind Superior and Huron. It is the only Great Lake totally contained within the United States. The shoreline is densely populated with small resort towns and medium-size cities like Green Bay and Traverse City in the north and large metropolitan areas to the south. It is the most easily traversed of the upper lakes. The population network requires connecting highways, secondary roads, and numerous airports. The lake is a vacationer's paradise with mile after mile of pure sand beaches in close proximity to rivers, inland lakes, sand dunes, forests, and every conceivable tourist attraction.

Stocking programs in Indiana, Wisconsin, and Michigan waters supplement naturally reproducing stocks of predominantly Manistee-strain steelhead. These fish roam the long, narrow lake and feed heavily on alewives, herring, smelt, and immature salmon and trout. Offshore, charter boat fishing is very big business throughout Lake Michigan.

Steelhead are caught regularly within sight of Chicago's Lake Shore Drive and all along the northward coast past Milwaukee, Sheboygan, Green Bay, and into Michigan waters southward to the short Indiana shoreline.

Just north of the Illinois border, Wisconsin's Pike River has a reasonable run of steelhead and provides good fishing at times. A bit farther north, near Racine, the Root River hosts very large runs both in fall and spring. In September, October, and early November this river can be very crowded and take on the aura of a minor circus or rock concert. This is due to a combined run of spawning brown trout, Pacific salmon, and steelhead. Again, in the spring, when steelhead numbers swell, the concentration of anglers can be overwhelming. But the runs are huge and the fish are willing. A visit to the Root in midweek or a bit ahead of, or behind, the peak runs is the best choice if a measure of peace is important to enjoyment.

The Manitowoc River enters Lake Michigan at the town of Manitowoc about 20 miles north of Sheboygan. This is a fine river that receives large runs of anadromous fish from September through April. Steelhead follow brown trout and salmon from September through early November and make their serious spawning run beginning in late March. Between the river's mouth and the upstream barrier at Clark Mills Dam, steelhead have access to more than 20 miles of river. The main problem in fishing the Manitowoc is that a flush of water is required to bring steelhead into the flow, and the upper Manitowoc is plagued by sediment-bearing soils that quickly cloud the water and reduce visibility to near zero during and after any precipitation that is significant enough to attract migrating steelhead.

At the base of the Door Peninsula, the Keewaunee River enters Lake Michigan at the town of Keewaunee. This river is very popular with local anglers due to its large numbers of very big steelhead. It is a "brood stock" stream with a steelhead control weir. If the Keewaunee is not to your liking, try Stoney Creek just a few miles farther north. This is a small, short river with a steep hydraulic gradient and water levels that fluctuate severely after a rain or during snowmelt, but it has good numbers of steelhead in the spring and can be a real jewel if conditions are right.

The Oconto River enters Lake Michigan's Green Bay at the town of Oconto. Between the river's mouth and the upstream barrier at Stiles, steelhead can access about 10 river miles. Several roads with good public access parallel and cross the river west of Oconto. Take a drive along North River Road, County Road J, Airport Road, and Funk Road and see for yourself. The Peshtigo River has a short run of water below a dam that attracts large concentrations of steelhead (and anglers) during the peak of the spring run. If it is not too crowded, fishing here can be superb.

East of Escanaba and just a few miles southwest of Manistique, Michigan, the small town of Thompson straddles US 2 within sight of Lake Michigan. Thompson Creek crosses the highway and dumps into the lake near a large public parking area. The creek is tiny, too small to fish, but the flats fishing along the shoreline is often fantastic. Steelhead, salmon, and some of the largest brown trout in all of the Great Lakes prowl this flat in search of prey. The flat is wadable. Use a sinking-head line, a stout leader, and large baitfish streamers.

A few miles north at the town of Manistique, the river of the same name has a short stretch of productive steelhead water below a dam. This stretch is best in late spring and often has excellent fly fishing well into May. Surprisingly, this very productive short piece of water is rarely crowded.

South of "Big Mac," the Mackinac Bridge, Michigan's west coast is a gold mine for steelhead fly anglers. Driving southward, you'll first reach the Jordan River, which has very good fly fishing for several miles upstream from the town of East Jordan. This is a scenic river with ultraclear water and spooky but abundant and large steelhead. Check the water along Alba Road. Just a few miles north, the lower Boyne River has a fine fishery in the spring and a few steelhead in the fall that follow migrating salmon and brown trout.

South of Ludington, the Pentwater River has a large run of spring steelhead. This small river flows in a northwesterly run from Hart to Pentwater. It is mostly narrow and tight with long stretches of sand bottom and a smooth, pool-like flow. Access is limited and the fishing can be tough, but these steelhead run large and tend to be quite aggressive.

The Rogue River flows through the town of Rockford about 10 miles north of Grand Rapids. This small stream flows southward and joins the Grand River north and a little east of the big city. A small dam in Rockford halts the upstream movement of steelhead. Fly fishing is often excellent throughout the Rogue's short flow to the Grand River. A greenbelt parkway provides public access right in town.

The mighty Grand River lures thousands of steelhead and salmon from Lake Michigan. This is very big, dangerous water, and extreme caution is advised. Most successful wade fishing takes place right in downtown Grand Rapids below the Sixth Street Dam. You won't be able to miss this spot. Wading anglers are almost always in view. Please be very careful. Fishermen drown here every year.

The St. Joseph River is most famous for its heavy summer runs of Skamania-strain steelhead. This strain is lean and long and incredibly active when hooked. Many individuals exceed 20 pounds. Their aggressive nature and wild abandon when hooked make them a huge favorite. The "Saint Joe" enters Lake Michigan at a point between the two cities of Benton Harbor and St. Joseph. The beachfront lake area has excellent flats- and surf-style fly fishing for these big steelhead. The river proper is too large to fly-fish and too featureless to easily read the water, but the Dowagiac River, a tributary, can be very good and is often exceptional. This river has a classic, riffle-pool configuration with sand, gravel, clay, and deep corner holes. Skamania steelhead seem to like gaudy, flashy flies best. Be sure to bring large, fluorescent rabbit-strip leech patterns, Crystal Eggs, and white Zonkers along with more standard flies for the Dowagiac.

Milwaukee River

This river defines urban angling within the Great Lakes basin. Some of the best holding water for steelhead is "downtown." It might seem a bit strange to be fly fishing for steelhead in the middle of a major city, but by walking just a few minutes from parking areas it is possible to combine good fishing with relative peace and quiet.

The Milwaukee River watershed drains approximately 600 square miles of mixed urban, suburban, agricultural, and rural lands. The portion of river available to migrating salmonids extends from the mouth at Milwaukee Bay, upstream almost due north for 25 miles to an impassable dam at the town of Grafton. Except under extreme drought conditions, the large watershed and deep harbor entrance allow fish to access the entire 25-mile stretch to the dam. Flows of 750 cubic feet per second and above encourage steelhead to move out of the harbor and begin their upstream runs. At 750 cfs and more, steelhead can easily pass over a series of low dams on the way to Grafton.

Two of the factors that influence the size of yearly salmonid smolt plantings are human population and angling access. The Milwaukee fits flush with these criteria and ensures large plants. Another factor that lobbies in favor of large smolt plants is the extensive charter boat fishing fleet based in the city. Charter fishing for steelhead in Lake Michigan is very big business in and around Milwaukee, and large numbers of fish make for happy repeat customers. And it is not just steelhead generating these dollars. Pacific salmon, brown trout, and brook trout are also stocked in large numbers, ensuring spawning runs of a variety of desirable fly-rod species throughout the spring, fall, and early winter.

One of the best access points within the city is at Estabrook Park. The park is reached from Capitol Drive and provides access to about a mile of good fly-fishing water. There is an excellent mix of deep holding water and gravel-based riffles between the park access and an upstream, natural limestone falls. The salmonids use all of this water. Upstream from the falls you will find numerous pockets in the ledgerock bottom that hold fish, and a deepwater channel below a low-head dam holds staging steelhead that are resting before a run upstream.

The Milwaukee is a big river, with widths ranging from 100 to over 200 feet. Depths range widely, and caution is advised when wading. If a particular spot looks too deep to wade, it surely is. And the agricultural lands of the river's upper riparian zone introduce sediment to the flow, which means it usually carries at least some stain. This is mostly a good thing for fishing but can impair visibility to the point where extra care is required while wading.

MILWAUKEE RIVER

⸺⸺⸺⚫⸺⸺⸺

Location: Milwaukee, Wisconsin.

Airport: Twenty minutes from Milwaukee, one hour from Chicago.

Lodging: Extensive, all major chains.

Fly shops and Guides: The Flyfishers, www.theflyfishers.com. Bob Blumreich, www.silverdoctor. net, 608-637-3417.

Between Milwaukee and the dam at Grafton, access to good steelhead water is available at county parks and various road crossings. There are several east-west roads that cross the river off northbound WI 32 between Milwaukee and Grafton. County Line Road, Highland Road, Pioneer Road, and Falls Road are just a few that run close to good stretches of water. Maps of Milwaukee and Ozaukee Counties will show more numerous access points at smaller side roads and county parks.

Steelhead runs in the Milwaukee represent a mix of strains. Chambers Creek, Skamania, and Ganaraska fish make up the bulk of returnees, but a few strays from the Michigan side of the lake also show up in spring and fall. Some of these grow very large, entering the river after four or even five years in Lake Michigan. Steelhead reaching the middle teens in pounds are fairly common in the Milwaukee. The average weight, however, is closer to 7 or 8 pounds. These are usually two- to three-year-old fish. Precocious males, fish of 18–20 inches, complement these larger year classes during both spring and fall migrations. The combination of year classes with a variety of strains produces an exciting potpourri that provides an extended period of productive fly fishing as well as a mix of sizes and fighting characteristics. In the fall, from late September through most of November, Seeforellen-strain brown trout and large Pacific salmon—both silvers and kings—add spice to the soup. The brown trout are quite large on average, and some are enormous. These browns like the same flies that steelhead eat.

The agricultural lands along the upper river keep a certain level of suspended sediment in the river, and this stain demands visible flies. Dark flies with a strong silhouette are most productive when swinging Spey or streamer patterns. Black, black and purple, purple and red, chartreuse, and chartreuse blends are most effective in traditional Spey patterns and in the marabou ties such as the Popsicle series. Long, slithery leech patterns are also very good for searching large pools with a two-handed rod.

A standard assortment of eggs, nymphs, Woolly Buggers, and Egg-Sucking Leeches works well in the Milwaukee's seams and pocket water. Be sure to include some light-reflecting material such as Krystal Flash or Flashabou in some of your nymph patterns. The egg patterns should be on the bright side as well. Flame, chartreuse, and steelhead orange are good colors. If the water is dirty, with visibility in the 24-inch range, eggs with Estaz or Crystal Chenille bodies are the best choice.

Look for current seams and ledges or pockets when fishing nymphs and eggs. Both bottom-bouncing with additional weight and indicator techniques are effective on this river. Sink-tip lines in various densities can be very helpful in reaching bottom-hugging fish in the deeper pockets and runs, and when the water begins to cool dramatically in the late fall. The *sinking-leader technique* described in Chapter Three is a highly productive way to fish nymphs in the Milwaukee.

A long rod is very useful here. A 10-foot, 7- or 8-weight offers clear advantages in achieving distance and effective mending in such a large river. Two-handed rods between 12 and 14 feet are even better.

A current issue at the forefront of concerns for steelhead in the Milwaukee River is the excessive bag limit of five fish per day. This is too high. Anglers who fish the river have attempted to pressure authorities to lower this limit, but have been countered by the powerful charter boat industry. The fear is that a reduction in harvest within the river would translate to a similar reduction in the kill limit on the big lake. Charter boat captains feel that this would damage their business, despite the fact that a *five-fish-per-day-in-aggregate* limit could be comprised of a mix of lake trout, brown trout, salmon, steelhead, and brown trout. The good news is that catch-and-release is a common practice and is growing in acceptance within the sport angling community fishing the river.

The Milwaukee, despite the perhaps daunting mental image of urban angling, is a very good steelhead river for fly anglers. Its mixed bottom structure of ledgerock, gravel, sand, silt, and cobble is rich in aquatic food forms and is attractive to spawning salmonids in both spring and fall. Its long run of 25 miles of water accessible to steelhead and anglers means there is room to spread out and enjoy relatively pressure-free stretches of river. The river's mixed bag of species and its variety of steelhead strains presents a wide calendar of opportunity. And there is a real possibility that you may touch a 20-pound steelhead here.

Sheboygan River

The town of Sheboygan, Wisconsin nestles on the Lake Michigan coast about midway between Milwaukee and Green Bay on I-43. The river's headwaters are a short distance east of the village of Kiel. Flowing south by southeast, the Sheboygan meanders through Sheboygan Falls, then due east to its mouth at Breakwater Light in the town of Sheboygan. I-43 bridges the river midway between Sheboygan Falls and Lake Michigan.

Wisconsin's Department of Natural Resources classifies the state's steelhead rivers according to their size, flow, and accessibility. The Sheboygan is a Class I stream, which means that it receives regular plants of hatchery salmonids. These include Pacific salmon, brown trout, and steelhead. Specific strains of steelhead have varied over the years, and a mix of strains utilize the river at various times of the year. The Canadian Ganaraska strain is present, along with Chambers Creek, Skamania, and a few roaming fish from Michigan, the Manistee strain.

The best public access on this river is downstream (east) of I-43. Esslingen Park and the Taylor Drive boat launch are the two best access points. From I-43, take the WI 23 exit east to Taylor Drive, and turn south to the access spots. This is prime water for fresh fish from Lake Michigan. This stretch used to feature flat, slow current. Lake Michigan's previous high levels pushed lake water into this section and masked the contours of the gravel and rubble bottom. More recently lake levels have dropped, and the river shows its normal flow and gradient. Silt has been scoured from the gravel, and mint-bright steelhead seem to love this part of the river.

The very close proximity to Lake Michigan means that many of these steelhead are just a couple of hours from the big water. They are usually hungry and aggressive. This is a great area to swing Spey flies and strip streamers. When conditions line up favorably, waking dry flies in the surface film often results in jarring, visible strikes. Nymphing techniques are

Throwing a mend on the Sheboygan River.

also productive, of course. Most anglers fishing nymphs and eggs in this stretch utilize strike indicators, but because the fish are fresh and aggressive and the takes are usually dramatic rather than soft and subtle, the indicator system is not necessary to detect strikes. Scattered gravel reaches and cobble-studded bars and current breaks will hold some fish for an extended period, but most steelhead in this reach are resting and staging for migration farther upstream.

A bit farther upstream, the river flows through the corporate campus of the Kohler Design Center off CR PP. This stretch of river has excellent fly-fishing water but is entirely surrounded by the private holdings of the Kohler Corporation. A yearly pass to park and access this water is available from the company. An upstream barrier within the Kohler property holds steelhead in this reach in substantial numbers. The river channel here ranges from about 60 feet to 90 feet wide. There are many runs rich in ideal spawning gravel mixed with cobble, rocks, and boulders. The river twists and turns through a lovely pastoral setting alternating between manicured lawns and wild tangles of bankside trees and shrubs. For the most part the river is easy to wade. Its depth averages about 2 feet, but there are deeper pockets, runs, and holes at the corners. And it usually runs fairly clear, but a rapid snowmelt or heavy rain can stain the flow and reduce visibility.

Some years ago I had a stroke of good luck and was able to fish this stretch with Bob Blumreich. Bob is one of Wisconsin's preeminent fly-fishing guides, and one of his great passions is swinging elegant Spey flies in front of eager steelhead. It is only fair to add that he is one of the nation's finest and most creative tyers of Spey-type patterns.

We entered the Kohler property and parked in a designated space close to the river. The Sheboygan curled like a soft ribbon of black ink through an open area, then dumped into a hard riffle and disappeared into a tunnel of trees on both banks. It was mid-November and cold. Fresh snow had laid several inches of white carpet and pushed the visual effect to one of stark contrast.

> ## SHEBOYGAN RIVER
> ———⬤———
>
> **Location:** Sheboygan, Wisconsin.
>
> **Airport:** One hour from Milwaukee, two hours from Chicago, two hours from Green Bay.
>
> **Lodging:** Extensive, all major chains.
>
> **Fly shops and Guides:** See Milwaukee River; also Tight Lines (De-Pere), www.tightlinesflyshop.com, 920-336-4106; Latitude North (Green Bay), www.latitudenorth .com, 920-434-7240.

The sun broke through the clouds when we reached the river's bank, and I noticed patches of green grass poking through the snow, the protective cover of a tangled logjam on the far bank, and a clean spawning redd with three large, dark shapes near midstream.

"Salmon," Bob said. "Let's fish these riffle pockets a little downstream. A steelhead is probably lurking nearby."

Bob was using a long, two-handed rod of his own design, and a floating fly line. He showed me one of his favorite patterns. "This is the Purple and Orange Spey. I developed this for spooky fish in stained water," he said. The fly had a dark purple body with a silver rib, dyed pheasant rump hackle, and a layered wing of purple hackle tips and orange goose shoulder feathers. It was slim, intricate, and elegant; it seemed too beautiful to actually put in the water and fish, and I said so. "I tie these for steelhead. I fish them because steelhead eat beautiful flies," he said.

Through the afternoon and evening Bob taught me several effective Spey casts and even showed me how to execute variations of those casts with a shorter, one-handed rod. He explained his color choices and pattern types for various water conditions and showed me the obvious, and not so obvious, holding locations for fall steelhead on this stretch of the Sheboygan. He also demonstrated—with the help of eager, aerial-oriented steelhead—the power of added leverage in the long rod. The differences in results between master and novice were obvious, but Bob's patient counsel finally paid off when I hooked a silver giant. We did not stay connected for long. I had started to chase the running fish by hopping downstream through the rocks next to a high, grassy bank. Somehow I managed to lose tension on the steelhead and the hook came loose. Breathing heavily, I reeled up the slack line and took a backward step just as Bob, net in hand, reached my side. At that precise moment, a mature rooster pheasant erupted from the grass at my feet. I lurched forward and nearly fell in the river. Bob looked at the escaping bird, at me, at the river. "Hmm. Nice work," he said.

In addition to steelhead and fall-run salmon, the Sheboygan receives a substantial run of large brown trout in October and November. Many of these fish are Seeforellen-strain browns. They are very large, eager to eat flies, and magnificent fighters.

Bob suggests a mix of egg flies, some drab and pale, some bright with built-in flash, for the Sheboygan. He states flatly that you need only two nymph patterns for this river, dark stoneflies and wiggle (extended-body) Hex nymphs. For nymph- and egg-fishing methods, a 9-foot, 7-weight rod will cover the water effectively. He suggests practicing a one-handed Spey cast, as this delivery will pay dividends when you're backed up against tree-lined banks.

He prefers to swing Spey patterns, however, and has convinced me, and countless clients, that this is as effective and more fun than other tactics. When conditions are right—moderate flow, steady barometer, fresh fish—Bob recommends swinging dry flies in a waking presentation. The best pattern for this exciting method is the Dinner Mint Muddler, but other patterns also produce hits. Waller Wakers, deerhair Bombers, and large stonefly or caddis adult patterns are good choices.

The Sheboygan is within easy reach of millions of people. It is only minutes from Milwaukee and about two hours from Chicago, but still presents a semi-wild setting for fly anglers. It has a wide range of steelhead strains that prefer varying time periods for their upstream movements, so this means that fish are present in reasonable numbers for extended periods. In addition to steelhead, Pacific salmon and trophy lake-dwelling brown trout join the fall spectacle. That is a combination of positive elements that make the Sheboygan hard to resist.

Muskegon River

The headwaters of this great steelhead fishery are many miles from Lake Michigan. It begins as a cool seep in Dead Stream Swamp near the northwest corner of Houghton Lake in the north central Lower Peninsula. Flowing south and westward, the Muskegon grows with the infusion of feeder streams and springs through seven counties and several major dams. The lowest dam, the Croton, is a few miles east of the town of Newaygo in the west central portion of the Lower Peninsula. Croton Dam is impassable for migrating fish and marks the upstream limit of the Muskegon's steelhead water.

From Croton Dam to its multi-channeled mouth at Lake Michigan, the Muskegon has over 60 miles of productive steelhead fishing. The best fly-angling water is from Croton downstream to Newaygo. For the past several years the Muskegon has benefited from a "run of the river" mandate by the Federal Energy Relicensing Commission (FERC). Simply stated, the river's volume at Croton Dam must be the same as the flow immediately above the pond behind the dam. This stable flow has improved the gravel runs between Croton and Newaygo, benefited aquatic insects, forage fish, and stream trout, and greatly enhanced natural steelhead reproduction.

Many Great Lakes steelhead rivers are more or less affected by the infestation of zebra mussels, and the Muskegon is no exception. The most noticeable effects are the incredible clarity of the water and a decrease (at least for now) in the numbers of the river's diverse caddis populations. But mayfly, cranefly, dragonfly, and stonefly populations are healthy, and forage fish continue to flourish.

This is a big river by Midwestern standards. Its volume fluctuates from natural causes—rain and snowmelt—regardless of the FERC mandate, and can range from about 1,000 cfs to several times that number. It seems to produce the best fly-angling opportunities between about 1,200 and 2,000 cfs. Above 2000 cfs, the river becomes a bit dicey for wading anglers.

Walk and wade access begins at the boat launch at Croton Dam, and this is a popular spot that holds a high number of steelhead. A bit downstream there is a Department of Natural Resources access at Pine Road with good fishing that extends to Calvary Riffle. Additional access points include Henning Park, River Park, the New Bridge DNR access, Old Women's Bend, and Mystery Creek.

Many of the best runs on the Muskegon are in areas where the banks are privately owned. This, coupled with the fact that it is a large river with many unwadable approaches to prime stretches, suggests a stable boat for transport. There is no reasonable substitute for a guided trip for your first (or second, or third) visit to the Muskegon. I should emphasize a few points here. First, this is a popular river close to a major metropolitan area—Grand Rapids—and during the peaks of both the spring and fall runs, it can be crowded. The guides have worked out a particular set of acceptable moves and behaviors for boat traffic that cover movement, stationing, proximity, and relocation. It is best to learn these by observation; trial and error can fray tempers. Second, it is a big stream and although much of the best water will be obvious to an experienced angler, many productive spots are more subtle, some bordering on enigmatic. Third, this river's varying riffles, runs, and pools provide an opportunity to practice (or learn) a wide range of techniques that are best coached by a knowledgeable guide. These include special, adapted nymphing presentations, swinging wet flies, and innovative streamer strategies.

The Muskegon attracts some very large steelhead. Each year many fish (usually males) in the 20-pound class are caught. I have personally seen several in this range. My guess is that fall-run steelhead average about 7 pounds and springtime fish run close to 9 pounds. Along with the Manistee River to the north, the Muskegon probably presents the best chance in the Great Lakes basin for a 20-pound trophy.

We mostly consider fly fishing for *mykiss* to be a fall and spring activity in the Upper Midwest, but winter angling on the Muskegon is often superb. Granted, the temperature can be brutal at times, but both wade and boat angling pressure is greatly reduced and the fish tend to relax and congregate in deeper, slow pools where they eat nymphs and eggs despite the very cold water.

A few years ago, I had the opportunity to fish with river guide and author Matt Supinski in December. It was a midweek day and very cold, with alternating bright sun and dark clouds pushed by biting winds. My best guess was that we would freeze to death, my wildest hope was to hook one fish, maybe. We were joined by one of Matt's regular clients, Maggie, who lived in California at the time.

Wrapped in layers of fleece, sheathed in windproof jackets, and fortified with strong coffee and insanity, we began the day as a weak pewter band in the east pushed the black sky upward. It was cold and the wind was blowing.

"Whaddya think, Maggie?" I asked.

"Perfect. Absolutely perfect," she said.

Matt laughed. "We're going to catch fish. Hang in there."

We did. I was still fumbling and trying to knot one of Matt's creative nymph patterns to my leader when Maggie's indicator dipped and she set the hook. It was a fat, handsome brown trout of about 14 inches and it got our blood flowing. Maggie hooked another fish, a steelhead this time, while I was organizing cameras and pouring another mug of coffee. The fish pulled free when Maggie palmed her reel too firmly and she muttered a word ("frozen," I think) under her breath. Matt asked me if I planned to fish or just guzzle coffee.

We moved to a soft, smooth riffle at the head of a long pool on the north bank. Matt told me where to cast and suggested that I mend carefully. On the second or third drift, the line twitched and I was connected to a beautiful silver hen of about 12 pounds. Despite the very cold water—38 degrees F (3.3 degrees C)—she fought with speed and vigor. We quickly photographed and released her. I remember that she had an especially baleful look in her eyes when I removed the fly from the roof of her mouth.

Matt Supinski and Maggie with a nice winter buck from the Muskegon's famous Gray Drake Pool.

We moved downstream to a deep pool and Maggie lost another good fish. "Just too cold to do this right. I'll watch. You fish," she said. I was cold as well. When we stopped at the Gray Drake Pool, Matt pointed out the center run and said that there would be some large fish holding there. I looked at the minuscule temperature gauge on my jacket's zipper. It read 18 degrees F (-7.8 degrees C). "Show me how. I'll watch."

MUSKEGON RIVER

Location: Newaygo, Michigan – MI 82 west of I-131, west central Lower Peninsula.

Airport: One hour from Grand Rapids, three hours from Detroit.

Lodging: Grey Drake Lodge, 231-652-2868, www.greydrake.com. Plus several local motels.

Fly shops and Guides: Great Lakes Fly Fishing Company, 1-800-303-0567; Matt Supinski, 231-652-2868; Kevin Feenstra, 231-652-3528; Thornapple Outfitters, 616-975-3800; Hawkins Outfitters, 231-228-7135; Fred Lee, 269-323-2316.

Matt hooked up on the second drift. It was a magnificent buck that had been in the river for some time, showing deep coloration along the back and flanks. It fought deep and long but revived quickly after being photographed. We guessed his weight at close to 18 pounds.

We quit before noon. Not a bad day at all for a few hours of extreme conditions.

Streamer techniques are becoming more popular on the Muskegon River each year. Much of this can be credited to the teaching techniques and innovative fly pattern development of another Muskegon guide, Kevin Feenstra. Kevin's streamers look a bit disheveled in the hand but they seem alive and natural-looking in the water. They are typically constructed with opossum fur heads, dubbed bodies, flowing hackle fibers, feather wings, and marabou tails. Varying in length from 2 to 4 inches, his streamers represent an array of forage fish including sculpins, smelt, and chubs. Steelhead will definitely chase and slam streamers, and there are many areas along the Muskegon, not well suited to nymphing techniques, that hold good numbers of aggressive fish. These spots, typically those full of larger rocks and boulders, are ideal for streamers. The strikes are aggressive and jolting, a preview of the following mayhem of the battle.

You will see a wide range of tackle on the Muskegon, including bait rigs, spinning gear, and heavy back-trolling rigs. The typical fly outfit is a rod of 9 or 9½ feet for a 7- or 8-weight line. More often than not the setup is for chuck-and-duck nymphing with a shooting or running line and long leader. Right-angle indicator nymphing with traditional, weight-forward fly lines is becoming more popular and two-handed Spey rods are common, both for nymphing and for swinging Pacific Coast–style steelhead flies. You will want a rod with backbone for the larger fish, whether you're nymphing or stripping and swinging streamers. I occasionally see folks with 6-weight rods but I think—unless you are an expert—these are less suitable than stouter models.

Standard egg flies work well on the Muskegon. Add a few with Estaz or Crystal Chenille bodies for more flash, and you will be in fine shape in that category. Even though caddis populations have declined in the past few years, the green and olive caddis pupa remains a top-producing nymph. Fluttering Hex nymphs, Hare's Ears, Pheasant Tails, a few Sparrow Nymphs, and stonefly patterns will cover the basics.

Classic West Coast steelhead flies work just fine, but I would add some marabou Speys to the list. Schmidt's Autumn Spey is awfully good, and Kustich's Purple October is excellent. Streamers should represent available forage fish. Sculpin patterns are my favorite. Feenstra's Sculpins, Zonkers in black or white, alewife patterns, and plain old Woolly Buggers produce solid hits.

The Muskegon is a food-rich and scenic tailwater fishery that nurtures a tremendous run of Lake Michigan steelhead from September through May. It has sparkling, lively riffles with ideal spawning gravel, deep, foreboding holes, heavy runs, and sweeping, gentle pools bordered by sand and silt. Depth ranges from a few inches to several feet, the bottom from solid and secure to tenuous and slippery. Below Croton, the river averages close to 100 feet in width with many reaches exceeding 150 feet. It is a beautiful, happy, wild, and scary (in places) river ideally suited to a wide variety of steelhead fly angling techniques and preferences. It is certainly one of the very best steelhead rivers in the Great Lakes basin.

White River

Overshadowed by the Pere Marquette to the north and the Muskegon to the south, the White River receives considerably less angling pressure despite its strong run of steelhead.

The headwaters of the White form at the junction of several small feeder streams a few miles northeast of the town of White Cloud in Newago County. After flowing southward to White Cloud, the river turns west to the village of Hesperia, then southwest through Oceana County into Muskegon County, then through White Lake, then finally empties into Lake Michigan.

WHITE RIVER

Location: Hesperia, Michigan, on MI 20, west of MI 37, west central Lower Peninsula.

Airport: Ninety minutes from Grand Rapids.

Lodging: Several small local motels; also, the Pere Marquette River Lodge in Baldwin is about 35 minutes north.

Fly shops and Guides: Great Lakes Fly Fishing Company, Rockford, Michigan, 1-800-303-0567 or 616-866-6060, www.troutmoor.com. Also see listings for Pere Marquette River.

The river has a soft, gentle current in most areas, with an average hydraulic gradient of about 6 feet per mile. This can lull an angler into a false sense of security. There are areas where the river's current gathers power and picks up velocity. As always, first-time visiting anglers need to scope out and analyze a particular stretch before wading. Be particularly careful around deadfalls and curving riffle water where it dumps into a pool or bend hole.

Steelhead ascend the White during the late fall, winter, and into mid-spring. The fall-run fish follow Pacific salmon and gorge on eggs and nymphs dislodged by the salmons' furious spawning activity while on gravel redds. Spring fish start to show in good numbers as early as the first week in March if winter weather has not been too severe.

The lower river begins at the junction pool where the North Branch enters the main river. From that point downstream to White Lake, the river is fairly large and often takes on a dark color, which makes safe wading problematic. By far, the best steelhead angling is farther upstream along the curves and bends that parallel Cleveland Road, both up and downstream from the 184th Avenue Bridge and farther upstream to the dam in Hesperia. Most, but not all, angling pressure centers at the dam in Hesperia, and it remains fairly heavy for about a mile downstream. Between 198th Avenue and Garfield Road there is a series of tight bends with deep, resting pools intermingled with riffle water and runs over gravel and sand. Fishing pressure is typically lighter in this stretch. In my opinion, the best water is between Garfield Road and Pines Point Campground. Pines Point is on the west side of the river and is reached off Cleveland Road.

The White averages about 50 feet in width in this area and runs about 3 feet deep, with pools and holes that exceed 6 feet. The bottom is a mix of silt, sand, and gravel. In some stretches the banks are open and casting is easy, but many runs and pools are back-dropped with dense trees. In these areas, roll casting and/or chuck-and-duck delivery are about the only effective methods. It is important to monitor your energy level and the strength in your legs when fishing this part of the White. Although the current is usually soft enough, the depth and the constant push of water will gradually sap your strength and ability. And there are numerous obstacles under the surface. Watch for old stumps and tangled logs, especially as you round a bend into a deep pool or a corner hole with dark water.

The river in this area is big enough to float in a canoe or small driftboat, but be aware that the tight bends can clog with logs and debris during the spring runoff. An impassable turn miles from anywhere is an ugly surprise. Do not float this river alone early in the spring. Bring a friend and a saw.

Steelhead in the White River can run very large. Many fish reach the middle teens in weight, but the average is closer to 8 pounds. They feed heavily on nymphs as well as drifting eggs. The White is one of the few rivers where I have observed aggressive steelhead charge several feet to inhale my drifting nymph. Thankfully, when this has occurred, everything happened so quickly that I did not have time to think and screw things up by striking too soon.

This river is extremely food-rich, with excellent mayfly, stonefly, and caddis populations. It has brown drakes and *Hexagenia* nymphs in notable numbers. These big bugs are present throughout the river, and steelhead love them. Over the years my best fly on the White has been a Hex nymph tied with a pale yellow body and fluttering filoplume (aftershaft feather) tail and abdomen gill structure. I use Swiss straw over the top of the abdomen to hold the gills in place and fold the Swiss straw forward to form a wing case. A fine copper wire rib and a couple of turns of partridge hackle at the hook eye finish this pattern. Lots of fly tyers like to add small, black plastic eyes, but I'm not convinced the eyes make a difference. If I could have only one fly pattern for the White it would be this Hex tied on No. 8 and 10 hooks.

Because there is usually some color to the White's flow, carry egg patterns in fairly bright colors. Even when the river runs clear, the duller, more natural-colored egg flies should show a spot of fluorescent orange or chartreuse. The Nuke Egg pattern, with its soft halo of cream or white yarn over a chartreuse or orange egg, is especially effective on the White River's spring steelhead.

The White is only about a half hour from Muskegon, about an hour from Grand Rapids, and it can be busy on weekends but rarely comes close to attracting similar angling pressure to that found on the Pere Marquette or Muskegon. In the 21st century, solitude is a relative term and there will always be other anglers around, but the White offers a measure of peace to complement its healthy run of steelhead.

The North Branch of the White River is a much smaller stream that attracts a surprisingly large run of spring steelhead. It enters the main White south of CR B86 in southern Oceana County. The best steelhead fishing is several miles upstream in the area between 144th Avenue and its junction with Bear Creek, and from Bear Creek downstream through a series of tight loops and S curves to the area off the west end of Winston Road.

This is a much smaller stream with an average width from 20 to 25 feet. Steelhead tend to hide and rest in the darkest, deepest water under banks and in corner pools or under the prolific logs and snags. The North Branch has the same abundant insect life as the main White, and a lifelike Hex pattern is usually the best fly choice.

Be sure to check the fishing regulations. The North Branch usually opens on the last Saturday in April and closes on September 30.

Pere Marquette River

A National Wild and Scenic River, the Pere Marquette is probably the most famous of all Great Lakes steelhead streams and, arguably, one of the most beautiful. Tiny creeks come together near the village of Chase in eastern Lake County and form the Middle Branch of the "PM." The Middle Branch, the Little South Branch, and the Baldwin River join near the town of Baldwin to form the mainstem of this great fishery.

Steelhead, salmon, and lake-dwelling brown trout make the run from Lake Michigan up and through the entire system, often reaching far into the headwaters. Steelhead fly anglers do well in the upper reaches of the tributaries during the open season, but it is the flies-only stretch from the highway bridge at MI 37 to Gleason's Landing, and the reach from Gleason's Landing to Branch, that receives the most attention. Part of the reason is that this water is open to angling all year—check the Michigan Department of Natural Resources (MDNR) regulations for any changes. More importantly, this part of the river, and especially the flies-only

Winter nymphing on the Pere Marquette.

stretch, is a perfect steelhead nursery with clean, cool, oxygen- and nutrient-rich water flowing over miles of ideal spawning gravel.

This gravel is the attractor for thousands of salmonids from early August—when the first waves of salmon rush in—through late fall, when large brown trout and steelhead ascend the river, and into spring's welcome to the bulk of the steelhead spawning migration. This ideal spawning habitat attracts and holds fishable numbers of trophy-size salmonids for 10 months of the year. Not surprisingly, the Pere Marquette attracts significant fishing pressure. The gathering of anglers peaks in September and October for salmon and in late March through April for steelhead. The fishing pressure is heaviest during these periods on the flies-only water.

The flies-only reach is approximately 8 river miles in length with a few public access points, although most of the riparian zone is privately owned. Cottages and year-round homes sit on the banks throughout the upper stretch, and many of the landowners have become more than frustrated with poor, disrespectful behavior of trespassers through the years. You will find countless "no trespassing" signs along the river, and it is wise—and proper—to heed their warnings. Some irate landowners have formed coalitions and hired custodians to protect their property from trespass. It is best to stay in the stream when moving from spot to spot. In most cases, this is not a safety issue. The PM in this area ranges from 40 to 70 feet wide and is relatively shallow and easy to wade.

The upper part of the flies-only water—from MI 37 to the Green Cottage—receives the heaviest pressure from both walk-in/wading anglers and from private and guided float trips by driftboat. There are very heavy concentrations of steelhead in this area during both fall and spring, and

---

PERE MARQUETTE RIVER

Location: Baldwin, Michigan, MI 37 at US 10, in the west central quadrant of the Lower Peninsula.

Airport: Ninety minutes from Detroit, two hours from Midland.

Lodging: Pere Marquette River Lodge, 231-745-3972; Baldwin Creek Motel, 231-745-4401; and several local motels.

Fly shops and Guides: Pere Marquette River Lodge, 231-745-3972; Baldwin Bait and Tackle, 231-745-3529; Ed's Sport Shop, 231-745-4974; John Kluesing, 231-745-3792; Jac Ford, 989-781-0997; Walt Grau, 231-757-3411; Charlie Weaver, 989-348-3299; Ultimate Outfitters, www.ultimateoutfitters.com.

it is probably the prettiest steelhead water in the Great Lakes basin. But how do you deal with the crowds? Fishing at midweek helps, but during the peak seasons it is best to start early—very early—and fish late into the evening when the pressure is lightest. There is another alternative. Because there are fair numbers of the great fish in the river before and after the peak times, try your luck in late November through December for fall fish. Look at late February, early March, and early to mid-May for the spring run. For me, this is much more enjoyable than rubbing elbows.

I have had excellent results in mid- to late November, when snow blankets the countryside and the bank traffic consists of deer and mink. Not long ago, Kelly Galloup and I floated from the MI 37 access to the Green Cottage on November 15, the opening day of deer season. It was cold but not uncomfortable, and we wore blaze orange caps as a safety precaution. We saw only one deer hunter, who waved a greeting from his stand near the bank. Kelly caught two silver hen fish on green caddis nymphs near the railroad trestle and I managed to land a nice buck that ate a black stonefly nymph in a small pocket near the junction with the Baldwin River. We saw no other anglers and had a great day.

May angling can be superb. When Michigan's general fishing season opens on the last Saturday of April, most folks start pursuing other species and steelhead angling pressure drops dramatically. Leaves are out, bugs are hatching, and the weather is warm and comfortable. Water temperatures are warming into the ideal range for rainbow trout, and the steelhead are active. Some of the fish in the river will be drop-backs—those that have completed their spawning and are heading downstream to big water. These fish are usually hungry and are interested in a wide variety of prey, including large surface flies and streamers.

The Pere Marquette Lodge sits on the west side of MI 37 just north of the bridge—the upper stream limit of the special-regulations water. The lodge and fly shop owns property down to the river's bank, and I have never been refused access to the water there. Be sure to ask, and it would not hurt to buy something. The fly shop is well stocked and is run by knowledgeable, helpful people. Just south of the bridge, 72nd Street runs to the west. A short drive on 72nd Street takes you over a set of railroad tracks and, a bit farther, to a parking area on the right-hand side of the road that is well marked and bordered by a wooden fence. This spot is roughly in the middle of the upper part of the flies-only water between MI 37 and the Green Cottage. A well-worn pathway from the parking lot winds down a hill to the river. The fishing is excellent in both directions from this point. Driving farther west a short way on 72nd Street brings you to an intersection with a well-used road. A right turn takes you to the Green Cottage access. This is about the midpoint, or 4 miles into the special-regulations water. Again, the steelhead fly fishing is superb in both directions, but my favorite move is to walk upstream several hundred yards and fish back down to the access. Over the years I have probably caught (and lost) more steelhead here than in any other part of the river.

Another popular public access point for walk and wade anglers is near the Claybank Pools off 52nd Street/Claybanks Road in Baldwin. The water is a bit larger and deeper here, but still safe to wade with a measure of common sense. It has the typical graveled-riffle-to-pool configurations of the upper stretch but is a bit bigger and darker in the pools and holes and has more submerged timber. The downstream limit of the special-regs water is at Gleason's Landing. This stretch holds steelhead in good numbers but is a bit more difficult to fly-fish—at least for me. I much prefer the upper water.

There are miles of excellent fly angling downstream from the flies-only water, but walk-in access is limited due to extensive private property control of the riparian zone. I strongly suggest hiring a guide for a float trip through these lower runs of the Pere Marquette. The water is less pressured and there are extensive stretches of ideal spawning habitat as well as perfect holding and resting areas. Some of the best fly-fishing guides in the country work this water with high success. I have fished with several of them and have never been disappointed with the angling or the companionship. You will find magical places on the lower water. Rainbow Rapids, A-Frame Village, The "D" Cup, and the long gravel reaches through the big club properties all produce excellent opportunities.

Tackle for the PM is varied depending on technique. Long, two-handed, Spey-type rods are used both for precision drifting of nymph and egg patterns and for swinging classic flies. A growing number of anglers use beefy streamer rods to jerk-strip large sculpin patterns when the water temperature is in the 55 degrees F (13 degrees C) range. This seems to energize steelhead and make them eager to slam a big fly fished aggressively. The most popular and versatile outfit is a long rod of 9½ to 10 feet in length set up to drift nymph and egg patterns deep and drag-free. The rod needs to have some backbone, and a 7-weight is most popular.

The basic fly assortment for the Pere Marquette is simple enough. Carry egg flies from about 5 millimeters to about a half inch in diameter in chartreuse, steelhead roe, Oregon cheese, and cream. Try mixing these colors in one pattern—Oregon cheese with a spot of chartreuse, cream with a spot of Oregon cheese, or a blend that looks good to you. Because the PM is rich with insect life, steelhead often zero in on a specific bug. Early in the spring season, a small black stonefly nymph (No. 14 or so) is often your best choice. Green caddis nymphs, Hex nymphs, Hare's Ears, larger stonefly patterns, the Sparrow nymph, Schmidt's Antron Bugs, and Egg-Sucking Leeches with chartreuse or orange heads make up the core of a well-stocked nymph box. Additionally, the local fly shops carry specialized patterns that work very well at various points during the season. Be sure to check these out.

The Pere Marquette River rewarded my early, fumbling attempts to catch steelhead on the fly in the 1960s. It taught me patience, stealth, and humility. It has provided great joy in success and deep appreciation for its wild, natural beauty. Its happy current, scenic valley, and magnificent steelhead make it one of my favorite places on earth.

PHOTO BY JOHN KLUESING

John Kluesing holds a huge Pere Marquette spring buck.

Little Manistee River

Thinking back to my early days of fly fishing for steelhead when a few friends and I were trying to learn the rules of the game, warm memories of success and jubilation often involve the Little Manistee. We fished it hard—mostly in the spring—and tried a wide array of flies, various line and leader configurations, and multiple techniques with mixed (often poor) results. We were chided and teased by lure and bait anglers in those early days back in the 1960s. "They won't eat flies." "Hey kid, try spawn. They only eat spawn." "Wigglers work. Getcha some wigglers." Wigglers, a local term for the *Hexagenia* nymph, are harvested from silt banks and sold through bait stores. *If steelhead eat live wigglers, why not artificials? If steelhead eat spawn, why not egg flies? If steelhead eat some Hex nymphs, why not caddis and stoneflies?* We didn't give up.

I clearly remember one cold April morning with heavy clouds that promised fresh snow. Steve Nevala and I were discouraged. We'd been fishing hard for two days with only a few brief hook-ups on very large (quarter-size) egg flies. We drove west along County Line Road downstream from Nine Mile Bridge and stopped at a friend's streamside cabin, where we had permission to park and fish. Steve walked to the bank and yelled. I joined him. From where we stood, several steelhead were visible gliding into and out of dark pockets near gravel. Some were bright silver, some showed a bit of color. One large male wore a deep red band along his entire length. "Let's sneak down there," Steve said. Yes indeed.

Adrenaline helped me toss several casts into logs and bankside willows, but I finally calmed down enough to actually hit the water. I was fishing two egg flies, one orange and one chartreuse. After a few drifts through a dark seam I saw a fish turn and reject one of my flies. I stripped in to examine my rig, thinking perhaps there was a small leaf or something on a fly. Both were clean. I don't know why but decided to use my scissors to clip down both flies. With a few snips the flies were reduced and ragged, actually a bit smaller than intended. They were now somewhat smaller than a dime and shaggy but still egg-shaped. My first cast produced a solid take and I actually landed the fish, thanks to Steve's fine work with the net. We clipped several more flies down to a similar size and each of us landed several fish through the morning.

That evening back in our motel room we tied dozens of small egg flies in various colors and shades. We examined our nymph patterns and decided they were also too large. We had been fishing Hex and black stonefly nymphs on No. 2 hooks, about the size one might use just prior to the salmonfly hatch on the Madison River in Montana. Way too big, we theorized. I tied a few nymphs on No. 6 and 8 hooks for the next day.

At dawn we were back at the same spot, shivering as much from anticipation as from the cold. We caught fish. It was truly a breakthrough day. We were actually smug—for a while. Parts of the equation remained to be solved but we were on the way.

The Little Manistee is a productive, fertile trout stream throughout its course from the area upstream from the small village of Luther to its mouth at the south end of Manistee Lake, with much of the best steelhead water upstream between Six Mile Bridge and Nine Mile Bridge. Above Nine Mile Bridge, the river parallels Riverside Drive and Mitchell Road for several miles. This is also a good stretch for steelhead in both spring and fall. Spencer Bridge and the Old Grade Campground site are at the upstream limit for productive steelhead fly fishing, due more to the small size of the water and the heavy bankside alders than to fish numbers.

In the prime stretch between Nine Mile and Six Mile Bridges the river runs from about 40 to 60 feet in width but does vary on both sides of these numbers. It runs cold and clean in depths measured in just a few inches to several feet in the deep bend holes. The Little Manistee is a perfect steelhead nursery. The water is high in oxygen and is food-rich. Its bottom is a mix of sand and silt with long runs of perfect spawning gravel

A fat, prespawn spring hen from the Little Manistee.

protected by logjams, undercut banks, and deep, dark runs shaded with dense vegetation.

Both the fall and spring runs of steelhead produce significant numbers of fish in most years. The fall run usually begins in earnest by mid-October, but often begins to fish well a few weeks earlier. Good fly fishing typically lasts through November into December with the best fly fishing taking place between mid-October and mid-November.

The spring run begins to build between March 15 and the end of the month. By April 5 it is usually in full swing. A note of interest for the spring run is the quota of eggs taken at the DNR weir below Six Mile Bridge off Old Stronach Road. This is a major producer of fertilized eggs for the entire Great Lakes basin. Steelhead are held until the quota is reached and then released upstream. It is wise to stop in at the facility and check the progress of the egg-taking operation.

Little Manistee steelhead range greatly in size during both the fall and spring runs. The bulk of the fish are in that classic 5- to 8-pound range, but there are many smaller fish in the 3-pound class and enough monsters from 15 to 18 pounds to excite even the most stoic fly angler. This wide range is a near mirror of the run of fish in the much larger Manistee River. Both rivers enter Manistee Lake before hitting Lake Michigan. As fish enter Manistee Lake before heading for their natal spawning grounds, there is a natural division but I think a fair number of the monster fish found in the Little Manistee have wandered a bit. This is hardly scientific, merely my opinion.

Because it is a small river it is not usually necessary to make long casts. Accuracy is at a premium, however. The narrow, fish-holding runs and pockets are often tightly bordered by logs and other obstructions. The water is almost always clear, so relatively fine terminal tackle is required. Still, there are huge, electric fish in this stream and your leader needs to have adequate strength and your rod enough backbone to handle them. It is a delicate balance on a moving scale based on prevailing conditions.

Since that epiphany nearly 40 years ago I have been convinced that small flies are one of the main keys to success on this river. Egg patterns, in a variety of colors, should be the size of a natural, drifting egg, which is between 4 and 5 mm in diameter. And I prefer multicolored single eggs of this size or two Micro-Eggs of two different colors (orange and chartreuse) on one hook. Nymph size should vary just a bit between fall and spring. This little river receives a lot of pressure, and the steelhead—

particularly the big, repeat-spawning fish—get smart. Natural bugs are smaller in the fall, because the bigger nymphs have hatched the preceding summer. Use stonefly and Hex nymphs on No. 8 and 10 hooks, and caddis larvae in No. 10 and 12 in the fall. Go up one size in the spring. Hare's Ears, Sparrow Nymphs, Pheasant Tails, Egg-Sucking Leeches, and Schmidt's Antron Nymph all produce on the Little Manistee.

Manistee River

The headwaters of the Manistee nurture wild brookies, and its middle reaches support large, sulking brown trout that rise freely to a wide array of mayflies and greedily chase sculpin and crayfish fly patterns. As a trout stream, it is surely one of the country's best east of the Rockies. But its enduring fame is due to its prolific runs of large steelhead.

The most famous section of the river is its final push below Tippy Dam to Lake Michigan. This is big steelhead water without peer in the Great Lakes basin. Tippy Dam is just north of the village of Wellston, Michigan, about 100 miles north of Grand Rapids and roughly 200 miles northwest of the Detroit metropolitan area. It is close enough to Chicago—about six hours by car—to entice even short weekend visits by anglers from the Windy City. The Manistee is steelhead Mecca.

The fish are special. They are plentiful and big. Estimates vary from year to year, but an "average" year brings eight to ten thousand fish into the river during the fall run, and approximately twenty thousand show up in the spring. The latter figure includes holdover fall fish and early winter arrivals. The Manistee is stocked heavily with smolts, and there is significant natural reproduction and excellent survival of wild steelhead. Again, estimates and opinions vary, but an angler can reasonably expect to find a ratio of one-to-one of hatchery and born-in-the-river steelhead. Both hatchery and river-born Manistee steelhead are aggressive fly eaters and this makes them truly special. The river is rich in food, particularly invertebrates. It holds caddis, stoneflies, and mayflies in abundance, so the small steelhead smolts are conditioned to feed on insects. They make the conversion to a fish diet only after entering Lake Michigan, where they grow rapidly. Many of the Manistee's fish are repeat spawners, and a significant number of these steelhead reach tremendous size. Each year trophies over 20 pounds are caught and released by fly anglers. The average Manistee steelhead—both fall and spring—is close to 9 pounds. They are big, numerous, and like to eat flies—what could be better?

The small village of Wellston, about 30 miles west of Cadillac, Michigan, is the best base for this steelhead fishery. Wellston has an excellent fly shop (Schmidt Outfitters), accommodations, restaurants, and grocery stores, and is only two hours from Grand Rapids and less than four hours from Detroit.

This is a big river that can run as high as 3,000 cubic feet per second. It averages a bit more than 100 feet in width and has deep pockets and holes that reach depths of several feet. It has a large amount of underwater timber, and all of this combines to endanger a careless wader. Use some common sense. By far, the best area for the wading, walk-in angler is from the boat ramp just downstream from Tippy Dam for about 2 river miles. As one might reasonably expect, this area gets the most foot traffic and angling pressure. Even if you own a good driftboat, your best bet is to hire a guide, at least for your first few visits to the Manistee.

Because the river is large, a fair number of boating anglers and guides use motors, both prop- and jet-propelled. Generally speaking, most follow the established etiquette and slow down to a no-wake speed when approaching and passing other boats and wading anglers. The motorized craft allow anglers and guides to work prime stretches repeatedly, then move at speed to the next target, and finally, back to the take-out ramp at the end of the day. Driftboats without motors must make a longer float to reach a take-out point and do not have the luxury of being able to move back upstream to a prime run after they have followed a running steelhead downriver.

The first float section is from Tippy Dam to High Bridge, roughly 8 river miles. This run has wide, long, and plentiful gravel beds that are ideal for spawning salmonids. Popular spots include Rock Pile, Gravel Island, Tunk Hole, and Suicide Bend. Guides without United States Forest Service special permits can guide only on this stretch and must both launch and take their boats out at the boat ramp immediately below Tippy Dam.

This is a prime fly-angling area. The plentiful gravel holds spawning salmon in the fall, and steelhead congregate in close proximity to gorge on eggs and nymphs dislodged by active salmon hens. The steelhead often become very bold in this area. Most often, they lurk in the deeper pockets and riffles below active salmon redds, but I have sometimes seen them darting around the cleaned gravel right next to the (usually) larger, agitated salmon. The king salmon attract more then steelhead. Because they are very large—some exceed 30 pounds—they also draw large numbers of people. And a certain, if not dominant, percentage of these are so crazed with the bloodlust for big salmon that they practice ugly and illegal snagging tactics. It is best to wait until the salmon run is on the wane to avoid these hooligans. By November 1, the salmon craze is typically over and steelhead fly fishing begins to peak.

Another favorite fly-fishing stretch is from the access at Bear Creek (itself a fine steelhead fishery) to Rainbow Bend. This run of the river is less crowded for both spring and fall runs of steelhead. It has more difficult walk-in access, and guides must have the USFS permit. It is ideal for fishing from a boat, with dark, gravel-bottomed runs, slow resting areas, and deep, foreboding holes. From the Bear Creek access, guides can easily reach the key spots in this long stretch of water, even extending downstream from Rainbow. Some of the favored hot spots include Cemetery Run, Buck Horn, Geezer, and Power Line. The big curve just upstream from Rainbow Bend has also produced many fine steelhead for me.

The Manistee has a wide variety of water types that are suitable for different fly-fishing techniques. If you want to use a two-handed rod and swing classic Spey patterns, you will have success on the Manistee. The river also produces fish for anglers who prefer to use heavy sinking lines and jerk-strip leech and sculpin streamers. The chuck-and-duck technique is widely applied here. It works extremely well, particularly in short, deep pockets and runs. Outfitter and guide Ray Schmidt has developed and refined a new and extremely effective nymphing technique that utilizes long, two-handed rods and a float (strike indicator). The method allows for incredibly long, drag-free drifts. The cast and the mending technique are the keys, and it only takes a few minutes to learn. This method is outlined in Chapter Three.

Flies for the Manistee are fairly typical of those used elsewhere in Michigan, but there are a few that stand out. Green and olive caddis nymphs, black stoneflies, Hex nymphs, Hare's Ears, Pheasant Tails, and Sparrow Nymphs should be in your box. Be sure to have several of Schmidt's Antron Bug. This fly comes in dark, medium, and light colors as well as an all-white version that imitates the Mysis shrimp. The shrimp version is my favorite. Egg flies? Of course. Bring a variety of sizes and colors ranging from large chartreuse to small (life-size) pale cream. A common and effective terminal rig for Manistee steelhead combines an egg fly dropper with a nymph as the point fly. When in doubt, start with an Oregon cheese-colored egg above a caddis, Hex, or Antron Bug.

The sheer size and wild nature of these extraordinary steelhead require certain minimum capabilities in rods and reels. It is possible to hook

PHOTO BY BO BRINES

Bo Brines with a typical spring hen from the Manistee River.

fish into the mid-teens in weight every day of the season. They will leap, crash, and run for long distances. In order to land and release such magnificent creatures unharmed, a 7- or 8-weight rod and a *really* good disk-drag reel are mandatory. The rod needs to have some serious backbone for lifting and turning, and the reel must have a smooth, reliable drag with minimum start-up inertia.

One of my favorite memories is from just two seasons past. I hooked a large male steelhead on an Antron Bug in a deep run below Bear Creek. The fish made a wild leap, then ran downstream, fast and hard, past another boat anchored at midstream. It then turned at a right angle, around the anchor rope of the other boat, and dove toward a logjam. Miracles happen. The helpful guys in that boat carefully freed my backing from their rope, and I was again directly connected to the big buck steelhead. We pushed our boat downstream quickly to gain line and entered into a deep, bulldogging standoff for several minutes. The fish took off downstream again and ran close to 300 yards before stopping in a deep pool. Despite our hard rowing to keep up, this fish was often 150 yards away. We finally netted this great steelhead after—I'm guessing—about 15 minutes of joyous panic. He was 36 inches long, deep and thick, with a hateful gleam in his eye. My rod was a 9½-foot 8-weight, and the reel was a Ross Canyon 4 with 250 yards of backing. I don't believe we would have landed that fish with anything less.

The Manistee is a special river by any measure. It is handsome, powerful, and blessed with ideal habitat for steelhead. Because the river is rich in food and drains into Lake Michigan, probably the most productive food factory of the upper Great Lakes, it grows very large steelhead. We all have goals and dreams. One of mine is to land, photograph, kiss, and release a legitimate 20-pounder. I have come close, really close, several times. With this goal in mind, the Manistee is my first choice among all the rivers in the Great Lakes.

Bear Creek

Bear Creek empties into the Manistee River about 10 miles west of Wellston. The junction pool is just below a major USFS access site and boat launch facility used by area steelhead guides and anglers. Over the years I have fished this pool and the immediate downstream run often, usually with good results. From a vantage point near the junction pool, you will see the wakes of cruising steelhead as they nose into the soft current of Bear Creek and then dart upstream into the smaller river.

Bear Creek is one of the major nursery streams for the Manistee steelhead strain, with excellent gravel reaches that extend many miles to the north despite its unimpressive, low, and marshy appearance at the junction with the Manistee. In the area immediately upstream from the big river, the Bear runs slowly through twisting, convoluted bends. Its banks are soft and spongy, and the edges are littered with stumps and fallen trees. This area has a bottom mix of sand and silt and is excellent habitat for large burrowing *Hexagenia* nymphs. Steelhead often stage in this vicinity and a Hex nymph is the ideal choice for the angler.

The best areas for steelhead, both spring and fall runs, are upstream a few miles, where the hydraulic gradient washes silt and mud from spawning gravel. This is a small stream, too small for boats and nearly ideal for the wading angler. It has deep chutes and pockets, dark churning holes at the bends, highly oxygenated gravel, undercut banks, and lively riffles. It has some very large steelhead.

There are a few problematic access points between the mouth of the Manistee and the bridge on Coates Highway that require a rugged four-wheel-drive vehicle—that you don't care too much about—and a brush-busting slog through the woods. It also helps to have youth, energy, determination, and a compass to reach the fish that stage in this area. It can be worth the effort. Typically there are plenty of fish and relatively light angling pressure downstream from the Coates Highway bridge. The width of the Bear in this area runs from about 25 to 45 feet, and wading is relatively easy. The bottom here is a mix of sand and gravel with a few boulders thrown in. You will find trees, stumps, undercuts, overhanging vegetation for shade, and occasional large, sweeping curves with dark holes and deep slicks for cover.

Driving north from Coates Highway on High Bridge Road, there are access points at bridges on Kerry Road, Johnson Road, Milks Road, and CR 598 just west of the village of Kaleva. Steelhead continue their movement upstream above Kaleva all the way to the uppermost tributaries, but here the stream becomes very small and too tight for most fly fishing. Still, it is worth noting that I have seen (and hooked but not landed) several steelhead in this small water while fishing for stream trout during late May. The riparian zone is a mix of public and private lands. Be watchful and careful of private property notices and particularly so near roads and at the major bridges.

Steelhead in Bear Creek run larger than one might reasonably expect in such small water. In fact, they can be very big indeed. I have seen several that would push into the high teens in weight. The average fish in the spring is probably close to 8 pounds with fall fish running about 1 to 2 pounds lighter. They are dynamic, vigorous steelhead that run wild when hooked. A complicating factor on small water is the close proximity of heavy tangled cover. Runs are usually short as steelhead frantically dive for logs and other structure.

MANISTEE RIVER, LITTLE MANISTEE RIVER, AND BEAR CREEK

Location: Wellston, Michigan, MI 55 west, 5 miles from MI 37 in the northwest quadrant of the Lower Peninsula.

Airport: Two hours from Grand Rapids, one hour from Traverse City, three hours from Detroit Metro.

Lodging: Schmidt Outfitters, 1-888-221-9056, www.schmidt outfitters.com, plus several small, local motels.

Fly shops and Guides: Schmidt Outfitters, 1-888-221-9056 or 231-848-4191, www.schmidt outfitters.com. Chuck Scribner, 231-723-6193; Chuck Hawkins, www.hawkinsflyfishing.com or 231-228-7135. www.hawkinsfly fishing.com; Ultimate Outfitters, www.ultimateoutfitters.com.

It requires fairly stout tackle to safely land and release a good steelhead in small water. I normally like to use long rods to facilitate mending and for extra leverage in turning a determined fish, but shorter rods work better in close confines. I think a rod of 9 feet for a 7- or 8-weight line is about right for Bear Creek. That length is more than adequate, and the extra heft of the heavier line class assists in subduing a trophy.

Like all small streams, Bear Creek fishes best under low light conditions. Steelhead are nervous in skinny water, and bright skies make them downright neurotic. Cautious wading is an absolute necessity. Plan your first cast carefully. Take your time. That first delivery is your best shot for success. Low light offers an additional advantage in that you can use a heavier tippet—up to 8-pound test. This is extremely helpful in fighting heavy, electric fish close to snags and deadfalls.

A good mix of fly patterns for Bear Creek includes egg flies in cream, Oregon cheese, steelhead roe, and chartreuse. On bright days, use small flies. Under cloudy conditions, or if the water is tinged with color, larger egg flies can be used effectively, but I rarely tie one on that is larger than a half inch in diameter. Stonefly nymphs are very effective on this water. Black is the best color, and a No. 10 is usually right. Also, be sure to try a Hex nymph, Schmidt's Antron Bug, Green Caddis, Pheasant Tail nymph, and an Egg-Sucking Leech.

If you prefer walking, stalking, and wading to fishing from a boat, if you can apply patience and stealth, and if you don't mind losing a few big fish to obstructions, you will enjoy the intimacy of Bear Creek. It is best to fish Bear Creek during midweek if possible.

Betsie River

This lovely river begins at the outflow of Green Lake east of the village of Benzonia in southwest Grand Traverse County. It flows southwest into Benzie County, crosses briefly into Manistee County, then heads northwest to Lake Michigan. It is a wild river, particularly in its upper reaches, and has been listed as a natural river by the Natural Rivers Management Plan. This should afford protection by limiting development in coming years. In addition, much of the Betsie's flow is through the Pere Marquette State Forest, which affords a significant protective zone to the watershed.

Spring steelhead enter the river at the village of Frankfort and move through Betsie Lake and the Betsie River State Game area quickly. In early

March they begin to settle in slow, deepwater pools in the stretch that parallels River Road (west of MI 31) between Adams Road and the first River Road bridge. As the water temperature warms and approaches 40 degrees F (4.5 degrees C), the large push of fish moves farther upstream and begins to spread out.

Typically, large numbers of steelhead congregate in the span of river from River Road Bridge upstream to Homestead Dam. This area also has the highest concentration of anglers. There is easy park-and-walk access on the upstream side of the bridge at MI 31 south of Benzonia and at the access near Homestead Dam off Dam Road a short distance upstream. This is an easy area to fish. The river is small and welcoming. Between the dam and MI 31 it runs from about 30 to 50 feet wide in most places. The bottom is a mix of sand and gravel with some large rocks and areas of silt and mud. Downed trees, shaded banks, and deep pools provide shelter and security. Due to angler traffic, well-worn footpaths traverse the shoreline on both banks. Most of the spawning gravel in this stretch is in shallow water, and when fish are on their redds they are easy to see. Even when steelhead stay in the darker water in proximity to gravel, the active redds stand out like neon signs.

Steelhead are typically shy and easily spooked in this part of the Betsie. They sense a lot of heavy footsteps on the banks and see innumerable baits, lures, and flies. One or two careless casts will send a steelhead dashing for dark water.

Most anglers use terminal tackle that is too heavy, and flies that are too big. In almost all cases, and especially when the sun is bright and the water clear, size your tippet and flies downward. Rather than using a tippet of 8-pound test, try 6- or even 5-pound-test fluorocarbon. Nymphs should be no larger than appropriate to a No. 10 hook, and Micro-Eggs about 5 mm in diameter work best.

Stonefly nymphs are abundant in this part of the Betsie, as are most mayfly and caddis species. Black and dark brown stonefly patterns, green and cream caddis patterns, Pheasant Tail, Hare's Ear, and Hex patterns form the basic assortment. Sparrow Nymphs, Michigan (Spring's) Wigglers, classic Woolly Buggers in olive and black, and Egg-Sucking Leeches also catch fish with regularity.

The ultimate set of conditions for fishing the Betsie includes overcast skies, a slight warming trend, water temperatures between 40 and 50 degrees F (4.5 to 10 degrees C), and slight discoloration or stain due to light or moderate rain. This combination excites the fish and jump-starts activity. And they feel more secure in soft or subdued light. Equally important is the simple fact that cloudy days with rain, or the chance of rain, tend to mitigate angling pressure.

Steelhead that use the Betsie average close to 8 pounds, but there are many that come in much heavier weights. The largest Betsie River steelhead I've landed was about 14 pounds. It took a small egg fly in a dark, bankside run about halfway between the dam and the parking access at MI 31. The biggest fish I've personally seen landed was a huge, red-striped male that was more than 3 feet in length, deep-shouldered, and very heavy. It was taken on a small, black Woolly Bugger in the second deep hole upstream from MI 31.

Most often the heaviest fishing pressure runs from the base of the dam for about 200 yards downstream. For obvious reasons, fish stack up in this short stretch. When the Betsie is running low and clear, the low dam is a formidable barrier to upstream migration, but when the water rises from snowmelt or rain some steelhead do make it over the dam and move farther upstream.

> ## BETSIE RIVER
>
> **Location:** Benzonia, Michigan on US 31, in the northwest Lower Peninsula.
>
> **Airport:** Three hours from Grand Rapids, 45 minutes from Traverse City.
>
> **Lodging:** Extensive and varied in Traverse City, small local motels in Benzonia.
>
> **Fly shops and Guides:** Grouse Feather Fly Shop (Boyne City), 231-582-9950; Streamside Outfitters (Traverse City), 231-933-9300; Kelly Neuman, 989-848-5983; Pat Moore, 989-344-0605; The Northern Angler, www.the northernangler.com, 231-933-4730 or 1-800-627-4080.

The water above Homestead Dam is smaller and wild, best characterized by tight turns, log structures, long, sandy-bottomed stretches, and banks heavily lined with fly-grabbing bushes and trees. Steelhead tend to spread out in the upper river. They often stop and hold in a deep run or hole for a day or two, then move through long, sandy stretches to another position. There are fewer steelhead in the upper Betsie, and they are scattered rather than concentrated in specific runs. Several years ago I caught one in early May just downstream from Black Bridge, west of Thompsonville. I was fishing carelessly, exploring for resident stream trout with a black Woolly Bugger. I was shocked by a heavy jolt and pleased (and lucky) to land a 5-pound hen.

One might think that floating would be a decent way to explore this water. It is—with an experienced guide. There are stretches of unproductive water, tight turns, and enough obstructions to give pause if you are not familiar with the water. Old trees break and fall, currents move log-jams, and you might need a chain saw to proceed. If you can't get through or over an obstruction, there is a long hike in your future. That's the bad news.

The good news is that an experienced guide can put you on steelhead that are much less pressured than in most rivers. These upper-river fish behave naturally and readily eat flies. The fishing is in a natural, wild setting with light human intrusion. The surrounding countryside teems with waterfowl and wildlife, and the fly fishing ranges from good to excellent.

If you want to avoid the crowds and cast to wild fish in a primal setting, book a guided float on the upper Betsie. Both Kelly Neuman and Pat Moore run trips on this secluded part of the river, and they often work together to take a group of three or four fly angling friends. They will get you to the right spots at the right time with the right attitude.

Walk-in access on the upper river is reasonable but limiting, in that fishable numbers of steelhead may not be present in any given spot on a particular day. The Wollin Road bridge, Black Bridge, the Psutka Road bridge, and the Landis Road access are worth exploring.

The Betsie has a strong run of king salmon starting in August, followed by good numbers of lake-run brown trout in October. Steelhead follow these fish and feed heavily on their eggs, as well as nymphs, through early November.

Platte River

The Platte has been one of the region's premier steelhead streams for more than 50 years. All of its flow is through Benzie County, a short drive southwest from Traverse City. The Platte's headwaters are northeast of the village of Honor and close to the world-famous Interlochen Academy. The river flows in a southwesterly direction to Honor, then slightly northwest through Deadstream Swamp and into Platte Lake. From its exit from Platte Lake the river runs northeast to the mouth at Platte River Point on Lake Michigan.

The upstream limit for anadromous fish is the barrier at the Platte River State Fish Hatchery, a few miles east of Honor on MI 31. I think the best steelhead fly fishing for both fall and spring fish is from just below the bridge at MI 31 near the hatchery to the downstream MI 31 bridge west of Honor.

This stretch of the Platte is generally easy to wade and attracts large numbers of steelhead. The water is extremely clean, clear, and cold. It flows over a sand and gravel bottom with muck and silt edges. Its banks, except in the area right in the heart of Honor, are shaded and protected by cedar and spruce trees. There are undercut banks, submerged logjams and other woody debris, deep pockets, and dark holes. Long stretches and small patches of perfect spawning gravel are abundant. The average stream width is probably about 40 to 45 feet, but some smooth, shallow flats run considerably wider. It is, for the most part, a shallow river, easy to wade and explore. You would have to leave your brains in the truck to get in trouble while wading the Platte.

Clear, skinny water dictates a cautious approach. I was a bit clumsy on my first trip to the Platte back in 1965. Steelhead spooked and fled from the shallow pockets behind spawning gravel, and I became frustrated. Luckily, I was able to observe a more practiced, careful angler enjoy success. He stayed low, literally "duck-walked" into a casting position, and kept his fly rod low with a sidearm delivery. He hooked and landed a beautiful chrome buck of about 7 pounds on his third or fourth cast. I netted the fish for him and he thanked me with some pointers and several egg patterns that were smaller than those I carried. He suggested I use finer tippet and keep rod movement to a minimum on such a clear day. He said I should stay as low to the water as possible and wade very slowly and carefully. His tips paid off, not that day, but the next. I caught two beauties on those small egg flies. One was a slender, sleek hen of about 4 pounds, and the "trophy" was a large (for me at the time) buck of about 9 pounds.

Spring steelhead build to reasonable numbers in late March and accelerate through April. In a typical year the Platte will fish well later than many western Michigan streams, perhaps due to its cold, consistent flow. These fish get smart in a hurry. On a clear, bright day they will secrete themselves in the darkest water available. Look at edges, undercut banks, log tangles, and deeper broken water near gravel. If there is heavy angling pressure, try fishing at first and last light. The first hour or so at dawn and the last hour at dusk are usually the best on weekends or when skies are clear and sunny.

Fall-run fish follow Pacific salmon and will usually be found near active kings and silvers from late August (kings) through November (silvers).

My favorite stretch of river at this time of year is the northwesterly run from the Platte River Campground on Goose Road downstream to the bridge at Zimmerman Road. The river is typically at its lowest and clearest in the fall, and there is more shade and cover in this section.

Property owners on Platte Lake have lobbied hard to reduce the numbers of salmon in the past few years. A lawsuit against the Department of Natural Resources has been settled, and provides for a significant reduction in the total number of salmon in the Platte River. A weir below Platte Lake and close to the mouth at Lake Michigan controls the fall migration of Pacific salmon. One thousand kings and 20,000 silvers are allowed to pass. The larger number of silvers are needed at the upstream hatchery. Steelhead are allowed to pass without limit. Although greatly reduced from pre-settlement years, the salmon count is enough to provide a sport fishery in such a small river. In 2002 and 2003, fall steelhead numbers were lower than normal but are expected to rebound. In the fall of 2004, a gradual increase in steelhead returns was already evident. This bodes well for the future.

> ## PLATTE RIVER
>
> ———————●———————
>
> **Location:** Honor, Michigan, on US 31 between Traverse City and Benzonia.
>
> **Airport:** See Betsie River.
>
> **Lodging:** See Betsie River.
>
> **Fly shops and Guides:** See Betsie River.

There is some fishing available in the Deadstream Swamp run of river, but this stretch is typically silt-laden, dark, spooky, and hard to access and wade. I do not recommend it. And the run of river from the outflow of Platte Lake to the mouth holds fish but is not well suited to fly fishing. Most steelhead in this lowest section of the river stage in a couple of deep, slow pools just upstream from Lake Michigan that are better suited to bait fishing under a large bobber.

Although access is good throughout the best water, quite a bit of the riparian zone is privately owned, and you will see "no trespassing" signs along the banks. These must be respected. Stay in the water when fishing through these areas. You will find access points at Veterans Memorial Campground at MI 31, Platte River Campground on Goose Road, and at several side road bridges through Honor.

Tackle for the Platte is an interesting mix. You need a rod with enough backbone to handle fish in the 10-pound class and with a sensitive tip and upper section to protect light tippets. I suggest a moderate- or medium-fast-action rod in 6- or 7-weight. The best reel will have an extremely smooth drag with little start-up inertia to protect those fine leaders.

Take small single egg, Micro-Egg and Nuke Egg patterns in natural colors to the Platte. Be sure to have some in pale cream with a small dot

A big fall steelhead makes a run for it on the Platte River.

of orange or Oregon cheese in the mix. Aquatic insects are abundant here. *Hexagenia limbata,* brown drakes, Hendricksons, stoneflies, and caddis populations are strong throughout the river. One of the best nymph patterns for the Platte is a simple Pheasant Tail on a No. 12 hook. Schmidt's Antron Bug, in black, tan, brown, and white versions, is superb. Green Caddis Larvae, Black Stoneflies, and small Hare's Ears make a reasonable assortment.

If you like the thought of quiet stalking, actually hunting for trophy steelhead in small, challenging water, the Platte is ideal.

Lake Huron

Second largest of the Great Lakes, Huron covers 23,010 square miles. Its shoreline loops and curves through numerous channels and bays along Michigan and Ontario coastlines. Lake Huron is born in the cold rush of Lake Superior's water through the St. Mary's River. It blends with Lake Michigan directly beneath the big bridge at the Straits of Mackinac. At its northern end, Huron splits and curves around a series of large islands, creating a serpentine international border. The lake's North Channel forms here to the east of St. Joseph Island (Ontario) and Drummond Island (Michigan). Georgian Bay, itself large enough to qualify as a Great Lake, forms at the base of the North Channel and covers thousands of square miles southward past the Thirty Thousand Islands and the foot of the Grey–Bruce region of Ontario. This is the birth lake of freshwater steelhead. They have roamed Huron's icy caverns for more than 140 years and found the lake and its tributaries much to their liking.

Michigan's side of Huron has good steelhead fishing offshore and in a few tributaries, but does not match the number and variety found on the Canadian coast. Michigan's steelhead program for Lake Huron streams is managed primarily as a hatchery-sustained fishery. The Manistee strain, well adapted to Lake Huron, is the base genetic stock. The hatchery-raised fish are supplemented with natural reproduction in several rivers, but the actual percentage of wild fish is open to conjecture. Fin-clipped steelhead indicate hatchery origin. In the Au Sable River the proportion of fin-clipped fish seems to run about 60 percent. The Au Sable below Foote Dam gets too warm in the summer to nurture immature steelhead to the smolt stage. It is possible that unmarked steelhead

Monster brown trout, like this one from the Lake Huron surf, can be an unexpected bonus at the mouths of steelhead rivers.

with all their fins are roamers from Canadian rivers. Some people speculate that young-of-the-year steelhead in the Au Sable hightail it to the lake at a very small size—a peculiar and very specific adaptation.

Along Michigan's east coast steelhead are available offshore between Port Huron and Mackinaw City, but fishable numbers of steelhead in tributaries are limited to just a few streams. Good numbers of fish are found in the lower reaches of the Cheboygan River, Thunder Bay River, and Black River, but these are not classic fly-fishing venues.

The Pine River and Van Etten Creek are often overlooked by fly anglers. They are both tributaries to the Au Sable through Van Etten Lake, near the town of Oscoda, and receive significant runs of both fall and spring fish. Van Etten Creek joins Pine River just north of Van Etten Lake near Barlow Road and County Road F-41. Both the West and East Branches of the Pine River have good spring runs, with access points at several county roads and two-track fire trails northwest of Van Etten Lake. This is small water with large steelhead. Stalking skills are useful.

The Ocqueoc River enters Lake Huron's Hammond Bay a few miles northwest past the Forty Mile Point Lighthouse near Rogers City. This river has a good run of spring steelhead, and brown trout and Pacific salmon in the fall. Ocqueoc Falls, just off MI 68 is a scenic stop of interest. Many anglers congregate to fish the water immediately below the falls. Look at the river farther downstream for less crowded conditions. Public access is good through the Mackinaw State Forest along numerous gravel roads and fire trails.

North of the Mackinac Bridge, the Carp River crosses I-75 a few short miles past the town of St. Ignace and enters St. Martin Bay. This is another small, intimate stream. It has heavy runs of pink and king salmon in the fall and a respectable number of spring steelhead. Access points at the campground on MI 63 (Mackinac Trail), off the dirt road just off I-75, and along an unimproved gravel road running west from MI 63 to East Lake Road cover most of the best steelhead water.

The Canadian coastline offers more variety—and more high-quality steelhead rivers—than the Michigan side of Lake Huron. The Garden River enters the North Channel a short distance south of Sault Ste. Marie, Ontario. It has strong fall runs of Pacific salmon and a sizable spring steelhead run. Much of the best water on the Garden flows through native lands, and access is tightly controlled.

Much of the Ontario coast between Massey and Bayfield Inlet is extremely remote, with few roads and several large areas of Indian Reserves. The best rivers are along the southwestern edge of Georgian Bay, north along the Bruce Peninsula, then south on the Lake Huron coast, but the Hog River near Midland has prime steelhead habitat and is a favorite of local fly anglers. Check the river between its mouth and the town of Coldwater.

Both the Sydenham and Au Sable Rivers are close to the rivers covered in detail later in this chapter and have strong runs of predominately wild fish in fall and spring. They are within an easy drive of the Saugeen to the south and the Bighead and Beaver to the east. The Pottawatomi River is another fine stream and is favored by many local and touring fly anglers.

The Ministry of Natural Resources for the Province of Ontario emphasizes wild fish in its steelhead management programs. Habitat protection and restoration, safeguarding nursery streams, and reduced bag limits with an emphasis on catch-and-release angling are having a positive impact on angling quality throughout provincial waters. The positive impact is especially notable in the Lake Huron and Georgian Bay coastline tributaries.

East Branch of the AuGres

This small, picturesque stream has excellent runs of late fall and spring steelhead. The East Branch of the AuGres is formed at the junction of Hale Creek and Smith Creek near the town of Hale and flows nearly due south past the Iosco and Arenac County line.

Steelhead utilize the entire stream, but the best fishing—in terms of numbers of fish and the stream's fishability for fly anglers—is from the MI 55 access downstream to the general area south and east of National City in the vicinity of Turtle Road. The most productive steelhead water, in my experience, runs from Carpenter Road just north of MI 55 to Whittemore Road, a run of about 4 miles. In this stretch the East Branch runs from about 30 feet to 45 feet wide and has long, productive gravel sections that are ideal for steelhead redds. The fish congregate here and hide in dark creases and in pools near the prime spawning areas.

At the MI 55 bridge there is a well-maintained roadside parking and rest area with a set of wooden steps descending the steep bank to the river. This section of the AuGres is very easy to wade and offers enough

Fall is a great time to fish the picturesque AuGres River.

room for fly casting. And it has good numbers of fish in both spring and fall. Downstream from this point to the area of Whittemore Road the river supports its highest density of anadromous fish. Correspondingly, this area has the highest angling pressure during the peak runs, and particularly on weekends.

I prefer the fall season on the East Branch. After the salmon have died, fishing pressure declines dramatically. In most years the system has cleared of salmon by November 1. Steelhead numbers are strong and the fish are eager to eat faded, natural-looking egg flies and nymphs.

Black stonefly patterns in No. 8, Hex nymphs in 8 and 10, Green Caddis, Hare's Ears, and Pheasant Tails in No. 10 and 12 are the basics. Additionally, I have done well with Egg-Sucking Leech patterns. They seem to produce best with a small chartreuse egg at the head on dark cloudy days, and with an orange head on bright days.

> ### RIFLE RIVER AND EAST BRANCH OF THE AUGRES RIVER
>
> **Location:** West Branch, Michigan, MI 55 west From MI 33, in the northeast Lower Peninsula.
>
> **Airport:** Three hours from Detroit, two hours from Flint, one and a half hours from Midland.
>
> **Lodging:** Chain and small local motels in West Branch, local motels in Hale and Rose City.
>
> **Fly shops and Guides:** See Au Sable River.

Steelhead in the East Branch average about 6 pounds and there are a lot of small fish in the fall, usually males in the 3-pound range. There are big fish as well. The largest I have seen in the river was a huge, hook-jawed spring male with a vibrant and wide crimson band from cheek to tail. He was busy chasing smaller males away from a spawning hen and did not notice me until I had made several casts with a large streamer. On my second or third delivery, the big buck charged the streamer but did not eat it. I think I must have moved, or jerked, or done something that alerted him because he then just turned and drifted downstream to darker water. I waited for him to reappear for several minutes but he did not show and I moved on. My guess is that this fish was about 3 feet long. He was very thick in the body and probably weighed about 18 pounds. The largest fish I have landed in the East Branch of the AuGres was another male. He took a black stonefly nymph a few hundred yards below MI 55 in early November. I guessed him to be about 12 pounds.

Although the East Branch is small and easy to wade, there are a few points to remember. The holes at sharp bends are often quite deep. These spots usually have some tangled timber and often enough there are small clay patches that are extremely slippery. The combination can be problematic. Be especially careful in these locations. Sometimes the intensity of battling a large steelhead bent on running downstream can cloud judgment. On two occasions I've had to assist very wet, cold, and frightened anglers who slipped and dunked at a sharp turn in the river.

A rod of 9 or 9½ feet for a 6-weight line is plenty for the AuGres. Some folks use 5-weights, but I think that is just too light to beat a strong fish in close quarters quickly enough to ensure the fish's survivability. We owe a measure of respect to these trophy creatures, and a good way to show it is to use enough rod to do the job safely.

A side benefit to fishing for steelhead on the East Branch of the Au-Gres is the healthy population of resident trout. On those days when steelhead ignore your best efforts, it is likely that you will be entertained by numerous stream trout. Another bonus is the reasonable expectation of a huge spawning brown trout during the fall. These are lake dwellers up from Huron. Their numbers increase through November and into early December. Some reach extraordinary size—up to 10 pounds and more—but the average is smaller at about 5 pounds. The big browns will eat the same flies you brought for steelhead, and also like streamers.

This is a beautiful, bountiful little river that is easy to wade and fish. Its steelhead are lovely and rambunctious.

Rifle River

The headwaters of this small stream are found in the Rifle River Recreation Area about 4 miles east of Rose City in Ogemaw County. The outflow from Devoe Lake joins with several small streams including Gamble Creek and Houghton Creek within the recreation area's boundaries. From the junction with Houghton Creek downstream all the way to Lake Huron—more than 60 river miles—the Rifle supports steelhead runs in late fall, winter, and spring.

This entire run is unimpeded by dams. Steelhead, salmon, and large, lake-dwelling brown trout make their ascensions from the big water to spawning gravel quickly when the urge hits them. They move upstream through varied riparian zones including mixed hardwoods, cedar and balsam swamps, and rich, dark-soil farmland.

For the most part the Rifle is a clear, happy stream. It is easy to wade and the holding areas are fairly obvious, but the farmland areas in Ogemaw County push sediment into the stream during the spring thaw

Winter nymphing on the Rifle River.

and after heavy rains, and the river clouds quickly. In most cases it will clear in one day but a torrent can make fly fishing problematic for up to two days. It is worth waiting for this stream to clear. Very often superlative fishing kicks in as soon as the river's visibility begins to improve.

Peak fall fishing begins about the November 1. The steelhead are bright silver, rock hard, and fairly aggressive during this late fall period. They are in the river system to eat and are eager for salmon and brown trout eggs, as well as the drifting nymphs dislodged from spawning redds.

Look for polished gravel that indicates salmon or brown trout are actively spawning in the area. Most often (not always!) steelhead will lurk in the dark slots near cover or deep water immediately downstream from active redds, where they gobble the drifting banquet of eggs and nymphs. I like a tandem fly rig for steelhead and think it is particularly effective during the fall run on the Rifle. If the day is cloudy, a fairly bright egg fly showing some fluorescent chartreuse is a good choice. Team the egg pattern with a small black stonefly nymph as the point fly. On bright, clear days a more faded, natural color is best for the egg pattern. A mix of white with Oregon cheese produces a soft blend that closely resembles faded salmon and brown trout roe that has been in the gravel for a few days. On clear days, a Hex nymph or Hare's Ear is usually a wise choice for the point fly. The flies should be small under bright conditions; egg flies about the size of a pea and nymphs on No. 10 or 12 hooks are best. They can and should be bigger on dark days or when the water has color; egg patterns should be roughly the size of a dime, and the nymphs are best on No. 8 hooks.

You will have to change colors and sizes regardless. Some days the fish want just one color of egg and nothing else. Other days will produce takes on a particular nymph. You need to be ready. A fair assortment of flies for the fall season on the Rifle includes a variety of multicolored egg flies (emphasizing bright and subdued/natural) in both pea and dime sizes. The nymphs should be tied on hooks from No. 8 to 12. An assortment of Black Stoneflies, Hare's Ears, Hex, Sparrow Nymphs, Olive Caddis, and Pheasant Tails will cover the basics. Add black Egg-Sucking Leeches and a few standard Woolly Buggers.

When conditions are right—water temperatures close to 50 degrees F (10 degrees C) and fish fresh from the lake—streamers and Spey flies can be productive. This is an incredibly exciting way to fish the Rifle River. Alternately swinging and stripping sculpin patterns like Conrad's Sculpin or swinging undulating Spey flies through the runs and dark pools often produces an arm-jolting hit followed by a wild, acrobatic ride. You will need a heavy tippet for this work. Ten-pound-test Maxima is the lightest feasible for the wrenching strike of an agitated steelhead.

A gorgeous chrome hen from the Rifle River.

The spring run on the Rifle is fairly slow to build. More fish begin to show in mid-March but this is usually just a trickle. The run begins in earnest in early April and reaches a peak, in most years, around April 20 and often lasts well into May.

The first wave of spring steelhead move quickly and settle into the upper reaches of prime spawning gravel between Peters Road and Sage Lake Road. The second wave usually is more spread out, but often shows its highest numbers between Peters Road and MI 55. The third and final rush (very late in April) seems to prefer the downstream run from MI 55 to the Lake Ogemaw area and below.

Because the Rifle is for the most part a shallow river, there is little need for a heavy weight and the chuck-and-duck method of fishing. Fly anglers can fish pure fly lines—weight forward floating lines—with just a small split shot or a pair of beadhead nymphs and effectively put their offerings at the correct level to interest steelhead. A 7-weight rod of 9 or 9½ feet is the right tool for the Rifle.

Fly patterns for the spring run are the same as those used in the fall and winter, but perhaps a size larger. An assortment of multicolored eggs, stoneflies, Hare's Ears, caddis, and Pheasant Tails covers the basics. Add a few fluttering, filoplume Hex and Sparrow nymphs for the complete assortment.

The steelhead in the Rifle vary greatly in size, with 7 pounds a fair average. There are plenty of small, precocious males in the 2-pound class and a fair number of fish that come close to the 15-pound trophy category.

The Rifle's riparian zone is mostly privately owned and there are stretches of cabins and homes with lawns reaching right to the water. These are interspersed with long runs of cedar and balsam swamps, aspen and hardwood hillsides, and red pine- and jackpine-covered banks. Remember that many of the "wilderness" runs are still privately owned. Some property owners are friendly to anglers, others not so. Stay in the stream while wading and respect their rights. Carry a plastic bag and pick up trash. This helps in the obvious way and also assists good relations with landowners.

Although there are fall, winter, and spring steelhead throughout the river from the Rifle River Recreation Area to the mouth at Lake Huron, it is best to concentrate in the middle reaches where the mix of shaded banks combined with a varied bottom structure of cobble, gravel, sand, silt, and clay is most attractive to the highest number of fish. Key access points include Sage Lake Road, Peters Road, State Road, and MI 55.

If you want to float the Rifle by canoe or boat, be aware that the public access points are few and far between and you must have permission to land or take out at most points.

Au Sable River

The steelhead run on the beautiful Au Sable is short and sweet. Foote Dam, less than 10 river miles from the mouth at Lake Huron, is the upstream barrier for anadromous fish. By the time the river reaches the big lake it has drained over 1,700 square miles of northern forest land. Its volume ranges from roughly 1,000 cubic feet per second to over 2,000 cfs during the spring runoff. You can expect flows in the 1,000 cfs range during the fall and winter with 1,400 cfs being a fair expectation during the spring.

This is big water complicated by a vast array of drowned, underwater timber left over from the logging era of the late 1800s. Au Sable means "river of sand" and sand is the dominant bottom feature of the river. The sand is fine, pale blond in color, and often covers hundreds of yards of river without a break. Clay ledges, mud, and pure silt appear sporadically, most often along the banks and in deeper pools. Happily, the gravel reaches are ideal for spawning salmonids. Most of the gravel ranges from the size of a large garden pea to about an inch in diameter and occurs in areas with relatively steep hydraulic gradient.

Most of the best spawning gravel lies in the upper section, between Foote Dam near Rea Road and the US Forest Service access at the Whirlpool, about 4.5 river miles downstream. The lower section, from the Whirlpool to Oscoda, has less spawning gravel in fewer locations and is less suited to fly-fishing techniques. Most of the best gravel reaches lie at fishable depths ranging from 2 to 6 feet and are easily located when they are "washed" by active hen salmon and steelhead in the fall and spring. The best holding lies are usually the dark pockets up- and downstream from clean gravel.

The Au Sable below Foote Dam is incredibly clear; its flow is moderated by the hydroelectric power plant, and the water clarity is the direct result of the infestation of the exotic zebra mussel in the backwaters upstream from the dam. This has a direct impact on angling opportunity that has evolved over the past few years. One noticeable effect is the decline in caddis species. The zebra mussels eat by filtering the same minute lifeforms from the current as those needed by caddis. The decline in caddis has lowered the effectiveness of caddis nymphs, particularly the Green Caddis, for steelhead. Another obvious result that affects fly fishing is water clarity. It is as clear as mountain air. It is sometimes possible to read the old logging companies' faded brands stamped into the ends of logs at a depth of 10 feet or more. You can spot fish at similar depths from 60 feet away. And of course, they can see you, too. The environment favors the fish and requires technical presentation.

Long leaders with fine tippets of 6-pound test (or 8-pound-test fluorocarbon) are the norm for the Au Sable. You will need to be able to make long casts and mend precisely. A rod of 9½ feet will suffice, but one of 10 feet provides just a bit more control and precision when mending and feeding line to the proper depth. Flies need to be a bit smaller and more natural in appearance than you might use on other steelhead rivers. Combine all this—very strong fish that average about 8 pounds, clear water, light leaders, and a bottom littered with tangled logs—and you have a true fly-angling challenge.

> ## AU SABLE RIVER
>
> ───────●───────
>
> **Location:** Oscoda, Michigan on US 23, in the northeast Lower Peninsula.
>
> **Airport:** Three and one-half hours from Detroit, two hours from Midland/Bay City/Saginaw.
>
> **Lodging:** Redwood Motel, 989-739-2021; AmericInn, 989-739-1986.
>
> **Fly shops and Guides:** Au Sable Angler, www.ausableangler.com, 989-826-8500; Little Forks Outfitters (Midland), www.littleforks.com, 877-550-4668 or 989-832-4100; Flymart (Royal Oak), www.flymart.com, 248-584-2848; Kelly Neuman, 989-848-5983; Mike Bachelder, 989-826-8500.

Lake Huron streams tend to peak later for both fall and spring steelhead runs than Lakes Michigan, Erie, and Ontario. In fact, they seem to be (almost) on the same schedule as the much colder Lake Superior. The fall ascension begins in October, but near the end of the month. While fly anglers are enjoying great fishing on Lake Michigan tributaries early in October, the Au Sable faithful are still waiting. The run really kicks in about October 25 and seems to peak in numbers about November 10. Fall fish are bright silver and eager to eat salmon eggs and nymphs. They can be enthusiastic for Spey flies and streamers if conditions are right; they seem to respond best to swinging or pulsed flies when water temperatures are near 50 degrees F (10 degrees C). Strikes will be jolting and require a short, strong leader with a 10-pound-test tippet.

You should carry small (salmon-egg-size) egg flies in an assortment of colors. The hues should be muted by blending white or cream-colored yarn with cheese, orange, tan, or small bits of chartreuse. Fall nymphs need to be no larger than No. 8. I like Hex nymphs, Hare's Ears, Sparrow Nymphs, and a Mysis shrimp pattern (white or pale cream) on a No. 10 hook. Streamers that copy sculpins, leeches, and small lampreys are the best. They should be tied so they slither and undulate. Use marabou and/or rabbit strips for best results. Spey patterns should cover three basic color or shade types: dark flies with a combination of black and purple, medium/natural flies with tan, brown, gray, and gold, and light patterns with orange, chartreuse, and white combinations will effectively represent the necessary range.

The spring run can begin as early as late March with building fish numbers, but this is directly controlled by the length and severity of winter weather. More often it is mid-April, perhaps the third week, before large numbers of steelhead move into the better fly-fishing water between Rea Road and the Whirlpool. Numbers peak during the last few days of April and begin to decline quickly after May 1. Still, fishable numbers remain through about mid-May. Fishing pressure drops considerably at this time. Many folks are off in pursuit of other species and the result

A fine spring steelhead from the Au Sable.

can be wonderful—plenty of unpressured, fresh fish and little or no competition.

For the past several years, stocked smolts have had a pectoral fin clipped to signify a hatchery fish. My personal observations are that about 60 percent of the spring run will be fin-clipped. Below Foote Dam, the Au Sable becomes too warm in the summer to sustain juvenile steelhead, and survival is extremely low. I suspect that many of the "wild" fish may be wanderers from other Lake Huron tributaries. Whether they are wild or hatchery fish doesn't seem to matter much. I simply cannot tell the difference in strength, speed, or aerial display. These "hatchery" fish may be inferior animals to some people, but I have come to like them. They have survived time in the cold, dangerous caverns of the big lakes and made the run upstream triggered by an ancient, primal signal. *They* think they are wild and that is plenty good enough for me.

You can use the same core fly assortment in the spring as in the fall, and carry a few in larger sizes. Egg flies can be a bit brighter, and nymphs can go to No. 6. The Au Sable runs bigger in the spring from snowmelt and rain and will carry the slightest tint on some days, but you will still need long leaders and fairly fine tippets. I can't remember a day in the past few years when 8-pound test produced strikes.

A big river running deceptively hard with slippery clay and mud and tangled with large timber means danger to the wading angler. Combine this with the fact that gravel and holding lies are widely dispersed and you come to the obvious conclusion that floating this water is the best approach. And the best float, by far, for fly fishing is the upper float from the boat launch at Rea Road to the Whirlpool. This run has the best hydraulic gradient, gravel reaches, and fly-friendly pools and riffles. And, because of the gravel, this stretch attracts more steelhead than the lower run from Whirlpool to Oscoda.

If you want to walk in and wade-fish, be prepared to deal with a lot of company, particularly on weekends, and to do a bit of hiking. There are several "park and walk" accesses along the upper river. Check out the High Banks scenic overlook and several drive-in trails that exit north from River Road.

The lower stretch is best fished during the winter months. It is slower, deeper, and more difficult to fly-fish effectively with traditional methods. There are a few spots along this run that will hold steelhead in the fall and spring, but they are distant from each other. The gravel run at Three Pipes is one example, and the deep chute and pool at The Railroad Trestle is another.

Even the most accomplished steelhead fly angler, under the best conditions, will find the Au Sable's steelhead a challenge. You will not enjoy the numbers of hooked fish that are now common on Ohio, Pennsylvania, and New York tributaries but you will treasure the accomplishment when you bring one of these difficult, beautiful creatures to hand.

Maitland River

The mainstem of the Maitland River flows for more than 94 miles (150 kilometers) to its Lake Huron mouth at the town of Goderich. The best stretch of steelhead water is from the village of Wingham on Highway 86 southward through Auburn toward Holmseville, and then north and west to Goderich. The Maitland is a big river with a variable channel width from 120 to 240 feet. Depths in some of the larger pools can reach 20 feet and more. The surrounding valley is rich agricultural land (about 80 percent) interspersed with rolling hills, forests, and wetlands. Four main feeder branches join at Wingham to form the main river, and several small tributaries feed the system throughout its course to Lake Huron.

The lower Maitland valley is rich and beautiful and, therefore, under pressure from agricultural and development interests for additional deforestation and conversion of wetlands. In response to these concerns, the Lower Maitland Stewardship Group was formed in 1998 with goal of assisting in the protection of the valley and river resources. This group works closely with several authorities, including Ontario's Ministry of Natural Resources, to maintain and enhance the valley's natural ecosystem. This is vital to the protection of the forests and wetlands which provide cooling shade, bank protection, and groundwater springs for the river. All of this contributes directly to the robust health of wild steelhead runs in the Maitland River.

Like all Ontario rivers, the Maitland's management plan emphasizes wild fish populations sustained through natural reproduction in the main river and its feeder streams. The Maitland is primarily a warmwater/coolwater flow through much of the year, but has sufficient coldwater reaches, influenced by ground springs and tributaries, with good spawning habitat to maintain and grow significant salmonid populations. There are more than 30 species of fish in the river. Most angling activity centers on smallmouth bass, king salmon, and steelhead. Juvenile steelhead remain in the Maitland for up to three years before "smolting" to the lake. Steelhead runs have increased in numbers over the last decade as a direct result of vigorous habitat improvement programs, installation of fish ladders and passes, improved regulations and operations of several dams, and a growing awareness and acceptance of fishing regulations.

Because of the river's large size, a few words on precipitation and its impact on current strength and depth are worth noting. The majority of the precipitation in the Maitland watershed occurs from August through early winter; about three quarters of this is rainfall. But due to snowmelt and rain, the highest flows are usually in March and April.

The islands and streambed are owned by Ontario all the way from Goderich to Wingham, and the province controls the waterway as a navigable river. This results in mile after mile of accessible steelhead water. A good topographic map or a digital equivalent like SoftMap will greatly assist the exploration of this vast steelhead system. If you would like a break from crowded conditions and the resulting behavior of heavily fished steelhead, the Maitland has numerous long reaches of productive water that receive only token angling pressure.

> # MAITLAND RIVER
>
> ———————●———————
>
> **Location:** Goderich, Ontario, on Route 21, one hour north from Sarnia in southern Ontario.
>
> **Airport:** Two hours from Toronto, one hour from London.
>
> **Lodging:** Chain and local motels.
>
> **Fly shops and Guides:** See Saugeen River.

Access to one of the best stretches on the Maitland is just outside the city of Goderich at the Falls Reserve Conservation Area north of Highway 21. The access points within conservation area lands present miles of river with superb steelhead holding water. A few of the more popular pools will attract and hold the vast majority of anglers, but if you are willing to explore just a little you will have excellent water to yourself.

The river section from the railroad bridge upstream through Falls Reserve at Benmiller has a large number of water types ideally suited to a variety of fly-angling methods. Much of this stretch of the river has a moderate hydraulic gradient that features a series of small and large pools. Even with moderate current speed, it is best to be mindful of the fact that depths in some of these pools can exceed 15 feet. This depth can be a good thing. It is ideal for resting fish and particularly so in cold water temperatures of the late fall and through the winter. Steelhead that over-winter in the river find shelter and food in these softwater pools and do not have to exert themselves in strong current. In addition to the lovely, enticing pools, this stretch has many deep runs and hard riffles with productive pocket water. Whatever your preferred fly-fishing method might be, you will find nearly ideal conditions through this part of the river. The shallower tail-outs of the pools are perfect for swinging Spey and streamer flies on a floating line; the deeper sections of these same pools fish well with heavier sinking lines; and the runs and pocket water are ideal for nymphing techniques.

Dave Green is an avid steelhead fly angler and aquatic biologist who fishes the Maitland regularly. Dave has his best success with nymphs and egg patterns in the faster water sections. He targets the seams and buffer currents where fast water presses against slower current. He fishes troughs, depressions, and pocket water around boulders with special attention. He feels that nymphing techniques in these water types are most effective when steelhead are on the move upstream rather than holding in a specific area, and when the more traditional resting places in pools have been disrupted by angling pressure. He also targets the larger current seams along the main river channel with a combination two-fly rig. He prefers the dead-drift technique with a single egg fly as the dropper and a stonefly or caddis nymph as the point fly. When swinging flies out in the main current, Dave fishes his streamers and wets very slowly and thoroughly before taking a few steps downstream and repeating his casts.

Good-quality polarized sunglasses are a critical part of your equipment for the Maitland. Not only will they assist in spotting fish in holding water, but they will help you avoid trouble. You will certainly see stretches of vertical steps where current has scoured the river bottom down through layers of glacial deposits to bedrock. These form natural obstacles to navigation, but steelhead can pass them with relative ease under high water conditions. In moderate to low water flows, steelhead congregate in large numbers in the pools below these steps. Even when flows are high, fish will pause and hold in the pools before climbing through the steps. Look for large boulders near the tail-outs of these pool formations. These form the most attractive lies for fish and should be your first target. Dave recommends a long, two-handed rod and a sink-tip line matched to water volume as the most productive fly-fishing method for these spots.

Timing is critical to successful steelhead angling on all rivers, and the Maitland is no exception to the rule. Rising water on the Maitland is a key element in good fishing. And a gradual rise in water level is much better than rapid, severe increases in flow. Dave told me he once had a fantastic day using nymph tactics with a small, single-egg pattern. He managed to be in the right place—a run heavily used by migrating steelhead, at the right time—rising water levels had drawn fish upstream from the close proximity of Lake Huron. In the lower reaches of the Maitland, steelhead often move back and forth between the river and the lake, and on this day a trigger was pulled and fish were moving and hungry.

Rising water levels that trigger movement also increase water speed and pressure on wading anglers. Strong currents, large and small cobble, and exposed bedrock can be treacherous for the unwary. The deep water of many pools becomes more hazardous when the water rises. Cleated felt soles and a wading staff are quite helpful under these conditions.

Both Dave Green and John Valk recommend rabbit-strip and featherwing Spey flies, large strip leeches, and wet flies with long soft hackles for swinging-fly techniques. All black, black and red, and purple and red are the best fall colors. During the spring season, a tan or soft brown Spey fly with a copper body is the go-to fly. Caddis and stonefly patterns are the most productive nymphs. Bring an assortment of egg flies, both single and double egg, in large to small (5 mm in diameter) and in both bright fluorescent and pale natural hues to match water clarity and light penetration. Both Dave and John use large flies when the water is high and stained but do not hesitate to go to very small patterns on No. 14 and 16 hooks when the water is low and clear.

A fairly rare fly-fishing opportunity for Great Lakes rivers presents itself when water levels recede and drop-back fish move toward Lake Huron in May—steelhead actively feeding on the surface. This is an exciting combination of very hungry fish, clear water, and hatching insects. Because the river has prolific insect life throughout its long run from Wingham to Goderich and Lake Huron, heavy hatches of mayflies, caddis, and stoneflies incite steelhead to feed on top. This is dramatic, high-adrenaline fly fishing. Picture a 10-pound steelhead rising steadily in 3 feet of clear water. The fish eats every fluttering stonefly in sight with a crashing take. Tie on a large black caddis or stonefly dry, and try a drag-free drift first. If the fish looks but does not eat, try a waking, dragging sweep over its position. This usually succeeds. John and Dave both recommend large caddis and stonefly patterns as well as high-riding, bushy Irresistibles in varying shades of gray and tan.

The Maitland is a unique fly fishery, somewhat atypical for the Great Lakes basin. It has mile after mile of easily accessible, prime steelhead water. The fish are a naturally reproducing wild strain ideally suited to this big river and its tributaries. The riparian zone is an idyllic and picturesque valley cut through Devonian rock nearly 400 million years old. The floodplain vegetation is diverse. Deciduous forests of maple, beech, ash, birch, and aspen intermingle with white pine, hemlock, cedar, and tamarack. Tangled shrubs and wild grasses follow the banks. Here you will see wild grapes, ferns, goldenrod, and sedges. Wildlife is abundant. Woodpeckers, thrushes, tanagers, ospreys, eagles, herons, ducks, and geese are common sights along the river. Deer, raccoons, coyotes, beavers, mink, and muskrats are numerous and seen regularly throughout the valley. The combination of all this is a scene we fly anglers think of as more typical of Pacific Coast steelhead rivers—big water and wild fish in an unspoiled valley.

Whether you prefer nymphing tactics, two-handed rods and Spey fly techniques, or salivate at the thought of catching steelhead on dry flies, the Maitland should be high on your list.

Saugeen River

This giant steelhead river empties into Lake Huron at the southern Ontario port town of Southampton on Highway 21. This is the endpoint of a varied and superb fishery that runs for productive mile after mile in a north-by-northwest direction from the town of Walkerton. It is a big, healthy river. In its lower reaches the Saugeen will run between 100 and 200 feet wide, with average depths in the 3- to 5-foot range. The hydraulic gradient varies as the river moves through different geological forms, but averages a drop of nearly 19 feet per mile. The Saugeen flows through rich agricultural areas, hardwood forests, low swamplands, and picturesque villages. A significant feature of the Saugeen's extensive steelhead water is its twisting, curving route. Moderate curves and tight turns in all directions lengthen the actual river miles considerably over "crow-fly" miles and present an ever-changing and fresh set of holes, pools, runs, and lively riffles.

The Saugeen is food-rich, with mayflies, caddis, stoneflies, midge, dace, shiners, sculpins, immature salmonids, and much more. It has the highly oxygenated flow and rocks necessary to support heavy populations of stonefly species, especially the golden stonefly, fine and course gravel for mayflies and caddis, and marl reaches to nurture the burrowing nymphs of *Hexagenia limbata*. Between the towns of Walkerton and Southampton, the Saugeen is a free-flowing river with no dams that

The author nymphing on the upper Saugeen River.

would adversely affect invertebrate populations or obstruct the upstream movements of fall and spring steelhead. This is a very good combination—miles and miles of prime steelhead water that includes a prolific natural food base. And spawning habitat is ideal throughout. Gravel, both coarse and fine, seems to be everywhere.

Most of the fishing pressure on the steelhead is from Denny's Dam at Southampton downstream to Lake Huron. This stretch features a series of rapids, runs, and pools that are both attractive to steelhead and relatively easy to fly-fish. One spot, the first island, has a build-up of faster current, and fish congregate in this area. There is good access from both sides of the river, and the best pools and current seams are fishable from either side. The steelhead that stop and rest here are bright and fresh from the lake. They are silver demons packed with high energy and explosive attitudes. It seems that each group of fish beginning their upstream migration stop and hold here for at least a brief period.

All methods of fly fishing are productive in this stretch. Work the current seams with an array of stoneflies, caddis, mayfly nymphs, and egg patterns. If you like to swing flies, classic steelhead wets and Spey patterns work well in this area, with the added benefit of covering a lot of the best holding lies with long, sweeping drifts.

The next key area upstream is named Big Rapids. It is fast and deep, and steelhead also stop here for a period to rest. Fish the current lines and seams where fast water meets a slower flow, and cast also to spots below rocks and boulders that create softwater pockets. Nymphing techniques are best in this area, and added weight is necessary to sink the fly to a fishing depth. Be careful wading here; the current is strong and deep. Make sure your reel has plenty of backing. A hooked steelhead knows how to use the heavy current to its advantage and will quickly run more than 100 yards.

Another good stretch is just upstream from Big Rapids. It is called "the flats." Here the water runs from 3 to 5 feet deep and the current is moderate. It is a resting place for fish that have just worked their way through the rapids. They hold along seams and near boulders from the tail-out to the shallow head of the pool. This is an excellent area for swinging marabou and rabbit-fur Spey patterns as well as more traditional streamers.

The Graveyard Pool is immediately upstream. The river makes a hard, wide turn at this point, creating a bend pool that holds steelhead in good numbers. This is a very large pool with varying water depths to about 8 feet. Steelhead hold throughout and are often very aggressive in response to a swinging Spey, streamer, or leech pattern.

Upstream from the Graveyard Pool, you will find a fast rapids on one side of a small gravel island and a riffle on the other side. This run is called Little Island. Fish hold on both sides of the island and both sides are worth your time. Nymphs and egg flies work best in this pocket water.

Continuing upstream, you come to Steelheaders Flat and the Abutment Pool, where two old concrete bridge relics create ideal holding water. All methods work here, but swinging flies with a long Spey rod is probably the most enjoyable and productive. Steelhead rest again and hold in the Dam Pool immediately below Denny's Dam before entering the fish ladder and continuing their upstream odyssey for another 70 miles.

This lower river section is short and sweet. It has a variety of water types, large numbers of aggressive, healthy steelhead, and easy access. It is conducive to all fly-fishing methods and fly pattern types. Obviously, it is quite popular.

The run of river from Denny's Dam upstream to Walkerton, a distance of close to 70 river miles, is a whole new ballgame played in a different world.

Some notable exceptions to the issue of access upstream from the dam are near the junction of River Road (off County Road 3) and Port Elgin

Road not far from the dam. This is an easy public access point with great fishing water. At this point, the Saugeen averages about 90 to 100 feet in width and has superb steelhead holding lies. The best way to cover the water in this stretch is with Spey techniques and patterns, but there are a lot of in-stream rocks and boulders, so nymphing techniques will also produce fish. One of the keys to success in this area is the timing of a run of fish. It usually takes about 48 hours for a wave of steelhead to reach this section from the mouth of the river.

Between River Road access and the town of Paisley, public access to the Saugeen is minimal. A floodwall surrounds this town, pushing the river into the confines of a small valley. Here the channel averages about 85 feet wide with a fast current and deep pockets that hold good numbers of steelhead. Access within and near Paisley is easy enough, but be careful of the current's speed and depth. Concentrate on pockets near boulders and on current seams in the faster water. There are a few large pools—easily identified—in this stretch, and they also fish well. Two other rivers join the Saugeen at Paisley. The Teeswater enters the larger river right in town and is visible from Main Street. The North Saugeen also joins here and creates a nice pool at its junction with the mainstream.

Between Paisley and Walkerton, access is limited to small sections of the river near bridges on country roads. This area is mostly farmland, and the river's channel follows a fairly tight ravine. Walk and wade opportunities are few.

At the town of Walkerton, access improves considerably. Several of the river's best pools are here and within a short walk of convenient access points. This area is the upper limit of Ontario's extended steelhead season for the Saugeen. Truax Dam currently stops the upstream migration of

---

SAUGEEN RIVER

Location: Port Elgin, Southhampton, Ontario, Highway 3, Highway 11, and Highway 21, in southern Ontario north of Sarnia and northwest of Toronto.

Airport: Two hours from Toronto, two and a half hours from London.

Lodging: Extensive motels and very nice bed-and-breakfast establishments. Contact Saugeen Country Travel Guide for complete listings by town, www.saugeencountry .on.ca. or the Southhampton Chamber of Commerce, 1-888-757-2215. Garham Hall in Paisley is very nice. Call 519-353-7243.

Fly shops and Guides: Grindstone Angling (Waterdown, Ontario), www.grindstoneangling.com, 905-689-0880. Also, some local tackle stores carry limited fly-fishing supplies.

fish. The dam has a fishway—a vertical slot cut into the side of the dam—but this is often blocked by logs and there is no regular, official maintenance to remove the clogs and allow fish access to the upstream reaches.

From the pool at the base of Truax Dam through Walkerton, the river has a wide variety of water types and all are good for fly fishing. There are pools, deep troughs, boulder-strewn pocket water, fast riffles, and deep runs with softer current seams. It is a diverse set of fishing opportunities. Pick your method. Wading anglers have access to almost 4 miles of river in the Walkerton area, and all fly-fishing methods are effective.

John Valk is an avid steelhead fly angler and guide, and the owner of Grindstone Angling in Waterdam, Ontario. John brought the first fly-fishing driftboats to Ontario in 1997, and began to explore the Saugeen River in areas previously unavailable to anglers. His fly shop and guide service now has four McKenzie-style boats and employs a cadre of energetic, knowledgeable, and friendly young guides to take clients to the best steelhead and trout water in southern Ontario.

Over the course of my fisherman's life I have been blessed with many opportune situations, moments in time when circumstances came together to produce indelible memories. One such happy stroke of luck came in the late fall of 2003. John volunteered to take me on a float trip on the Saugeen and show me the quiet wild of the untrod upper Saugeen. In addition to nymph fishing the appropriate water types, we would use big rods and swing elegant Spey patterns designed for Ontario's steelhead rivers.

"There are fish in the river and we won't see another boat or angler. Let's go, eh?" John said. Indeed, let's go.

John and his guides have taken the time and made the effort to cultivate relationships with private landowners and have secured a series of access points that make several different float trips—on nearly virgin steelhead water—available to fly-fishing clients who happily release all their fish.

We launched John's driftboat early on a gray November morning from a parcel of private property at the edge of a small village on the upper river. At this point the Saugeen was close to 100 feet wide and flowed over mixed rock and gravel through a riffle that ran from bank to bank. The water was lightly stained with clay and other sediment from a moderate rainfall the preceding day, but there was certainly enough clarity for steelhead to see our flies.

We rounded a wide bend in the river and left the small town behind us. An elderly man waved at us as we entered the curve. That was the last sight of another human, or human impact on the river, for many hours. Below us, a handsome riffle ran straight through a tight channel, heavily forested on both sides, before curving hard to the right. It seemed we had entered a wilderness tract with nothing but a natural river in a wild land under the sky.

I learned a lot on that float trip. John coached me to an understanding of and appreciation for his sunken-leader technique. He demonstrated, then taught me, several mending procedures to swing undulating Spey flies more artfully with long rods, and to effectively control the depth and speed of my presentation. All of this, combined with complete solitude on a lovely, wild river was a fine reward for our efforts. Hooking steelhead was a bonus.

We stopped and beached the driftboat at the head of a narrow but long gravel island below a large, smooth pool. I fussed with cameras and asked John to start fishing. He started at the head of the island and fished a deep trough that extended from the island to the far bank. He used his sinking leader rig and began working the pockets near large rocks at the head of the trough. I noticed that John fished very thoroughly and that his attention was truly riveted. He had stepped downstream several times and was working a current seam when I ran out of film and opened my camera for the changeover.

"Here's one, Bob," he said. Based on the severe arc of his rod and the high-speed sound of his reel I guessed it to be a big fish. It was a lightly shaded buck of about 7 pounds. John eased the hook out of his jaw and it swam away quickly. "Oh, did you want a picture?" he said.

John demonstrated great skill and landed two more fish that day. I managed one very nice hen to the net. She ate a small stonefly nymph and fought with real fire. We had several good tugs swinging Spey flies but only managed to drive the big hook into one fish. This was a dark buck that had been in this upper part of the river for some time. Still, it fought the leverage of the long rod with abandon and determination. It was probably close to 9 pounds, with a crimson band from cheek to tail.

Steelhead that run the Saugeen average a bit more than 7 pounds in weight, but often grow much larger. John's biggest fish to date is a buck of 38½ inches with broad shoulders and heavy girth. That steelhead certainly pushed the 20-pound mark. The annual combined run is somewhere around 8,000 fish. John estimates that about 40 percent of these run the river in the fall, with the remaining 60 percent coming in stages from late March to early May. They spread out along the extensive gravel reaches throughout the entire system from Walkerton to Southampton.

The Saugeen's run above Denny's Dam is all wild fish. John praises the Ontario Steelheaders Association for their diligent, yearly efforts in transporting wild fish upriver to protected spawning tributaries. He said that this is the key to further development of natural reproduction in the upper river.

"The Saugeen drains a vast area, nearly 3,200 square kilometers [almost 2,000 square miles] of watershed, and much of the best spawning habitat is in small, remote tributaries. Ontario is emphasizing natural reproduction, a wild steelhead fishery throughout the province, and we are seeing wonderful returns. The results so far are extremely positive in Lake Huron streams and in the Grand River that feeds Lake Erie."

The Saugeen is a good-size river with a variety of holding water throughout. I would recommend the longest rod you can comfortably handle as the best choice for both nymphing and swinging-fly tactics. Seven- or 8-weight rods are fine, and I think a length of 10 feet is right for a single-handed model.

All the standard nymphs and egg flies seduce fish on the Saugeen. I would emphasize large, dark mayfly patterns, stonefly nymphs, and caddis pupae in the nymph category, and egg flies with a small amount of built-in flash in a range of hues from bright to pale. John recommends big marabou or rabbit-strip Spey patterns in black, black and red, and purple and red during the fall season. For spring steelhead he adds a tan featherwing pattern with a bright copper body. When steelhead start to drop back to Lake Huron after spawning, they are ravenous and can sometimes be caught on large dry flies. John suggested carrying a few deerhair flies, like Bombers, for these occasions.

"This is basically an untouched, unspoiled river with pure, wild steelhead. Please ask your readers to handle and release all of them carefully," John said.

Beaver River

Formed by gigantic pulses of the Niagara Escarpment and scouring by glaciers more than 10,000 years ago, the beautiful rolling hills of Beaver Valley belie its violent but gradual formation. These sloped and forested outcroppings blend softly into open fields and lowland ravines that appear as foliage ribbons gently wrapping the landscape. The ravines shelter running water hurrying to Georgian Bay. The traveler's view, spring and fall, is reminiscent of New England's countryside panorama. In fact, during the fall months, it is a tourist Mecca, and October's blazing maple, quaking aspen, and glowing oak foliage is the main draw.

Knowledgeable steelhead anglers also make the pilgrimage to Beaver Valley. Cutting through the heart of the valley, Beaver River winds northward for many miles from south of Kimberly through Heathcote and Clarksburg to its junction with Georgian Bay at the town of Thornbury. It is a medium-size stream throughout its course, and its sweet, highly oxygenated water and ideal spawning gravel make it attractive to steelhead from mid-fall through early May.

BEAVER RIVER

Location: Thornbury, Ontario, Highway 26, in southern Ontario's Grey–Bruce area.

Airport: Two hours from Toronto.

Lodging: Local motels and bed-and-breakfast facilities. Contact Beaver Valley Accommodations at 1-888-439-2659 or www.beavervalleyaccommodations.com.

Fly shops and Guides: See Saugeen River.

In 2002 a $5,000,000 dam rebuilding project began at Thornbury. This project included an element of keen interest to steelhead anglers. The old fish ladder at the dam was inefficient and had become derelict over the years. The fish ladder has been completely revamped and is now a state-of-the-art facility. Before reconstruction, only 400 to 500 steelhead were able to move upstream in any given year. The new fish passageway has virtually unlimited capacity, and approximately 2,000 fish made the transition to upstream gravel in 2003. This is a remarkable improvement with dramatic and immediate positive results. Like all rivers in Ontario, the emphasis for Beaver River steelhead is on wild fish and natural reproduction. Five times as many wild fish can now access the prime spawning reaches of the Beaver River and production will soar, with a noticeable impact in returning numbers expected in 2006 and 2007.

This bodes well for anglers. In past years steelhead were forced to stage and congregate in a very short stretch of river between the dam and the mouth at Georgian Bay. This created extremely heavy fishing pressure during peak steelhead movements. Shoulder-to-shoulder fishing is not attractive to most anglers, but this short piece of river has great cover and had so many fish stacked in such tight confines that the pressure remained nearly constant.

Several years ago these conditions were in full effect when I had an open day to fish the Beaver. There were lots of people everywhere along the lower stream section. They were laughing, joking, and having a fine time catching fish, but it was far too crowded for my taste. I rambled around a bit and found a place to park close to the river's mouth. Two fellows were spin-casting lures to the side of the boat channel. While I watched, both men hooked fish and one was landed. After a short while they reeled in and waded back through knee-deep water to the parking lot. The harbor mouth was open now, obviously wadable, and fish were present. I put on waders and a short vest and grabbed a streamer setup with a 250-grain, sink-tip line. Reasoning that large baitfish would be the preferred menu item, I tied an olive and white Deceiver to a short leader and waded out toward the edge of the boat channel.

Several casts through a 180-degree arc went unrewarded. I remembered an earlier visit to this spot with Bud Hoffman, when a large Grey Ghost produced fish. I changed flies and cast into the boat channel, then across the channel to the edge of a pier. A solid hit came on the first strip, and a steelhead was in the air in a heartbeat. It was a bright silver male of about 5 pounds—a rough guess on the weight because the fish unbuttoned before I got a good look. I fished there until it started to get dark, landing two steelhead and one brown trout of about 6 pounds on the Grey Ghost.

Driving back toward the dam, I noticed that there were still multiple anglers fishing the Beaver between the dam and the beginning of the boat channel. It seemed as though I had had all of Georgian Bay's wealth and beauty as my private pond for a short moment in time.

Steelhead numbers are now building upstream from the dam at Thornbury to near Kimberly, a distance of about 12 miles by road. Through this reach, the Beaver twists and turns back upon itself and winds through tight corners and wide curves. There is a reasonably straight run of river near Kimberly, but for the most part the stream runs a serpentine course with constantly changing water types. This is a free-stone river and somewhat volatile in response to precipitation. Extended dry periods shrink the flow to the point that it is virtually unfishable, and the steelhead are captive in pools and corner holes and cannot move until a spate raises water levels. And the reverse is true. Major rainstorms or rapid thaws quickly swell and stain the water. This is fine for migrating steelhead, but it may take a day or two for the water to clear enough for decent fly fishing.

For the most part this river is fairly shallow, with many fast riffles studded with rocks and boulders. Nymph fishing the pocket water is usually productive in both fall and spring. Deeper runs and pools are interspersed throughout the best steelhead water and can be fished with a variety of techniques including swinging Spey and streamer flies. Width varies of course, but a typical range is from about 45 feet in deeper pools to about 60 feet in wide, shallow riffles. The rocks are slippery. Be sure to wear felt-soled waders; studded felt is even better.

Insect life is varied and prolific. Mayflies, caddis, and stoneflies are present in large numbers and are the main components of a steelhead's in-stream diet. Drifting eggs and baitfish are also important. A fly assortment for the Beaver should include the same patterns as recommended in this book for the nearby Bighead River. In addition, carry a few smelt-type streamer patterns such as the Joe's Niagara Smelt and the Grey Ghost.

Several country roads and bridge crossings in the area lead to productive steelhead water. As you follow Road 13 north from Kimberly toward Thornbury, there are several side roads heading westward on the approach to Heathcote and again near Clarksburg. These roads lead to the river. Be aware of and respect private property. Much of the waterside lands are privately owned. A combination of year-round homes and vacation properties are spread throughout the riparian zone. Public access through the area between Kimberly and Clarksburg is problematic. If you are not absolutely sure you are welcome, do not enter the river before asking permission. If no one is available to ask, go elsewhere.

This is a lovely stream with an intimate, friendly feel and rapidly building runs of wild steelhead from October through May. Grindstone Angling is now in a "research" phase and will begin offering *zero impact* steelhead float trips in inflatable rafts beginning in the fall of 2005. The guides will have found the best water and made the necessary arrangements with landowners to assure a productive, hassle-free experience. That is the way to fish this water, and I plan to book a spot on one of these float trips as soon as possible.

Bighead River

The Grey–Bruce Peninsula juts northward and forms the southern landmass arm that separates Lake Huron proper from Georgian Bay. The Grey–Bruce area is a mix of rich agricultural lands, forested valleys, and high rolling hills that are part of the vast Niagara Escarpment. A short drive from Toronto, it is a tourist haven with festivals, scenic lighthouses, museums, hiking and cycling trails, canoe and kayak routes, golf, beautiful scenery, and friendly people.

Steelhead are the main attraction for touring anglers, both from Canada and the United States. They nose into the Peninsula's bays, inlets, and river mouths throughout the year with peak activity in April, May, October, and November.

The Bighead River runs in a northeasterly direction pasts Bognor and Elmhedge before reaching its mouth at Georgian Bay at the lovely village of Meaford. My most recent trip to the Bighead was in early November 2003. It was my first return trip visit in nearly nine years and when I looked again at the water I wondered why, oh why, had it taken so long to return.

My hosts were John Valk, guide and owner of Grindstone Angling in Waterdown, Ontario, and Rob Heal, a talented fly-fishing guide on John's staff. At my request we just stood next to the vehicle for a short time and watched the river after meeting Rob at streamside. He had been scouting and fishing earlier in the morning as John and I drove up from Waterdown. The river's hypnotic trance broke when a bright steelhead slid out from behind a rock and pushed upstream.

"Well Bob, do you want to fish or just hang out here?" John said.

We decided to fish and hiked upstream several hundred yards after suiting up. The first place we stopped was only about 2 river miles from the big lake and maybe a half mile upstream from the village of Meaford. We passed an angler during our short walk; he was using a Spey-type, two-handed rod and swinging a fly through the tail-out of a smooth pool. Rob asked if had had any luck, and the man replied with a laugh, "Two on, none landed."

John led us to a spot where the Bighead ran through a tight chute, pounded against a logjam, and spread into a deep pool that curved gently from left to right against the far bank. The pool ran for about 40 yards before it shallowed and the current quickened and slid into a long, choppy, boulder-strewn riffle. At this point the river was approximately 50 feet wide; the upper part of the pool, next to the logjam, was about 5 feet deep.

"Steelhead rest here after swimming up through that long rapid stretch," John said. "We'll fish here a bit. You should get a few decent pictures and a fish or two."

I loaded a fresh roll of film and asked John to start fishing. Rob said he would move downstream a bit and try a couple of deep pockets in the riffle. John rigged up for his sinking-leader technique (see Chapter Three) and tied a small stonefly nymph to the tippet. For some unknown reason, perhaps a cosmic charge, we both turned at the same time to look downstream. Rob's head and shoulders were just visible above a large boulder on the bank about 70 yards below us. Instantly his head and shoulders disappeared and were replaced by his lower legs and feet sticking straight up into the sky. They too, quickly disappeared. We ran, slipping and sliding in mud, to where we had seen Rob crash. He stood up just as we arrived.

> ### BIGHEAD RIVER
>
> ────────●────────
>
> **Location:** Meaford, Ontario, Highway 26 between Thornbury and Owen Sound, in southern Ontario's Grey–Bruce area.
>
> **Airport:** Two hours from Toronto.
>
> **Lodging:** See Beaver River.
>
> **Fly shops and Guides:** See Saugeen River.

"Are you all right? What happened, Robby?" John said.

"My feet just went out from under me. I was standing still, getting ready to cast. The next thing I knew I was upside down. I'm okay."

John turned and said he should have warned me about the super-slippery mud along the Bighead's banks. It has caused many nasty falls. He turned back to Rob to make sure he was not injured. Rob grinned.

"I'm a hockey player. I'm fine," he said. When we walked back upstream to our pool we did so very carefully.

John concentrated on the deepest water as it came through the chute and widened against the logjam. Rob fished the tail-out with an egg pattern. Both used small, brightly colored strike indicators. John was first to hook a steelhead. The fish was supercharged. It made several hectic, high-speed dashes back and forth across the pool, charged downstream, then turned back to the deeper water. It thrashed at the surface once then made several shaking leaps. It seemed to be extremely angry and aggressive rather than frightened and trying to flee. Rob honored the fish with a careful, precise scoop of the net and we posed a photograph before releasing the bright chrome, nasty-minded hen.

Before we moved on John landed another kinetic steelhead, and Rob caught one that we chased far downstream through the riffle. We ran fast over rocks, then tiptoed carefully through the slick mud stretches. That chase would have made an amusing video. I hooked two that just tore me up with speed and quick changes in direction. In both cases I just lost control, and slack line allowed these fish to come unzipped from barbless hooks.

We fished wide smooth pools, tight pocket water, and churning riffles through the day. John and Rob continued their success at landing steelhead and I carried on by losing every one I hooked. At the end of the session I was "0 for 6" but a better angler for the experience. Even after so many years in rabid pursuit of steelhead, the learning process was high reward. I watched two fine fly anglers employ a deadly nymphing technique and closely noted their quick reactions in rod movement and ultimate control of these especially wild, acrobatic fish.

Steelhead water on the Bighead runs from Meaford upstream to near the town of Bognor, a distance of about 12 miles. In the upper reaches the stream is smaller, more "troutlike," with both fine and coarse spawning gravel. As it flows toward Georgian Bay it is fed by several small tributaries and gathers size and velocity as it passes the village of Elmhedge. The best steelhead holding water is probably the stretch between Route 12 and Meaford. In this section the stream varies from about 35 feet in width in tight chutes and deep plunge pools to perhaps 70 feet in more shallow riffles. Depths run from ankle- to nose-deep, but the average is

John Valk and Rob Heal with a classic fall fish from the Bighead River.

about 2 feet. The rocks and ledges, and particularly mud patches, are slippery. Felt soles are an absolute necessity.

John and Rob recommend a variety of flies for the Bighead. The standard nymph patterns work well enough but a few stonefly adaptations are special (see fly plate 4). Egg flies in a wide spectrum of colors produce solid takes by both spring- and fall-run fish. Carry chartreuse and hot orange for cloudy days or when the stream has a bit of color. Use small, pale eggs on bright days when the water is clear. Spey-type patterns are very effective on the Bighead. John likes to swing them on a floating line with a sinking head. He recommends both marabou and rabbit-fur ties in black, black and red, purple and red, and tan and copper in clear water. He uses fluorescent colors when the river is stained. Bighead steelhead are mostly wild, born in the river, and are incredibly strong and fast for their size. A 7-weight rod is about as light as I would use, and the longer the better. A rod of 10 feet is a long lever and helps control the kinetic dashes typical of these great fish.

Access is quite good along the Bighead's prime steelhead water. There are several easy park-and-walk spots in the town of Meaford as well as at most country roads upstream toward Elmhedge and Bognor. All this water offers fantastic fly fishing.

St. Mary's River—The Rapids

A powerful current lives in Lake Superior. Deep and cold, it flows slowly but inexorably from west to east. Superior's tributaries continually recharge the giant lake and push water from shallow bays and deep caverns toward Sault Ste. Marie. The mass of water condenses at Whitefish Bay and enters a narrow funnel between Ontario and Michigan. At this point it forms the short but mighty St. Mary's River, which drains Lake Superior into Lake Huron. Here the world-famous Soo Locks raise huge freighters from Lake Huron to Lake Superior. The mass of moving water is difficult to comprehend both in width and depth. Almost directly below the International Bridge connecting the two nations, the St. Mary's Rapids begin. Looking downstream less then a mile from the bridge, a traveler can see the termination of the Rapids and the beginning of Lake Huron.

The hydraulic gradient in the Rapids is severe, 28 feet in less than a mile. This is a giant, formidable riffle carrying tens of thousands of gallons of ice cold, pure water onward. The depth and volume of the flow are dependent on the natural level of Lake Superior. If the big lake is high, so is the rushing drain of the Rapids. If Superior is low, this too is reflected in its discharge. The water is as clear as mountain air. It flows over gravel, shale, rocks, and boulders of varying size. The bottom color is a mix of tans, grays, soft blues, and pinks dappled with spots of brown and black. Moving clouds adjust the palette, alternately modifying the bottom's pastel hues with shade and bursts of sunlight. Accurately judging the depth for your next step can be confusing. Add to this the problem of force created by heavy water moving quickly around and over slippery boulders. This is not a safe place for the foolhardy.

Food and gamefish are plentiful in this immense rapids. Resident rainbow trout, brook trout, and whitefish are joined by migrating Pacific salmon, Atlantic salmon, brown trout, sturgeon, and steelhead from Lake Huron. They seek pockets of cobble and gravel for spawning redds and feed on a wide variety of forage fish and aquatic insects, as well as the drifting eggs of their spawning brethren. The St. Mary's Rapids nurtures immature members of all these fish species and supports suckers, crayfish, sculpins, and more in addition to prolific numbers of caddis, mayflies, and some stoneflies. Due to the scouring power of the current there is little silt along the edges, but gamefish enjoy the benefits of drifting *Hexagenia* pulled into the flow from Lake Superior's edges a short distance upstream.

Steelhead follow spawning runs of salmon into the Rapids beginning in August, and fishing remains good until the wind-driven cold weather becomes unbearable in November. During late summer and early fall, fly anglers are often rewarded with an exciting bonus in the form of *Salmo salar* (*salar* is Latin for "leaper"), an Atlantic salmon. The Atlantics attain significant size and eat the same fly patterns favored by steelhead. They have about the same power and speed as *mykiss* but do, indeed, leap higher and more frequently.

Lake Huron steelhead entering the Rapids are a mix of strains from both Ontario and Michigan stocking programs, with the characteristics of Ganaraska and Manistee strains appearing to be dominant. They are big, powerful fish with brash color, wide powerful tails, and thick, muscular bodies. They are fast and pull very hard when hooked. In my opinion they are, pound for pound, second only to the purest, wildest strains of Lake Superior steelhead in fighting ability. Of course, the current speed and the simple fact that it is difficult to quickly follow a running fish here add to the impression of awesome speed and strength.

Access to the fishing water of the Rapids is only from the Canadian side of the river, and you must have an Ontario license. There is an access road that runs past the Ontario information and welcoming building to a hard right turn that leads to a small parking area in a walking and cycling pathway park. A path runs from this point across a short canal bridge through a low wooded area with multiple paths, benches, and observation points for nature viewing. The path continues through to the edge of the Rapids. Here you will see the current divided by a concrete berm. Steelhead rest and spawn on both sides of this berm. The current speed and the size of the flow are larger, by far, on the outside. You can wade across the inside current to the berm and fish either side as you desire. The larger number of fish will be spread throughout the much larger flow, but the current is softer and the wading easier on the inside of the berm.

ST. MARY'S RIVER

Location: Sault Ste. Marie, Ontario.

Airport: Minutes from Sault Ste. Marie, Michigan and Sault Ste. Marie, Ontario airports; five hours from Detroit; two hours from Traverse City, Michigan.

Lodging: Extensive chain and local motels on both sides of the international border.

Fly shops and Guides: Closest fly shops are in Traverse City, Michigan. Local sporting goods stores carry limited fly-fishing tackle. Karl Vogel, 705-649-3313; John Giuliani, 705-942-5473.

A common tactic for fishing the Rapids is to stalk along the top of the berm and spot fish before entering the water and presenting the fly. Steelhead, especially those silver shadows fresh from Huron, are very difficult to see in the crystalline flow over the multihued, jumbled rocks and boulders. It can be mesmerizing. I had an accident here a few years ago. While walking upstream along the berm attempting to locate a fresh group of steelhead, I lost track of where I was. The moving water shaded by clouds, and the search for wisps of smoke in the shape of a fish hypnotized me and I walked off the narrow concrete berm into thin air. I landed, quite quickly, on a pile of rocks at the edge of a shallow-water stretch. It was good luck to land in a shallow area, because I was severely bruised and stunned by the rocks. On subsequent trips I have been extremely cautious while walking the berm.

Long rods are the best choice for this water, and two-handed, Spey-type rods are popular here. They allow careful, precise mending for drag-free drifts of nymphs and egg patterns, the necessary reach to swing Spey and streamer patterns. And the long, powerful fulcrum is a distinct advantage in turning and ultimately controlling a heavy steelhead in such powerful current. Still, the initial run of these steelhead is often long as well as fast. Use the very best reel you can afford. It must have a smooth disk drag and a capacity of at least 150 yards of backing.

Polarized glasses with super optical quality are necessary. Most of the time you will be casting to sighted fish rather than fishing blindly to productive-looking water. Under the best of conditions these steelhead are difficult to locate, sometimes appearing only as faint shadows in the rough shape of a fish. Felt soles are an absolute must. Felt soles with carbide studs are best.

Bring a mix of fly patterns to the Rapids and be prepared to change often. If the fish you see are dark in color, it means they have been in the river for several days at least. This also means they have probably been spawning over this period and that drifting eggs are now a bit older and more pale in color and shade. If the fish are bright silver, or if the day is heavily overcast, use brighter eggs. A nymph selection can be pretty simple. Hare's Ears, Pheasant Tails, Black Stoneflies, Hex nymphs, Green Caddis, Brown Caddis, Brown Drakes, and Sparrow Nymphs on No. 10 and 12 hooks have all worked for me over the years. The most consistently productive streamers are sculpin patterns in soft, natural colors, but a large white Zonker will often bring jarring hits.

The volume and velocity of the clear water hamper your ability to accurately gauge depth, and this is an issue in safety. It also hinders the ability to spot fish. For these reasons I suggest hiring a guide for your first visit to the St. Mary's Rapids. Only licensed Canadian guides are authorized to work here. Both Karl Vogel and John Giuliani are residents and know the water intimately. They are expert fly anglers with highly trained, and sharp, vision. They will steer you to fish and away from danger. Despite all I have written here about the necessity for caution you should note that Karl has had hip replacement surgery—fully recovered now—and still manages to wade safely by exercising common sense. I have fished with both men and recommend them without reservation.

The scenery, the sense of place, along the Rapids is not what you might expect. The view to the west presents lumbering freighters, a massive hydroelectric plant, and the smokestacks of urban America. To the north a railroad bridge and the International Bridge dominate the scene. A look to the south is more pleasing. The rapids crash over a last upwelling of boulders and smooth into the large river channel. Behind you, eastward, a low tangle of trees and shrubs shields the shore from city noise. This is Canada, but urban. It is the water that will firmly hold your attention after just a few moments. Looking hard, concentrating on shapes and hues, anticipating the cast, the take, the pure adrenaline of wild fish in the rush of nature's purest power will do that.

Within the larger frame, several smaller scenes stand out. I remember my son's first steelhead from the Rapids. It was mid-May and the spring run was at its peak. The fish, a slender bright silver hen, ate a small dark Hare's Ear and ran and leaped with wild abandon. We photographed and released her and smiled widely.

Twice I have seen anglers simply disappear, sink out of sight, while chasing fish recklessly. Both incidents ended happily; the anglers were wet and cold, but safe. The more impressive of these cast a very large, heavy man in the starring role. He wore a derby hat and was puffing on a cigar. I heard him whoop with excitement and watched him raise his rod high overhead as he chased a running steelhead downstream. Then he vanished. Only his hat, raised arm, and bowed rod were visible. He had entered the upper edge of a deep hole. It took two of us to pull him to safety.

He gasped and panted. "Fish got away," he said. It was late May and the weather was warm. He sat on the berm quietly for several minutes to compose and dry himself. "This is beautiful, wonderful. I love you," he said. He was talking to the river.

Nottawasaga River

The run of wild steelhead in the Nottawasaga River is the largest and probably the most genetically diverse in Ontario waters. Rainbow trout were first introduced into the watershed with an accidental release into the Pine River, a Nottawasaga tributary, more than a century ago. These fish formed the base population through natural reproduction. Today, the Nottawasaga has one of the most dynamic fisheries in the entire Great Lakes basin.

The river's steelhead fishery covers approximately 45 miles from the junction of the Boyne River with the mainstream at Alliston, Ontario northward to the mouth at Wasaga Beach on Nottawasaga Bay, the southernmost arm of Georgian Bay. Wild steelhead use this entire flow and reproduce in the upper mainstream, the Pine River, Boyne River, Mad River, Noisy River, Sheldon Creek, and several other small feeder streams. Access to this extensive, high-quality spawning and nursery habitat sustains the wild fish population and provides superb sport angling.

Wild steelhead begin to stage in Nattawasaga Bay in early September and typically enter the river between September and May. Even mild weather periods in the dead of winter will induce fish to begin the upstream migration. The majority of the fish enter the lower river at Wasago Beach in September, October, and November. Many of these fall-run steelhead will hold in deep pools and holes in the main river and in the lower sections of tributaries until increasing daylight hours and warming water trigger the push to spawning gravel. Actual spawning activity may occur as early as February and last well into May, but the peak flurry usually takes place during April.

NOTTAWASAGA RIVER

———————●———————

Location: Wasaga Beach, Ontario on the Nottawasaga Bay of Georgian Bay in southern Ontario..

Airport: Ninety minutes from Toronto.

Lodging: Numerous local facilities. Check the Wasaga Beach Chamber of Commerce Web site at www.wasagainfo.com.

Fly shops and Guides: See Saugeen River.

Wild fish in this river system usually complete two summers of growth in Georgian Bay before their initial spawning run. These steelhead are called "maiden spawners" and average between 20 and 26 inches and 3 to 6 pounds. Repeat spawners are larger depending on their year class. Many exceed 10 pounds in weight, and a few have been documented up to 10 years of age and have made seven spawning runs! It is worth noting that the largest steelhead taken in Ontario waters weighed 29.12 pounds. It was caught on May 13, 1975 at the mouth of the Nottawasaga River. This is only 4 pounds shy of the Canadian sea-run record, a 33-pound fish from the Kispiox River in British Columbia.

The first 3 miles of river upstream from the mouth holds a good number of steelhead throughout the fall months, and it is also a good stretch to fish for hungry drop-backs during the spring. The water here, in fact throughout much of the river, is more subtle in defining the pools and pockets most attractive to steelhead than in most Great Lakes rivers. The current here is generally slow, moderate at best, through a series of pools and runs with deeper, hidden pockets.

Because of the strength of the run, the river's close proximity to Toronto, and easy access along the east bank, this lower section can be a bit crowded at times. Swinging Spey and streamer patterns is an effective method here, but may not be the best choice if there are other anglers trying to fish within a small stretch of water. Because the current speed is relatively slow and the holding lies less than obvious, the better approach is often with nymph and egg patterns under a strike indicator. A growing number of Nottawasaga anglers employ a center-pin reel and long, limber rod. The center-pin reel is free-spooled and facilitates an extremely long, drag-free drift under a float or bobber. They usually use bait in the form of salmon eggs or insect larvae, but occasionally use artificial flies.

But, even with flies, this is not fly fishing. The method does not use fly-fishing tackle and can be disruptive and annoying to other anglers. Sometimes the *drift* with these outfits can reach to nearly 200 feet of river in the hands of a skilled practitioner. However, this tends to monopolize and disrupt a large section of river that otherwise could be enjoyed by more people.

The run of river immediately upstream from the bottom stretch at Wasaga Beach is through a lowland swamp area that affords virtually no fly-fishing opportunity.

The best range of fly-fishing prospects is in the stretch of river from near the town of Alliston downstream past the village of Angus to the stretch below the Nicholson Dam and its fishway just north of the town of New Tecumseth. The Nottawasaga is smaller here, more narrow and shallow, and the water has greater clarity than the lower stretch, which receives suspended sediment from the swamp. This is a popular area for year-round and vacation homes, and much of the surrounding lands are privately owned. This is a double-edged sword. Public access is limited and you must obtain permission to reach the river in many locations, *but* fishing pressure is significantly lower. Even so, there will be other anglers spread through this part of the river. Remember, these are big, wild fish and highly prized. And the city of Toronto is just a short drive to the southeast.

The pools, runs, riffles, and pockets are more easily identified in this free-flowing run of the Nottawasaga but remain, for the most part, less obvious than what many of us are used to in other watersheds. Patience and a thorough approach to the water are the keys to success. The fastest and easiest way to shorten the learning curve is to fish with a knowledgeable host or to hire a guide. The width and depth of the river channel vary widely. Average depths run from about 2 to 4 feet but many pools and holes run considerably deeper. From bank to bank, the width variance can exceed 50 feet, depending on location.

The Nottawasaga is a clean, cold river rich in food forms with diverse and prolific aquatic insect life, baitfish, and crustaceans. It is a low-gradient stream with a modest current throughout its course. These factors, in combination with wild fish, produce fairly selective feeding habits. This tendency is particularly noticeable in the upper river as steelhead become reacquainted with the riverine environment.

The best fly patterns are those that are similar to natural foods in both size and color. When the water is clear, egg flies should be quite small. Micro-Eggs, tied one, two, or more to a hook, are a good choice. The actual size of the individual egg should be about 5 mm in diameter, close to the size of a natural steelhead egg. Soft, natural colors are best. Use soft orange and yellow colors when spawning activity is at its peak. Paler shades that represent "aged" eggs—those that have been in gravel for several days—are better after the main spawning period.

If there is one constant reaffirmation in my experience it is that wild, selective steelhead prefer smaller nymph patterns when the water is clear. Mayfly, stonefly, and caddis patterns work best on No. 10 and 12 hooks; often No. 14 and 16 hooks are even better. Include Hare's Ears, Pheasant Tails, Sparrow Nymphs, and Woolly Buggers in your assortment.

Nottawasaga fish put on an incredible display of chaos and power when hooked. Some of them are very large. A 7-weight rod is about right for the average steelhead in this river. A long fly rod of 10 feet facilitates mending and the execution of drag-free drifts demanded by picky fish in soft, clear current.

Swinging flies will also produce on the Nottawasaga, and this method is growing in popularity on the upper river. Classic Pacific steelhead patterns, Spey flies, streamer patterns that represent smelt and herring, and large slithering rabbit-fur leeches are popular.

One of the specific identifiable threats to the wild steelhead population in the Nottawasaga and its tributaries is overharvest. For years this river had one of the most liberal creel limits in Ontario waters. In January 1999, the Ministry of Natural Resources implemented a bag limit reduction from five to two steelhead. Additionally, the MNR specified seasonal closures and sanctuary areas to further protect breeding populations. Catch-and-release angling is emphasized and gaining in acceptance. Repeat spawners may be as high as 50 percent of the total run when angler harvest is low. These repeating fish are the most effective in sustaining the population; they produce larger and healthier eggs, in greater quantities. Without the contribution of adult, repeat-spawning steelhead, a modest or weak year class of maiden spawners will not be able to produce enough offspring to maintain the population at a reasonable level.

Steelhead returns are tracked at the Earl Rowe Fishway on the Boyne River—a tributary—and the Nicholson Dam Fishway on the main river near Alliston. The Earl Rowe facility monitors steelhead using the Boyne River and its feeder streams, and the Nicholson Fishway tracks steelhead using the upper Nottawasaga drainage. Steelhead scale samples from these two sites are used to determine, among other things, the DNA profiles of these wild fish ideally adapted to the specific characteristics of this unique river. Sample surveys taken at the Earl Rowe and Nicholson facilities in the fall of 1996 and the spring of 1997 counted approximately 3,500 steelhead. Out of this significant number, only three fish were stocked steelhead showing clipped fins; the rest were pure and wild.

Canadian research tells us that the survival rate for released fish caught by sport anglers in a coldwater environment is roughly 93 percent when steelhead are caught with a rapid hookset and are hooked in the jaw. This is the standard profile for steelhead caught with artificial flies.

Steelhead in the Nottawasaga are special. They exhibit the widest genetic diversity of all the populations within the Great Lakes basin, even more than wild steelhead in nearby Georgian Bay streams such as the Bighead River. These fish must be safeguarded to the best of our ability. The Nottawasaga Steelheaders formed in 1993 to help protect and enhance steelhead runs throughout the watershed. They work closely with the Ministry of Natural Resources and other conservation organizations to protect and enhance habitat for juvenile and adult steelhead and to ensure the continuation of this great fishery for future generations. If you visit the "Nott" please carefully release these wild beauties and tip your hat in salute.

Lake Erie

Lake Erie receives much of its volume from the Detroit River, the outlet of the three upper lakes. Its northern shore is in Ontario; the southern shore touches Michigan, Ohio, Pennsylvania, and New York. Three separate basins or pools of varying depths separate distinct habitats within the lake. The western basin is quite shallow and is famous for world-class walleye and smallmouth fishing. The central basin is deeper and it is here, and in the even deeper eastern basin, that steelhead thrive. Lake Erie is 239 miles long from west to east and covers 9,940 square miles of surface. The lake is named for the Erie tribe of Native Americans, whose historic homelands covered the range of its southern shore.

Canadian and American fisheries professionals have taken different approaches to steelhead management in Lake Erie. Ohio and Pennsylvania programs are built and sustained by stocking hatchery-reared smolts. The bulk of New York's short Erie fishery is also hatchery-based, but is supplemented by growing successes in natural reproduction in the Cattaraugus River and its tributaries. Ontario has recognized the viability of a self-sustaining, wild steelhead population based largely on the superb spawning and nursery habitat of the Grand River and its feeder stream system.

In Canadian waters the Grand River stands head and shoulders above all other Lake Erie tributaries, but there are a few other streams that deserve mention. Big Creek enters Erie at Long Point Beach, Ontario. The section of river between Teeterville and Lynedoch has good numbers of fish, and the area near Delhi is probably best for fly fishing. Close by, Venison Creek and Young's Creek also have reasonable runs of spring steelhead. Venison Creek is a tributary to Big Creek. Young's Creek is very small and delicate.

There are some feeder streams to the Grand River and one or two local streams near Waterdown that are productive in fairly narrow time windows. My best advice is to check with the pros at Grindstone Angling for current prospects and conditions.

When the Cuyahoga River caught fire in the 1960s, it burned more than sludge and trash. The blaze awakened the nation to the pitiful state of Lake Erie and its tributaries. It shamed us all. The rolling smoke and searing heat fused a new resolve to clean first, then protect and preserve the Great Lakes and their sustaining watersheds. The Cuyahoga fire sparked the cleanup. In hindsight, it may have been one of the best things to happen to the Great Lakes. It was certainly a defining moment for North American rivers.

The results of the fusion of environmental groups, concerned citizens, and governmental action have been nothing less than remarkable. Today, Lake Erie is recovering. It is a food-rich fish factory with spectacular walleye, perch, and smallmouth bass sport fishing. Local and touring anglers now generate a tremendous revenue base for local economies in Michigan, Ohio, Pennsylvania, and Ontario. This financial benefit is still growing.

Steelhead are now a vital part of the sport fishing "product mix." Put aside the notion that Erie is suited only to warm- and coolwater species such as bass and walleye. Stocking programs in the border states and in the Province of Ontario have produced a magnificent opportunity in many of the lake's tributaries for fly anglers. This success is not an overnight sensation. It is the result of hard work and careful planning by dedicated organizations and individuals.

Driving south to the Buckeye State and east toward Cleveland in late November 2004, I wondered how much fun a boy from the Michigan "sticks" could have fishing in a big city. I envisioned traffic jams, smokestacks spewing clouds of dirt, and shoulder-to shoulder "combat fishing" with tense confrontations and harsh words. I could not have been more wrong.

My hosts in the Cleveland area were Jerry Darkes and Jeff Liskay, both avid fly anglers and guides. As part of my education, they introduced me to Steve Madewell, steelhead angler and Deputy Director of Lake County (Ohio) Metroparks.

The first revelation came during an afternoon tour on the day of my arrival. Jerry and Jeff drove me to the major steelhead rivers in the metro

Cleveland area. It had rained hard for two days, and the Ohio streams—all spate rivers—quickly stain and get downright muddy after a major precipitation event. Happily, they also clear very quickly. Jerry and Jeff were looking for fishable water for the following day, as well as showing me the true nature of the riparian zones along the steelhead streams.

I was amazed. The haunting visions of ugly cityscapes and burning sludge were erased as we looked at the "greenbelts" that shelter the steelhead streams. They showed me the Rocky River and both its East and West Branches, where steelhead can utilize over 20 river miles, and the Vermillion, Chagrin, Grand, and Conneaut, where over 400,000 smolts are planted each year. They talked about the "Emerald Necklace," a greenbelt ring around the metropolitan area formed by Metropark areas. It was exhilarating, inspirational, lovely.

"The Ohio Central Basin Steelheaders are working hard to promote and preserve this fishery through education and continuing the fight for clean water. We're making progress," Jeff told me.

"A lot of our work is with landowners. Much of our steelhead water is owned privately. We stress good relations by asking permission and cleaning up the riparian zones and parking areas. Tomorrow morning we'll introduce you to some of our fall-run fish," Jerry added.

"I'm ready," I said.

The next morning my hosts took me to the eastern edge of Ohio's steelhead range, because the water there was clearing more quickly and would be fishable, with a visibility range of approximately 24 inches. We met for breakfast well before dawn and I noticed stars overhead. We thought this to be a good omen after the days of dark drizzle. We were right.

Steve Madewell joined us for breakfast, and we talked about the struggle to protect watersheds in a compact geographic area with 3.5 million people and no forested land blocks. The rivers flow through protected corridors for part of their journey to Lake Erie, but also traverse agricultural and other private lands. He described Ohio's participation in the Great Lakes Initiative and said that what Ohio really needs are dollars to buy more corridor property for watershed protection. He stressed positive results so far, but added that much work remains for the immediate and long-range future. I was in the invigorating company of dedicated angler-conservationists who are in the game and the struggle for the long haul.

In addition to the Ohio rivers covered here in some detail, be sure to check out the Vermillion River between the mouth and Birmingham, and the Cuyahoga River upstream from the harbor between the OH 82 dam and Edison Dam. The Chagrin River between the soccer fields and Daniels Park draws large numbers of steelhead and has fine fly-fishing stretches.

In January 2005, torrential rains and flooding breeched the Daniels Park Dam, opening an additional 4 miles of river to steelhead. This stretch of the Chagrin River runs through a heavily wooded valley and has some of the prettiest water in northeast Ohio. This will likely be a very interesting and productive reach for fly fishing. Even if all the rivers in the area are high and dirty from rain, all is not lost. Try the surf along the beach of Arcola Creek.

In Pennsylvania, several small "mile marker" creeks are worth fishing. East of Erie, between US 20 and PA 5, Four Mile Creek, Six Mile Creek, Seven Mile Creek, Eight Mile Creek, and Twelve Mile Creek all attract good numbers of fall and spring steelhead.

Rocky River

Much of the best steelhead water on this lovely stream flows through the "Emerald Necklace" Cleveland Metropark, which affords a measure of watershed protection and a rural, if not wild, halo-like shield for anglers.

This elegant buffer zone extends for many miles from the Emerald Necklace Marina near the mouth of Lake Erie to the access at Cedar Point and farther upstream along the East Branch beyond Bagley Road. There are 13 public access areas along this 10-mile stretch of river. Although steelhead ascend both the East and West Branches, the most productive angling is downstream from where these two tributaries form the mainstream at Cedar Point Road and Valley Parkway.

After an unsuccessful experiment with Pacific salmon many years ago, Ohio's Division of Wildlife converted to a steelhead program, and this has been refined to the present day. Ohio has worked out an arrangement with Michigan for fertilized eggs of the self-sustaining population of wild steelhead from the Little Manistee River system. These eggs are hatched at the Castalia Hatchery and stocked as smolts (6 to 9 inches long) in Ohio streams. The Manistee strain of steelhead seems ideally suited to Lake Erie and its Ohio tributaries.

In 2000, the Rocky River system received 100,923 smolts; 106,000 in 2001; 90,110 in 2002; 106,736 in 2003; and 90,000 in 2004. A "first return" Rocky River fish that has spent one year in the lake will be 16 to

20 inches long. A second-year steelhead will average close to 24 inches, and third-trip fish usually exceed 28 inches. Some of the biggest steelhead caught in Ohio streams come from the Rocky River. When the Manistee-strain fish reach the 30-inch mark they typically are at, or exceed, 10 pounds.

For much of its flow to the lake, this river runs at about 30 to 40 feet in width and carries 2 to 4 feet of depth. The bottom is largely shale and ledgerock with pockets of sand, cobble, and gravel.

Steelhead congregate and hold in deeper runs, bend pools, near ledges, in slight depressions, and in pocket water near larger rock formations. Look for color changes. The best water is often obvious, but sometimes that color change is subtle, merely a different shade or hue that signals slightly deeper water.

Successful fly anglers in Ohio use smaller flies, on average, than those employed in the upper Great Lakes. Jeff Liskay and Jerry Darkes use an assortment of nymphs tied on stout hooks ranging from No. 12 to 16. Egg flies, even "cluster" egg patterns like the Sucker Spawn, are smaller than those in common use for Lake Superior, Lake Huron, or Lake Michigan steelhead. These diminutive flies are extremely productive, even in discolored water. There might be a lesson here. I plan to use these Ohio patterns in my home rivers soon.

The Prince Nymph, and some interesting variations, is a staple for the Rocky River. My hosts carried black- as well as olive- and brown-bodied versions with red, green, and black goose biot "wings." Small Black Stonefly nymphs, Olive Caddis, and Hare's Ears (again, in a variety of shades) are important. Most of these nymphs should be tied in beadhead versions.

ROCKY RIVER

Location: Southern Cleveland metro area west of I-480 and I-71 off Brookpark Road (Hwy 17)

Airport: Thirty minutes from Cleveland.

Lodging: All major chains within minutes of the river.

Fly shops and Guides: Back Packer, 440-934-5345; Anglersmail, 440-884-7877, Chagrin River Gillies, 440-423-1291; Grand River Tackle, 440-352-7222; Rodmaker's Shoppe, 440-572-0400; Erie Outfitters, 440-949-8934; Jeff Liskay, 440-734-7098; Jerry Darkes, 440-846-8864; Mad River Outfitters (Columbus), 614-451-0363; The Rusty Drake (Dayton), 937-4388-0707. Monitor conditions in Ohio streams and carry appropriate tackle and flies.

The most productive egg pattern seems to be a small Sucker Spawn fly tied in a range and mix of colors. The basics are cream, pale yellow, orange, and chartreuse. Blended colors work well. Try cream and orange, yellow and orange, and orange and chartreuse. When wet, these colors seem to merge and glow, giving a natural, lifelike appearance to the fly. Small, single-egg patterns also produce fish. The same base colors apply. A small dot of contrasting color helps visibility when the Rocky is stained.

A 6- or 7-weight rod is the basic tool here. I used one of Jerry's rods, 9 feet in length for a 6-weight line, and thought it performed very well. Still, a longer rod is better for mending line and provides more leverage when fighting fish.

Because these steelhead hold in relatively shallow water, very little additional weight is required to sink flies to the proper depth. Often, the weight of the beadhead nymph was adequate to the task. The addition of a small, BB-size split shot or two is sometimes necessary. The really nifty thing about this arrangement is that it allows true fly casting with weight-forward floating lines and long leaders. Adjustable strike indicators that can be easily moved up or down the leader according to water depths are integral to success. This is particularly true when the stream is stained by rain or snowmelt.

Moving from up- to downstream, Jerry and Jeff recommended a series of access points: Cedar Point, the picnic area off Grayton Road, Mastic Woods (including the Blue Bank Pools), Morely Ford, Horse Ford, and Madison Pool.

All things considered, the Rocky River may well be the best bet for a first-time visiting angler. It is close to downtown Cleveland and Hopkins Airport, but has unlimited access to the water that flows through Cleveland Metroparks. A business trip to Cleveland? Just rent a car at the airport and you can be fishing the river in a matter of minutes. Despite its urban location, the river's setting is picturesque as well as productive.

The Rocky hosts a very strong run of steelhead, and some of Ohio's largest fish are caught here. The best angling starts in November when the numbers of returning steelhead start to build. The peak period is usually from mid-March through mid-April when there is a balanced mix of both pre- and postspawn steelhead in the system. The only drawback to this river is that it can take a few days to clear after a significant rainfall or especially rapid and heavy snowmelt.

Grand River

This is the largest Ohio tributary to Lake Erie, with a large run of fish that begins to reach appreciable numbers in November. Steelhead spread out over many miles of river as the run builds through April. The Grand's flow fluctuates with precipitation but usually runs about 90 feet in width over depths from 2 to 4 feet.

The Grand can be frustrating at times, especially for fly anglers, because it always carries some suspended matter and color. It originates in a series of lowland swamps, then flows through farmland, and the constant influx of decaying vegetation and other matter continues even during low water conditions. A unique characteristic of this river is that it clears first in the downstream reaches. Visiting anglers should check the lower river for water clarity if upstream areas are too dirty.

Steelhead smolt plants in the Grand have been heavy the last few years. In 2001, 112,225 were planted; 90,131 were put in the river in 2002; and 116,151 were released in 2003. The Ohio DNR, Division of Wildlife estimates an 8 percent return for the Grand. The numbers are impressive, producing a massive run of two- and three-year-old fish ranging in length from 25 to 30 inches.

The fish spread out and use most of the river from the Mentor Headland and Breakwall at the mouth to Harpersfield Dam near OH 307 and

A beautiful steelhead from Ohio's Grand River.

South River Road. Lake County Metroparks provides numerous public access points throughout the best steelhead water, a stretch of approximately 20 river miles. Moving upstream from the mouth, first check the public access points at Helen Hazen Wyman Park at OH 86, Mason's Landing off Madison Avenue, and Indian Point Park. Farther upstream, check the water at Hidden Valley Park at OH 528, Riverview Park at Bates Road, and Hogsback Ridge Park.

GRAND RIVER

Location: East of Cleveland in Lake and Ashtabula Counties, between I-90 and OH 84.

Airport: One hour from Cleveland.

Fly shops and Guides: See Rocky River.

The river's bottom structure is consistent with the smaller Ohio Streams, largely shale and ledgerock. And nutrients from swamps and agricultural lands provide a substantial food base for aquatic insect life. The Grand has an excellent population of stoneflies—particularly golden stones—and mayflies, including brown drakes and caddis.

Fly fishing is best on this river when the water begins to fall and clear after a rain or a period of snowmelt. Clarity is ideal when you can see your boot tops in 2 feet of water. If fish can see your fly at this distance, you are in business. When the Grand's color shifts from tannish silt (at this stage it looks very much like glacial runoff) to a light green shade, steelhead turn on and feed aggressively.

The best rod for the Grand is probably one of 10 feet for a 7-weight line. The reel should have a smooth disk drag and capacity of at least 150 yards of backing. Because the Grand is wide and open, a hot fish can and will build up steam and speed in a hurry. The most common terminal rig for Grand River fly anglers includes a strike indicator, a long leader tapered to a tippet of 5 to 8 pounds, and one or two small split shot to sink the fly.

Favorite nymph patterns for the Grand include the Golden Stone, black stonefly, Prince, Cream Caddis, and Green Caddis, in about that order of preference. These patterns produce good numbers of large fish in both standard and beadhead versions. When the Grand is stained, use egg patterns tied with blended fluorescent yarns. Orange, yellow, chartreuse, salmon egg, and Oregon cheese are good. When the water is clear, fish prefer more natural colors like cream and even white with a dot of color. For many years my best luck in clear water has been with a pattern called the Rotten Egg. It is a blend of about 60 percent white and 40 percent Oregon cheese with a "sparkle dot" created by pulling ten strands of pearl Krystal Flash up to the top of the egg.

Streamers work extremely well in the Grand. White Zonkers and Woolly Buggers catch fish when stripped, swung, or drifted. Try a variation of the standard Woolly Bugger. Add a small "egg" of root beer Estaz at the hook eye, a pair of long white rubber legs through the body and hackle, and two or three strands of pearl Krystal Flash in the tail. Swinging streamers with a sink-tip line is especially productive with dropback steelhead in the spring. Fish the deeper holes and pockets carefully. Flashy patterns are best with these fish. Two local patterns, the Hackle Flash Streamer and the Grand River Bleeding Minnow, are outstanding. And classic feather and hairwing Spey-type patterns along with traditional Pacific Coast steelhead flies like the Skunk, Freight Train, and Thor also produce Grand River steelhead.

Several sizable tributaries enter the Grand and support steelhead in fishable numbers. This is particularly true under high water conditions, when the Grand may be too discolored for decent fly fishing. Mill Creek and Paine Creek are the best of these. Both flow through Lake County Metroparks property with good public access. Mill Creek enters the Grand near Doty Road and flows through Hogback Ridge Park. Paine Creek is farther downstream. It joins the Grand after flowing through the Hell Hollow Wilderness Area and Paine Falls Park. Because they are smaller and usually run quite clear, you may want to add some smaller nymphs to your box when fishing these creeks. Copper Johns in No. 14 and 16, and natural and black Hare's Ears in No. 14 are good choices.

The Grand attracts more than steelhead in the spring. Both walleye and smallmouth bass ascend the river at this time, and it is not unusual to catch a fat walleye, a trophy smallmouth, and a wild, silver steelhead on the same day.

There is plenty of room for anglers on the Grand. Its width and volume attract large numbers of steelhead and its length and ease of access naturally spread angling pressure. Lake County Metroparks are worth visiting in their own right. The fact that they provide easy access to fabulous fly fishing makes them, in my opinion, a regional jewel.

Conneaut Creek

This stream receives steelhead smolt plantings by both Ohio and Pennsylvania, and this creates true blue-ribbon fly fishing for both fall- and spring-run fish. I do not have numbers for the Pennsylvania stocking program, but the Ohio volume is impressive enough. The Conneaut received 99,910 smolts in 2000; 110,134 in 2001; 75,005 in 2002; and 108,024 in 2003. In 2004, Ohio planted about 75,000 fish, with Pennsylvania contributing approximately as many. The Ohio fish are the Manistee strain, and with a projected return to the river of 8 percent, the run is enormous. The numbers of steelhead congregating in pools, glides, crevices, and along ledges throughout a run of more than 40 miles is staggering.

Conneaut Creek is on the east side of the metropolitan Cleveland area in Ashtabula County, hard near the Ohio-Pennsylvania state line. The river flows from Pennsylvania westward into Ohio south of the city of Conneaut on the shore of Lake Erie. The creek continues its westerly meander for several miles to a point close to the intersection of I-90 and OH 84. At that point it loops north, then turns back in a northeasterly run to its mouth at Conneaut Harbor.

The average stream width through the best steelhead water is from 35 to 65 feet. The average depth is a bit more than 2 feet, but there are chutes, pools, and holes with much deeper water. There is some limited natural reproduction in Conneaut Creek, but the water level fluctuates and often becomes too low and warm in the summer to produce a wild, self-sustaining fish population. The current level of fantastic steelhead fishing is dependent on the stocking program and the growing practice of catch-and-release.

Like the Grand River, Conneaut Creek has a stable and extensive aquatic insect base. Most important are stoneflies. Both black and golden stonefly nymphs are prolific throughout the river. Caddis, mayflies, and dragonflies all add to the soup.

Beadhead stonefly nymphs, both black and golden, tied on heavy hooks in No. 10 and 14, are critical for Conneaut Creek. Caddis larvae on No. 12 through 16 hooks, Hare's Ears on No. 10 through 14, and Copper Johns with green, red, black, or copper wire bodies on No. 14 and 16 hooks are also important.

Carry the same egg fly patterns in the same colors, both solid and blended, as listed for the other Ohio streams. Streamers work as well here as they do on the Grand. White seems to be the most productive color. Zonkers and Woolly Buggers, along with locally developed patterns like the Bleeding Minnow and Hackle Flash Streamer, bring jarring strikes. At times it seems as though a steelhead was moving at great speed when it slammed a pulsing streamer or Spey pattern. They often hit on the swing when the fly begins its arc toward you. Sometimes they hit on the pause during a jerk-strip retrieve. And occasionally they engulf the fly when it is directly downstream. Remember to let the streamer hang in the current a few seconds, perhaps pulse and let it drop back a time or two, before picking up for the next cast.

There is no designated public access along the Ohio section of Conneaut Creek, but the lower portions of the river, arguably the best steelhead water, flow through property owned by the Lake Erie & Bessemer Railroad and the city of Conneaut. This provides several miles of accessible water. The upstream stretches flow through private property. There is some access at bridge crossings, but some are posted and others require landowner permission. One of the paramount objectives of everyone involved with Ohio steelhead fishing is to establish and maintain good landowner relations to ensure future access. If you have any doubt about a specific stretch of river, always try to secure landowner permission. Carry a plastic bag and pick up any trash you see along the banks or in the river. Be extremely careful around lawns, structures, and fragile banks. Be courteous and smile. It will surely help the cause.

> # CONNEAUT CREEK
>
> ———————●———————
>
> **Location:** East of Cleveland in Ashtabula County to the Pennsylvania state line.
>
> **Airport:** One hour from Cleveland, one hour from Erie, Pennsylvania.
>
> **Lodging:** Major chains nearby; also, the Dave-Ed Motel in Kingsville is close to Conneaut Creek and the Ashtabula River, and they welcome fly anglers, waders and all. Call 440-224-1094.
>
> **Fly shops and Guides:** see Rocky River.

The best holding and spawning areas are in the lower river. This is lovely, medium-size water in a picturesque setting that is ideal for fly fishing. The upper reaches are typically long and flat over a smooth shale bottom and often require a good hike between productive spots.

Conneaut Creek drains a large watershed and it usually rises and colors more slowly than many area streams, so angling remains good for a longer period of time after a rain or snow event. Conversely, this stream takes longer to clear and drop after it does rise and stain. It may take two or three days to become fishable after major precipitation.

Be sure to bring your camera when fishing Conneaut Creek. Some of the riffles and pools curl near the base of high ledgerock ridges. Coupled with the aqua-green water color, the scenery is often dramatic. Although our best steelhead fishing often occurs during dreary weather through the late fall, winter, and early spring when bankside foliage is sparse and

Jeff Liskay with a steelhead from Conneaut Creek.

drab, beautiful photographs are achievable along Conneaut Creek. Have your partner kneel and gently lift that chrome hen just a few inches above the water, and use the shale cliff and the shining black spring seeps as a background. If you prefer film to digital pictures, use a film with enhanced, vibrant color. I think the best currently available is E100 VS, a Kodak slide product. VS stands for "vivid, saturated" color. It puts life and snap into pictures taken under gray skies.

Fishing pressure is fairly heavy on Conneaut Creek but spreads out reasonably well along many miles. Even during the peak of the run in April and early May, when both ascending and drop-back fish are present in very large numbers, there is usually plenty of room to fish. Check both the Ohio Central Basin Steelheaders Web site at *www.ohiosteelheaders.com*, and the Ohio Department of Natural Resources, Division of Wildlife Web site at *www.ohiodnr.com* for helpful information on current conditions.

Ashtabula River

Several rivers along Ohio's Lake Erie coastline host runs of steelhead even though they are not stocked with smolts. These roamers, or strays, enter the Huron, Cuyahoga, French, Euclid, Cowles, and Ashtabula Rivers. Angling pressure tends to be a bit less on these streams. That, coupled with the growing practice of catch-and-release angling, is a major contribution to the quality of the sport on these rivers and creeks.

The Ashtabula River is on the far eastern edge of Ohio in Ashtabula County, just a few miles from the Pennsylvania state line. The river proper forms at the junction of Ashtabula Creek and the combined flows of the East and West Branches near Kelloggville, a few miles east of the town of Ashtabula. From that point the river curves and loops westward, passes under I-90, turns north past the Olin–Dewey Road Bridge, then loops back westward to Indian Trails Park and finally north through town to the big lake.

Much of the riparian zone along this stream is privately owned but there is public access at both Cedarquist Park and Indian Trails Park. Happily, both these access points are along stretches of the river that are both serenely beautiful and attract good numbers of steelhead when conditions are favorable. Steelhead use other portions of the Ashtabula, of course, but you must have landowner permission to access water that flows through and over private property.

I fished the Ashtabula on a late November day not long ago. Heavy rains had pounded northern Ohio, and most of the steelhead streams ran dark and heavy. The chance of a steelhead being able to see a drifting fly was zero. But the rain had been lighter on the east side, and the Ashtabula was dropping and clearing. My hosts, Jerry Darkes and Jeff Liskay, said this would be our only reasonable chance on this particular day. They reminded me that this river does not get the same volume of fish as the stocked rivers, cautioned that conditions were still not ideal, and added that pressure might be higher than normal because anglers would be drawn to the Ashtabula due to poor visibility on the other rivers.

> ## ASHTABULA RIVER
>
> ———————●———————
>
> **Location:** Ashtabula County, east of Cleveland and north of I-90.
>
> **Airport:** One hour from Cleveland, one hour from Erie, Pennsylvania.
>
> **Lodging:** See Conneaut Creek.
>
> **Fly shops and Guides:** See Rocky River.

There were several other vehicles in the parking area when we arrived at Indian Trails Park. I could see anglers, perhaps 10 or so, spread out along roughly 300 yards of river. It was cold, cloudy, and misting as we rigged rods and suited up. Jeff said that the weather should improve and that the river would have decent visibility. Jerry handed me a box of flies he had tied for the day. It contained small, dark nymphs on No. 14 and 16 hooks, mostly stoneflies, variations on the Prince, a few bright caddis larvae, and an assortment of cluster- and single-egg patterns. I thanked Jerry and noticed that Jeff had walked down to the river for a closer look. When he returned he suggested we move upstream to a spot where the water might have more clarity, a place where he knew the landowner and had received prior permission to fish. Aspen, Jerry's Lab, barked approval and we noted her consent as a good omen.

It pays to have a knowledgeable guide, or two experienced guides in this case. The first place we stopped to fish looked no different to me than several hundred yards of water we had bypassed. It was a long, flat-looking pool with a subtle curve at the far bank. A double foam line formed below an overhanging tree and ran for about 50 yards before dissipating near the tail-out of the pool.

"There's a depression just off that foam line, a deeper groove through the ledgerock. Steelhead should be along that line and a bit to each side of it." Jerry said.

I wanted to take some photographs as a first priority and asked Jerry and Jeff to start fishing. They separated, up- to downstream, about 50 to 60 yards. Jeff fished the foam line below the overhanging tree, while Jerry and Aspen waded to the middle of the pool. I watched both men cast their floating lines and small nymphs and egg flies, carefully tracking the fluorescent tops of their strike indicators. It was mesmerizing for about five minutes. Jeff lifted his rod and it quickly throbbed.

"Fish" he said. It fought well with high-speed dashes, surface rolls, and strong determination. Jerry, with Aspen's coaching, netted the male and we made a few careful photographs before the release.

A few minutes later Jerry hooked and landed a fine, bright fish. This was quickly followed by another steelhead for Jeff. They insisted that I make a few casts, and I hooked up shortly thereafter. It was a handsome female of about 8 pounds. "That's enough for this pool. Let's leave them alone and look at some new water," Jerry said.

As we walked downstream we passed an angler sitting on the bank. His fly rod was lying across his knees and he was staring at his fly box. He looked frustrated and forlorn. Jeff stopped and asked if he could help in any way.

The man looked up and smiled. "Gee, would you? I've been watching you guys catch fish and I can't seem to figure this out. It's my first trip for

Jerry Darkes, Jeff Liskay, and Aspen admire a fine fish on the Ashtabula River.

steelhead." Jeff sat down next to the young fellow and pulled out his own fly box. Jerry beckoned me to follow him downstream, but I could hear Jeff explaining how to rig terminal tackle and which fly patterns to use before the river's song begged attention. I thought that these Ohio lads were pretty fine fellows.

We fished a series of chutes, deep riffles, pools, and ledgerock drop-offs through the rest of our brief time on the Ashtabula. We had hook-ups, if not a landed steelhead, at nearly every likely spot along the way. My guess is that we covered a bit less than a mile of river. The stream became more clear as the day progressed. Clouds thinned and bright sunshine broke through, sending beams of warmth to the tight valley. Water temperature moved from 39 to 42 F (3.8 to 5.5 C). The Ashtabula's tannish, morning color began to take on a soft, light green tinge and its steelhead responded.

I landed an acrobatic fish that ate one of Jerry's small nymphs next to a severe drop-off at the base of a high rock cliff. It was warm, the sun was shining, my friends were smiling, and a Lab was woofing approval. It was the perfect time to quit for the day.

Sixteen Mile Creek

In the fall of 2004, CNN reported the results of an economic impact study for steelhead fishing in Erie County. For every steelhead caught along the short Lake Erie coastline and in its tributaries, approximately $90 flows into the local economy. It is my understanding that this is the first such study within the Great Lakes Basin. Ninety dollars per fish—whether kept or released—is a very significant number, but not at all surprising to those of us who travel to fly-fish. Both touring and local anglers spend lots of money in pursuit of *mykiss*. This dollar value per fish will likely be duly noted throughout the Great Lakes region.

My companions and hosts in Pennsylvania represented a mix of backgrounds and experience levels that seem to mirror a cross section of today's steelhead fly angler. Ed Devine grew up in Pennsylvania and began fishing the Erie streams in 1993. He now lives in Indianapolis but returns several times each year, fly rods in hand. Jeff Conrad, a highly regarded professional trumpet player, is an avid fly angler who also lives in Indianapolis. He also makes frequent trips to fish the Erie area. Mike Conrad, Jeff's brother, is a novice fly angler from southern California.

It had rained heavily the day before and was still damp and cold with a biting wind when we met at our motel in the early afternoon. Our in-

Jeff Conrad readies the net for Ed Devine and a fall steelhead on Sixteen Mile Creek

tention was to concentrate on Elk Creek and sample its many miles of steelhead water over a two-day period. But Elk Creek was unfishable. It was running high and cloudy with, at most, 3 or 4 inches of visibility, certainly not enough for safe wading or for steelhead to see our flies.

"The weather forecast is for clearing skies later today and cloudy but no rain for several days after. Elk Creek only takes a few hours to clear, a day at most. We'll be fine there by noon tomorrow. Let's look at Sixteen Mile Creek today, maybe Twenty Mile. They are smaller and retain good visibility longer than Elk, and they clear more quickly. They both hold plenty of fish," Ed said.

Sixteen Mile Creek flows through the village of North East, Pennsylvania. It ranges from about 25 to 35 feet in width and runs shallow over ledgerock and shale, with an average depth of about 2 feet. Steelhead hold in deeper cuts and channels carved by the current and along well-defined shale ledges where they "tuck" under for security. Much of its riparian zone is privately owned, but I talked to two different groups of local anglers who said that access is not too much of a problem. They stressed care in walking along the banks and obtaining permission.

The creek has steelhead in fishable numbers for much of its course, but most people concentrate on the water from the parking area at

Wellington Street past the railroad trestle to the bridge at US 20, the run from Sunset Drive to the parking spot at North Mill Street, and the stretch from US 5 to the public access at Halli Reed Park near the Lake Erie shore.

After a rain event, Sixteen Mile Creek will be one of the few games in town, at least for a few hours. Under these conditions the little creek will likely get a lot more pressure than normal. We pulled into Halli Reed Park off Freeport Road at 2:00 in the afternoon on a late November day. There were four other vehicles in the lot, and I noticed a license plate from Michigan, one from New York, and two from Pennsylvania.

SIXTEEN MILE CREEK

Location: North East, Pennsylvania, east of Erie on I-90.

Airport: Twenty minutes from Erie.

Lodging: See Elk Creek.

Fly shops and Guides: See Elk Creek.

As we assembled our gear and donned waders I watched a fly angler working the midstream current about midway between a small dam outflow to my right and the Lake Erie surf on the left. During the few minutes it took to get ready, this angler fought two fish, losing both. There were fish in the creek, no doubt at all.

Ed instructed me to tie on a small beadhead Copper John as the point fly with an orange Sucker Spawn Egg Fly above. He pointed to a subtle current seam that formed below the small dam and ran to midstream.

"They should be holding along a ledge that buffers that seam. You can't see the ledge right now because of the stain, but that's where you should fish. We have about two feet of visibility and that's plenty," he said.

We had about two hours of daylight remaining, so I spent the first few minutes taking photographs of downstream anglers silhouetted against the leaden sky and the crashing waves of the big lake. Before I put my camera away Ed landed and released a handsome buck steelhead of about 7 pounds, Jeff Conrad had two hook-ups, and Mike had battled his first steelhead ever.

I switched back and forth between camera and fly rod during the remaining time before full darkness. Jeff landed two fish, Mike caught another, Ed caught three, and I managed to land two. During this period several fish jumped the low dam and headed upstream. I talked to three young men who had waded down to our position from the access near the intersections of Sunset Beach, Curtis Road, and US 5. They reported very good fishing with small, black stonefly nymphs, Hare's Ears, and beadhead Prince nymphs.

Both Ed and Jeff stressed the point that although Sixteen Mile Creek is a small stream, it should not be discounted. It receives a heavy run of steelhead through the fall and into the spring and, because many anglers opt for bigger water with easier casting, it is often less pressured. The fish behave naturally and eat nymphs and small egg flies with enthusiasm. Ed did point out that when water levels drop, this creek becomes very clear and the fish will tuck even deeper into depressions and under shelves. Very small flies are required under these conditions, often as small as No. 18. Almost everyone I watched fished with small indicators above their flies. Both Jeff and Ed like a fluorescent orange or chartreuse top over a white bottom on their indicators.

"It's easier to track the fluorescent color on top, and the white bottom looks like a spot of drifting foam to the fish and doesn't alarm them." Jeff said.

Twenty Mile Creek

This stream is a bit larger with more flow and is perhaps one third wider than Sixteen Mile Creek. It is a few miles east of the town of North East. Along with the now familiar ledge pools, midstream channels, and slate shelves there is classic pocket water in stretches with a more severe hydraulic gradient.

Steelhead use the river from the mouth through the reaches between OH 5 and I-90 and upstream past the railroad trestle south of US 20. It has a large run of fish that typically starts in September and fades in March. I asked Ed if he had noticed any changes in the fishing over the past years, and he said that the fish are bigger now, about 2 pounds heavier on average, with a typical steelhead weighing between 7 and 8 pounds. He added that there is a higher percentage of fly anglers than in the "old days," there are many more catch-and-release anglers, more out-of-state anglers, and more posted land. About 70 percent of the folks I saw on Twenty Mile Creek were fly anglers.

Ed and Jeff talked about their many great days at several different access spots on Twenty Mile, and I was foaming at the mouth with anticipation. Jeff cautioned us to be especially careful about private property. On his last visit he had received a bullhorn summons to "Come to the bridge!" from an officer of the law. There were two small "no trespassing" signs on either side of the bridge. Jeff had assumed that they referred to a specific section of water. He was slightly off—a few feet—in his calculation and this cost him, in the form of a $70 ticket.

TWENTY MILE CREEK

Location: East of North East, Pennsylvania, between I-90 and OH 5.

Airport: See Sixteen Mile Creek.

Lodging: See Elk Creek.

Fly shops and Guides: See Elk Creek.

"The officer was understanding and sympathetic. He said he knew it was an honest mistake, but it still cost me seventy bucks." Jeff said. He pointed at the bridge at OH 5. "That's it, right there. We need to stay well downstream from the bridge." We did.

There is public access on the downstream (north) side of OH 5, at the curve where Hirtzell Road joins Middle Road, at Hirtzell Pond, and at Gulf Road near the railroad trestle. A word to the wise. Watch for and respect posted sections.

Top flies for Twenty Mile Creek include Sucker Spawn Egg clusters in pink, yellow, and blue; small, single-egg patterns with a dot of contrasting color; and beadhead Prince, beadhead Hare's Ear, Flashback Hare's Ear, Black Stonefly, and Pheasant Tail nymphs. Your nymph selection should range a bit in size relative to water clarity. Use larger sizes if the visibility is 2 feet or less, smaller flies (down to No. 18 hooks) in clear water. Both Ed and Jeff also like soft-hackle wet flies like the Green and Partridge, and Woolly Buggers in both all black and all white. After taking a few photographs and making notes, I decided to swing a white Woolly Bugger next to a ledgerock shelf near midstream. In three casts I had two solid, jarring hits and managed to land one beautiful 8-pound buck on the white Bugger. This served as a reminder of the obvious—always listen to your guide.

We fished pocket water, pools, ledges, depressions, and dark water seams. We threw tiny nymphs and egg flies and swam soft-hackle wets and Buggers. Jeff landed several fish on Copper Johns, Ed did well with a small Mysis shrimp pattern, and Mike lost his rookie status by landing five handsome steelhead on a variety of nymphs and eggs. Even I managed to touch a few fish between taking photographs of my joyous colleagues. I used an indicator over a small Hex-nymph-and-egg-fly combination with some success, but had better luck with a beadhead Prince and small, red-bodied Copper John combo. And the white Woolly Buggers worked, but I lost the two in my box to particularly rambunctious, hard-running fish.

Ed Devine with a chrome steelhead from Twenty Mile Creek.

"We changed patterns, techniques, and locations a few times in order to stay successful," Ed said as we prepared to leave. "Too often people get in a rut and keep fishing a favorite fly, stay with a particular technique, or anchor themselves on a favorite run too long. The key to success on Pennsylvania streams is simple. Do not keep doing the same thing over and over if you are not having success. Change something. Move your location. Adjust the depth of your indicator. Change fly patterns. Mend your line and change your drift line."

Elk Creek

This is the prime steelhead river in Pennsylvania. It is a classic spate river that is almost totally dependent on snowmelt and rain for its volume of flow. Its width ranges from a tiny trickle of just a few feet at mid-channel during dry periods to well over 90 feet in the wet season, typically from September through March. Like other spate rivers on Lake Erie's southern coast, it stains and rises quickly during and immediately after any measurable precipitation event. The good news is that it also drops and clears quickly, usually within just a few hours. When the water color changes from brown to a light tannish olive and the clarity provides 2 feet of visibility, Elk Creek is fishable with flies. When it clears a bit more and takes on an emerald tint in the deeper pools, it is ideal for the fly angler.

Steelhead have access to many miles of the river from the mouth to and above its upstream junction with Lamson Run near US 79. The upper steelhead water from US 79 through the village of Sterrettania to US 20 and beyond is picturesque with tight, winding curves, deep bend pools, lively riffles, and even a handsome covered bridge.

Elk Creek's many fans refer to the run from Legion Park to the mouth as the lower river. This run has more straight riffle water, smooth glides, and fewer curves and deep pools, but it holds good numbers of fish and has several convenient access points with excellent fishing along the way. Legion Park, Boro Park, and Whiteman's Bridge are just a few.

Ed, Jeff, Mike, and I fished the upper water, an area called Struchen Flats, and the lower run above the Trestle Hole upstream from Whiteman's Bridge, in late November. The river was clearing and we guessed that steelhead would be able to see our flies at a distance of more than 2 feet. Ed felt the conditions were very good and improving.

"There are no sure things in fly fishing, but this is pretty close," he said.

At the main parking area at Struchen Flats, the river runs from left to right and the channel is approximately 100 feet wide. We waded slowly across, taking care to give plenty of room to several anglers intently working seams and pockets.

"Once we get a short way upstream we'll have the river pretty much to ourselves. Elk Creek is like anywhere else. Human nature puts the heaviest fishing pressure closest to convenient parking," Ed said. True enough. We moved upstream less than 200 yards, and the competition evaporated. Only one other angler in sight. I looked at a high shale cliff, and a deep, long, curving pool with a lively riffle at its head. I wondered why nobody was fishing here.

Maybe no fish? Jeff read my mind. "They're here, Bob. It's a deadlock certainty. Start with a pale Sucker Spawn Egg as a dropper and a small beadhead Prince as the point fly," he said.

I waded to a point where the water was about knee-deep. The casting distance to reach the deep run near the base of the cliff was about 40 feet. On my third drift, the indicator jumped about 6 inches and I was greeted with a surge of power and speed. A large bright steelhead thrashed at the surface then ran upstream about 50 yards before turning and jumping. After a few minutes of happy violence, the big hen tired and came to the net. She was beautiful, very thick and heavy. We photographed and carefully revived her. Ed guessed her to be between 12 and 14 pounds.

"The water temperature is only 39 degrees Fahrenheit. Can you imagine what she would have done if the temperature was a few degrees warmer?" he said. I thought that fish bordered on spectacular and wondered how much better it could get. I didn't have to wait long.

My reverie was interrupted by a holler and a splash. Jeff was hooked up on my left, and Mike was chasing a running fish to the right. I sloshed back to the bank, put my rod against a bush, and grabbed my camera. Ed had the big net at the ready and was grinning widely. He feinted right toward Mike, then jerked left in Jeff's direction.

> ## ELK CREEK
>
> ———————●———————
>
> **Location:** Lake City and Girard, Pennsylvania, 10 minutes west of Erie.
>
> **Airport:** Ten minutes from Erie, two hours from Cleveland, two hours from Pittsburgh.
>
> **Lodging:** All major chains—the Microtel at Exit 24 is value-priced and welcomes anglers. Call 814-864-1010.
>
> **Fly shops and Guides:** Lake Erie Ultimate Anglers, www.theultimate angler.com, 814-456-3035, or 1-888-456-3035.

"Help Mike first," Jeff said. At that moment Jeff's fish came unbuttoned and Ed moved upstream to net a handsome buck for Mike.

The fishing remained almost too good to be true throughout our session at Struchen Flats. We moved upstream around a severe bend to the right and crossed the river to fish a wide, straight run. I saw pockets, ledges, midstream cuts, and small depressions. At nearly every subtle color change that indicated a change in depth or a shadow from a protruding ledge, there were steelhead. A few were dark and had been in the river for some time. More fish were bright, appearing as vague shapes formed by nearly clear smoke. These were chrome fish just in from Lake Erie. There were small steelhead groups of three to five fish, duos, and a few singles here and there. This would be sight fishing that required precision fly placement and careful mending.

After some bungled casts we sorted things out. I managed to conjure up enough luck to hook and land a large male that ran up and down, back and forth, repeatedly. Jeff and Mike had more than one double hookup, and Ed ran his legs to nubs with the net. I kept the camera cranking and took countless shots of bent rods, splashing leaps, and goofy grins before we quit for the day.

Fly fishing is by far the most popular method among Elk Creek steelheaders.

"We've had enough fun here," Ed said. "Let's leave them alone." We all agreed. Enough is enough. And we were dog tired.

The following morning we went to the Trestle Hole near Whiteman's Bridge on the lower section of Elk Creek. There were fewer fish there on that particular day, and Ed guessed they probably had taken advantage of the high water to move farther upstream. Jeff and Ed each caught one but Mike was skunked and, since it was his last day before returning to California, the decision was made to move back upstream to Struchen Flats so he could have a better chance.

"We've got to keep the rookie well hooked," Jeff said and smiled.

"I'd say he's pretty much in the net," Ed replied.

Close to 90 percent of the anglers I saw on Elk Creek were toting fly rods. All released their fish carefully. Ed said he saw one fish on a stringer that first day, but I did not see any. Most of the rods were quite long and several were two-handed models. I asked Ed what he thought was the ideal setup for Elk Creek. He told me that his favorite is a 7-weight, 10 feet long with a medium tip and a powerful butt section. He and Jeff both use weight-forward floating lines in a neutral color. They like long leaders with a stiff butt section tapered to—depending on water clarity and hook size—2X, 3X, or 4X.

Favorite flies for Elk Creek are pretty much the same as for Sixteen and Twenty Mile Creeks, with a couple of minor adjustments. Ed's go-to nymph is a small, fluttering Hex. His favorite egg fly is a single-egg pattern in pale orange with a small red dot. Jeff favors the Copper John tied with a red, green, or black abdomen and the Sucker Spawn Cluster Egg in pale hues. I caught fish on beadhead caddis nymphs, Pheasant Tails, Princes, and an assortment of small egg flies. Lulls in the action were few and momentary. Whenever I would retreat to the bank, open my fly box, and appear befuddled either Jeff or Ed would magically appear, point, and say: "Try that one." I do what I'm told.

Elk Creek—and to a lesser extent the other steelhead streams on Erie's southern shore—produces an interesting hazard during the cold weather/cold water months. A peculiar-looking brown algae forms on some of the ledgerock slabs and is *extremely* slippery. Felt soles are not good enough to provide any traction at all—even in the most gentle current. Wear studded soles or chains for safety during the late fall and winter. This stuff is deceiving. The clean, almost creamy tan rocks are the safe ones with a good firm grip. The slabs with a brownish, speckled cast look as though they would provide more secure footing, but those are dangerous. It is exactly the opposite of what you might expect. Be careful.

Elk Creek has fantastic fishing from September through March in most years. It has abundant easy access and parking. The people are friendly and helpful, and the anglers are sportsmen. The fish are big, aggressive, and bountiful. What more can we ask for?

Cattaraugus Creek

Cattaraugus Creek drains a relatively long watershed by South Shore Lake Erie standards. It offers nearly 35 miles of steelhead water with good to excellent fly-fishing opportunities between Lake Erie and the upstream barrier at Springville Dam. One of the most popular sections to fish is from the town of Gowanda downstream to I-90 and on to Lake Erie. This run of river attracts high numbers of both fall- and spring-run steelhead and is a favorite of many fly anglers. This lower section of the "Cat" is entirely within Seneca Nation of Indians Lands—specifically the Cattaraugus Indian Reservation—and a special license, available for $10 at the reservation administration building, is required in addition to the New York license.

This section of river is quite large, averaging between 80 and 100 feet in width. The depth varies widely from about 2 feet at the tail-outs of long, wide pools and runs to 6 feet and more in corner holes and at the bases of heavy chutes. The current slows as the river nears the big lake but presents a nice, interesting variety of riffles and pools farther upstream on reservation land. The river usually carries at least some color in the form of sediment from clay banks and in-stream clay deposits spread throughout its course. Under normal flow conditions this is a very good thing. There is enough visibility for steelhead to see flies, but the water is not so clear that ultrafine leaders are required. Under spate conditions created by heavy rain, or even light rain combined with a spring thaw and snow runoff, the Cattaraugus can cloud quickly to the point of near zero visibility. This usually lasts at least a day or two before the flow clears and good fly fishing resumes.

The steelhead that run up Cattaraugus Creek are vibrant, aggressive, and handsome. Although the majority of the population base comes from smolt stockings by New York State, supplemental increases in steelhead numbers come from "roamers," fish stocked in Pennsylvania, perhaps even in Ohio waters. More importantly, as much as 25 percent of both the fall and spring populations are wild fish, born in the river. This unanticipated windfall from natural reproduction is an important contribution to the overall health of the population as well as to the enjoyment of fishing the Cat. Various projects designed to increase natural reproduc-

Rick Kustich with a fine Cattaraugus Creek steelhead.

tion and survival of wild fry and smolts are now in the planning and implementation phases.

Several small to medium-size tributaries to Cattaraugus Creek contribute to this growing base of wild fish. These include Clear Creek, the North Branch of Clear Creek, part of the South Branch of Cattaraugus Creek, Derby Brook, Coon Brook, and Spooner Creek. At this time, both the North Branch of Clear Creek and Spooner Creek are closed to fishing from January 1 through March 31 to protect spawning steelhead.

These fish, both wild and stocked, average about 5 pounds, with a few fish running much larger. Eight- to 12-pound steelhead are caught with regularity, and a few monsters go into the mid-teens in weight. New York's Department of Environmental Conservation encourages catch-and-release for all steelhead in the Cattaraugus system.

> ## CATTARAUGUS CREEK
>
> ⬤
>
> **Location:** Gowanda, New York, south of I-90.
>
> **Airport:** Thirty-five minutes from Buffalo.
>
> **Lodging:** All major chains in Buffalo, local motels in Gowanda.
>
> **Fly shops and Guides:** Buffalo Outfitters, www.cattaraugusflyshop.com, 716-631-5131.

My friend Rick Kustich fishes the Cattaraugus often. He is one of our sport's leading fly-fishing conservations and writers, as well as a respected, knowledgeable advocate for this unique river. Rick feels that the Cattaraugus is one of the best venues in the Great Lakes basin to swing flies with traditional (Pacific/Spey) methodology and enjoy high success. The Cat's long, wide pools and runs of moderate depth and its light stain are ideal for this approach.

Rick guided me to a long pool within reservation lands on my first day on the river. Unfortunately we hit a moderate spate condition that followed a day of rain. The water was dirty and visibility was less than 12 inches. Pretty tough, but workable with patience. Rick tied a purple and black marabou Spey pattern to my tippet and suggested I start at the head of the pool with a short cast to cover the nearest water first, then gradually increase the length of the casts to cover the entire width of the pool before stepping downstream several feet and repeating the process.

"If we go through the pool without a hit, we'll move back up to the head and try a smaller, lighter pattern," he said. To be perfectly honest, I did not have much confidence because of the dirty water, but I followed Rick's instructions. After fishing through the pool without success

I trudged back upstream and Rick replaced the large, dark fly with a smaller white marabou Spey pattern.

"They're here, Bob. Try it again the same way." As I waded back into position, a steelhead rolled on the surface some distance below me. This was an energizing catalyst to actually *fish* rather than just *cast*. I put my mind to the task and started to pay attention to position, cast, and swing. As I approached the area where the fish had broken the surface, my concentration increased. On the first swing through what we both thought would be the "sweet spot," a heavy, sharp take pulled slack line created by an untimely mend to a straight connection. I felt the fish for only a second or two before it was gone. I had more hits that day, but for whatever reason could not manage to maintain a solid connection with my fly at the moment steelhead decided to eat it. There was no fault with the river, fish, or method—it was all my error and poor luck. I've since corrected the percentages of solidly hooked fish to a more favorable level.

Spey flies tied with rabbit fur—like the Purple, Black, and White Bunny Spey—do a fine job with Cattaraugus steelhead. Marabou Spey patterns are also good on this river. Bring some in purple and orange, purple and black, chartreuse, and white. Swinging traditional streamers is also effective. If the water is warm—in the high 40s and 50s F (8 to 12 degrees C)—the streamers can be twitched and otherwise moved to excite fish. Otherwise, swing them without added movement. Basic sculpin patterns, Woolly Buggers, and streamers tied to represent smelt, such as the Grey Ghost and gray (natural) Zonkers, will produce solid hits by aggressive fish.

A nymph and egg fly selection for the Cat should include the basic patterns for Lake Erie tributaries described elsewhere, but I would add some larger flies in the egg category and go heavy on dark stonefly and Hare's Ear nymphs.

On occasion, fishing pressure within the reservation lands can be fairly heavy. This is particularly so when a light rain swells the river without turning it too dirty to fish. The spate flow quickly draws a fresh run of steelhead from nearby Lake Erie, and they first congregate in reservation water. The upper river has excellent steelhead water and is typically less crowded. There are access points upstream from the reservation and the village of Gowanda. Check the water within the Zoar Valley Multiple Use Area (extremely beautiful countryside!), the fishing access sites at North Otto Road and Hammond Hill Road, and farther upstream at Scoby Hill County Park. All these sections provide excellent fly-fishing opportunities. The river is a bit smaller here but still large enough to fish with your method of choice. There is an abundance of near perfect water for nymphing techniques as well as swinging classic western Spey patterns, and streamers.

The Cattaraugus has a substantial run of steelhead that are most receptive to fly-fishing techniques. Both ascending and drop-back fish seem always hungry and on the prod for action. This river is my first choice for learning—or practicing and refining—new techniques and fly patterns. It may well be the best river in the entire basin for two-handed rods and swinging flies. If you have tired of chuck-and-duck or other methods of delivering nymphs and eggs, if you are interested in widening your experience and developing new skills, consider a trip to this river. Guides and instructors are available in the area, and the river will not disappoint you. If I had to pick one period within the calendar year to fish the Cat, it would be from the last half of October through the middle of November. Fish populations are high and spread out through the system, and water clarity is generally more dependable than in the spring, when both snowmelt and rains often combine to confound fly fishing.

Grand River

Steelhead in Ontario's Grand River are the region's most recent fly-fishing bonanza. Anglers began to take notice of this big Canadian river in the mid-1990s, when its dry-fly fishing for large brown trout began to make headlines in fly-fishing journals. Prolific mayfly and caddis hatches and very big, free-rising trout lured anglers from throughout the United States and Canada. And many Europeans have also made the pilgrimage to friendly Canada for Grand River dry-fly action.

The Grand is a large river that drains a significant watershed, roughly the size of Connecticut, in southern Ontario. From the headwaters, north by northwest from Toronto near Dundalk, the river flows southward toward its mouth at Port Maitland on Lake Erie. Tributaries and spring-water feed the flow as it passes the Luther Marsh and moves toward Elora Gorge. From this point the Grand winds on and picks up volume from significant tributaries such as Conestoga Creek and Laurel Creek. The river skirts the eastern edge of the town of Kitchener, continues due south for a few miles, then bends to the southeast past Brantford, Caledonia, Dunnville, and on to Port Maitland.

Accumulating natural deterioration of the old Lorne Dam in the city of Brantford came to a critical point in the early 1980s, and the dam was removed in 1982. The elimination of this obstacle to upstream migration opened the upper Grand and its coldwater tributaries to spawning steelhead. Previous to this removal, natural reproduction by the Grand River's steelhead was limited to a very small area of the main river and two or three small coldwater tributaries downstream from Brantford. This minimal spawning was not nearly enough to sustain a wild population appropriate to the size of the river. But nowadays natural reproduction in the upper sections of the mainstream, and in a multitude of coldwater feeder streams, is the main source of the river's steelhead population.

In the year 2000, the Ontario Ministry of Natural Resources completed a study of Whiteman's Creek, a productive trout stream and steelhead nursery. The study estimated an annual production of 55,000 steelhead smolts from this single source. And Whiteman's Creek is but one of many. Several other small creeks serve as spawning refuges and steelhead nurseries. Current estimates suggest that as many as 15,000 purely wild steelhead survive the perils of big water to return to the Grand each year. This number builds annually. If the trend continues, the Grand will surely take its place as one of the top two or three wild fisheries in the entire Great Lakes basin. There is no reason to expect otherwise; steelhead now have free access to approximately 85 miles of the main river and nearly 40 miles of cold, pure feeder streams rich with ideal spawning gravel.

One of the best fly-fishing areas on the Grand is at the town of Dunnville on the lower river. Steelhead congregate and hold below the Dunnville Dam before ascending the fish ladder and continuing their upstream migration. The stretch of water between the dam and Lake Erie is short, so the fish are extremely bright, vigorous, and aggressive. It is big water in every sense of the term—wide and deep with a heavy current. It is best, and safest, to fish this area from a boat.

Both fall- and spring-run fish stack up in significant numbers below the dam, and the fishing is often spectacular. This is an exceptional piece of

---

GRAND RIVER (ONTARIO)

Location: Southern Ontario, Brantford–Port Maitland, west of Hamilton, southwest of Toronto.

Airport: One hour from Toronto.

Lodging: Extensive and varied, from large chains to small bed and breakfast and motel facilities.

Fly shops and Guides: Grindstone Angling, www.grindstoneangling.com, 905-689-0880; Oak Orchard Fly Shop, www.oakorchardflyshop.com, 716-626-1323.

water for swinging Spey flies and streamers with a sink-tip line. Look for current seams, soft eddies, and smooth cuts that blend into runs and pools. A long, two-handed rod offers many advantages here. Longer casts allow anglers to cover more productive water without repositioning the boat. Precise mends are more easily made with the longer rods, and they provide much more leverage when fighting fish. Remember that these steelhead are not only big, but they are also very fresh from Lake Erie. They are extremely powerful and energetic. This combined with heavy, big water makes for an exciting fight that usually lasts beyond just a few minutes.

Nymphs and egg patterns also produce fish here, but nymphing techniques are a bit more difficult to employ in the big water. Considerable extra weight may be required to put flies at the proper fishing depth. Pinch-on, nontoxic weights can be added to a leader as one alternative. Another approach is to experiment with the sinking-leader techniques covered in Chapter Three. This allows a cleaner drift, a bit more distance for pure fly casting, and more likelihood of a strike as the fly swings and stays directly downstream from the angler's position. Use the heaviest leader tippet appropriate to water clarity, but do not use anything lighter than 3X in this stretch of the Grand.

Another good fly-fishing area is near the town of York, approximately 20 miles upstream from Port Maitland. The river runs along the town's western edge and has a wide variety of productive water all the way upstream to the village of Caledonia. This whole section of the river has multiple access points that are on or very near areas with good fly-fishing opportunities. Do not be afraid to do some exploring. You will find a multitude of riffles with deepwater pockets, runs, and slower pools throughout.

The run of river between Caledonia and York is still big, impressive water. The average width is probably close to 200 feet and the average depth is around 4 feet, with many spots that are much deeper. The river bottom is bedrock and usually presents sure footing for felt-soled waders, but beware of strong current and medium to large boulders strewn along the bottom.

There is some excellent nymphing water in this stretch. Look for seams and shallower riffle water. A strike indicator is very helpful here. Use fairly big nymphs in this section. Stonefly and buggy, breathing mayfly nymphs tied with aftershaft feathers on No. 10, 8, and even 6 hooks are usually best. Use tan, gray, and olive nymphs if the water is very clear; black and dark brown are best if the water is stained. Caddis larvae in bright green, olive, cream, and tan also produce fish. Carry a few caddis nymphs tied with a Krystal Flash rib on No. 8 and 10 hooks. A range of egg fly colors should include bright fluorescent orange and chartreuse, as well as Oregon cheese and cream. Again, carry a few egg flies with built-in flash.

Still, as in the water below Dunnville Dam, the most exciting and productive way to fish this big water is with swinging-fly tactics and equipment. Rods between 11 and 14 feet that handle 9- and 10-weight lines are best. An assortment of interchangeable sinking heads for the fly line will give you enough flexibility to effectively fish all the best water.

The area between York and Caledonia has good access to productive water as well as light to moderate angling pressure, and this is an added benefit for those desiring a measure of solitude. Guided float trips are available on this stretch of river. It is a full day's float from Caledonia to York.

The next upstream area with good fly fishing is in and near the city of Brantford. Upstream a bit from the city, Wilkes Dam momentarily pauses the upstream run of fish. The run of river downstream from the dam to Brantford twists and turns through dedicated park lands with maintained walking trails and excellent public access. This section of the Grand has deep chutes and troughs interspersed with quicker riffle water. Fish hold in the troughs, the seams along deep chutes, and in the pockets formed behind large boulders within the riffles. Steelhead eat nymphs and eggs here, of course, but the most successful method is to swing large, bunny-type leeches and streamers.

Within the city limits of Brantford, the river channel narrows a bit. Logjams, large boulders, and current seams hold a surprising number of aggressive steelhead. With the exception of bridges, a few buildings, and the occasional honk of a truck horn, you would never know you were in the heart of a major population center. This stretch is best fished from a boat. Use extra-fast-sinking heads, a stout leader with a 10-pound-test tippet, and large leech patterns for best results.

Wilkes Dam is low to the water and is not a significant barrier; steelhead jump over the dam head and continue upstream after a brief pause. Upstream from this dam, you will find a short stretch of slow "frog" water, but above this the river quickly resumes its more shallow, lively pace. This continues all the way upstream to the town of Paris, Ontario. This stretch of the river is designated *no-kill* for all species, and terminal tackle is restricted to a single barbless hook. This part of the river recently disclosed some fish species that had been thought to be extinct, including a rare member of the dace family and another of the redhorse sucker clan. All fish must be quickly released unharmed, even if it is a chub or a sucker. The stretch between Paris and Wilkes Dam has more limited public access and is best fished from a boat.

Public access improves greatly close to Paris, with many roads and parking areas close to good water within the city limits. This stretch of river is full of fast runs and riffles with deepwater pockets. It is one of the best stretches of river for nymphing techniques. The river channel is still wide but not nearly as intimidating as farther downstream. Here the average width runs between 85 and 120 feet and the depths run between 2 and 4 feet.

The Nith River enters the Grand within the city limits of Paris. It is a fine steelhead stream in its own right, as many fish split away from the mainstream and ascend the Nith to their natal waters. The junction pool where the Nith joins the Grand is an excellent spot for steelhead during the early part of the fall run. Additionally, it is a superb place to fly-fish for drop-back steelhead in the spring. Depending on weather, this pool will hold fish as late as mid-June. Casting flies to hungry steelhead in short-sleeve weather is great fun.

The opportunity to catch a steelhead on a dry fly in the Grand River is best during the later stages of the spring run. Because of excellent water quality, relatively constant, moderate temperatures, and abundant aquatic insect life, immature steelhead hold in the river for up to three years before smolting to Lake Erie. Born in the river with little or no hatchery influence, they behave like resident rainbow trout during this extended period and feed heavily on insects. The adults are heavily imprinted, conditioned to eating bugs. When they return from the lake, this instinct quickly takes over and steelhead scour the current for nymphs and look to the surface for floating mayflies, stoneflies, and caddis.

It is a relatively common sight to see steelhead sipping on the surface once the weather has warmed and activated aquatic insects to hatch and mate. This is a wonderful time on the Grand. Fish are caught with the standard dry-fly dead-drift on basic, match-the-hatch patterns, and on large, waking flies like the Bomber and other bulky deerhair patterns. The take may be a gentle sip or an explosive, crashing surge.

Dry-fly fishing can also be effective during the fall run. In October, blue-winged olives hatch regularly throughout the river, and steelhead will eat them. This is pretty exhilarating, to say the least. Small dry flies

PHOTO BY JOHN VALK

A fabulous steelie from the Grand River.

and 10-pound steelhead are a volatile combination. John Valk told me he guided an Ohio client who hooked two massive steelhead on small *Baetis* patterns in 2002. The two big fish began to sip olives about 1:00 in the afternoon on a beautiful October afternoon. Both were stationed behind large boulders and sucking the little bugs creating large, breathtaking swirls.

The only dry-fly rig available that day was a light 4-weight rod. Both fish broke off quickly, but each had leaped clear of the water and gave a great view. Happily, John's client had landed two of six hooked earlier in the day on Spey flies, but the fish he continued to rave about were the monsters that ate tiny dry flies.

The Grand is long and mighty, with one of the healthiest wild steelhead runs in the Great Lakes. Its prospects for future improvement are superb. The Fisheries Division of the Ministry of Natural Resources continues to emphasize the qualities of wild fish, and this vision is shared and supported by local conservation groups and a growing number of dedicated catch-and-release fly anglers.

Lake Ontario

This is the smallest of the Great Lakes. Ontario is 193 miles long and covers 7,540 square surface miles. Its northern shore is Canadian land. Ontario's capital, and the nation's largest city, Toronto, is home to more than a million lakeside residents. The lake's southern shore nestles against New York, from urban Buffalo past Rochester to the narrows at Cape Vincent and the head of the St. Lawrence River.

Both New York and Ontario are now stressing the importance of wild fish in the balance of Lake Ontario's carrying capacity. Natural reproduction has improved on both sides of the lake in recent years. Nursery streams receive more protection. Successful spawning has increased dramatically and the subsequent survival of fry and smolts (recruitment) is significant enough to be recognized as a major contributor to steelhead stocks in Lake Ontario.

In Canada, moving eastward from the Niagara River, the Credit River enters the lake north of Hamilton and has strong runs of vigorous steelhead. The Credit is located on the fringe of Canada's largest metropolitan population center with nearly three million people. Steelhead have access to about 20 miles of river between the mouth and the upstream barrier at Norval Dam. Limited natural reproduction in the river below the dam and in Huttonville and Mullet Creeks provides some supplement to this primarily hatchery-based steelhead population.

A fishway at Streetsville, run by the Credit River Anglers Association, monitors the size of the run and provides brood stock for a small hatchery operated by volunteers. Approximately 200,000 fingerlings and 20,000 smolts are stocked yearly. In addition to steelhead, Pacific salmon

PHOTO BY RICK KUSTICH

Rick Kustich with a winter steelhead from New York's Salmon River.

are stocked annually. Stocking numbers range from 80,000 to 150,000 king salmon and from 90,000 to 170,000 silver salmon.

The Credit provides excellent but often crowded fly angling below the Norval barrier. The best access for sport fishermen is at Erindale Park. This section of the river has a steep hydraulic gradient and is typically riffle and chute water with productive pocket fishing. North of the town of Mississauga, human population density decreases. The river in this area has more classic water types with a variety of interspersed pools, runs, riffles, and pocket water.

The Credit fishes best from mid-September through early May. Steelhead success for fly anglers peaks in late October, but this time of year signals the height of the salmon runs and crowding can be an issue. All popular fly-fishing tactics produce steelhead here. The best flies are stonefly nymphs, single-egg patterns, Woolly Buggers, and Spey patterns in black and blue. Wait until the salmon run fades and cooler weather settles in for the best steelhead opportunities.

Bronte Creek north of Burlington, Sixteen Mile Creek upstream from Oakville, and Wilmot Creek near Oshawa and New Castle are worth exploring. Wilmot Creek is the highest-rated steelhead water for fly angling among these.

East of Port Hope and the Ganaraska River, look at the Moira River at Belleville. This stream has substantial runs of steelhead in both the fall and spring. The Napanee River at the town of Napanee has several stretches of good fly-fishing water and has a strong steelhead run.

About midway between Niagara Falls and Rochester, New York, Oak Orchard Creek crosses NY 105 and continues north to Lake Ontario. My first real success with Lake Ontario steelhead came on this river with the help of noted fly angler and author Rick Kustich. That was years ago. The fall and spring steelhead runs are still impressive, but the short stretch of river below Waterport Dam can be extremely crowded. This is especially true when fall Pacific salmon and huge brown trout make their spawning runs. If you can, wait until after salmon numbers drop in late October and early November, and fish in the middle of the week to avoid tight company. During the spring, steelhead run fishing is also best if you can avoid weekends.

I have a soft spot for Oak Orchard despite the crowds. The fishing can be truly excellent. I remember a magnificent silver hen steelhead that slammed a swinging Spey fly in early April. She jumped and ran and crashed wildly before tiring. She gave me a truly baleful stare as I removed the hook and pushed her back into the current. And I remember the biggest brown trout I have ever landed. He was 34 inches long and we guessed him at about 15 pounds. This fish ate a No. 12 Hare's Ear nymph. I was breathless when he swam away. A synthetic mount of this fish hangs on my wall.

A bit farther east toward Rochester, Sandy Creek and the Genesee River have sizeable steelhead runs and are worth a look if you are in the area. Continuing east, Grindstone Creek crosses I-81 north of Syracuse and a bit south of Pulaski. The south and north branches join a bit west of NY 11 and flow northwest to Lake Ontario. This river flows through extensive wetlands that mitigate the effects of rain and snowmelt. It often remains clear when nearby streams and the famous Salmon River are too high or dirty for effective fly flying. Grindstone Creek receives light angling pressure despite good public access and a strong run of steelhead. Some stocking takes place on Grindstone, but a high percentage of its steelhead are wild fish. This is a small river with an average width of about 30 feet. Stalking skills, careful wading, and precision casts are helpful.

Niagara River

Fly fishing is not the first thing that comes to mind when the Niagara River is mentioned. Honeymoon capitol of North America, the thundering cascade of Niagara Falls, a wonder of the world, tour boats and souvenirs, yes. Fly fishing? Yes. The magnificent roaring falls and the rapids immediately below create high oxygen levels in the flow that support a surprising variety of aquatic insects and attract massive baitfish populations. Alewives, smelt, herring, shiners, shad, and more flood the big river. The predators follow. Lake trout, brown trout, Pacific salmon, landlocked Atlantic salmon, smallmouth bass, muskies, northern pike, and steelhead feed on the bounty.

The Niagara River drains Lake Erie into Lake Ontario and the St. Lawrence River. It is the ultimate outflow of all the upstream Great Lakes to the Atlantic Ocean, and a "tributary," albeit the largest feeder stream in North America, to Lake Ontario. The flow from Erie to Ontario is approximately 20 miles. The river below the falls has numerous Class V rapids and one Class VI, which is totally unnavigable. This Class VI rapid is near the Whirlpool and it is off limits to boats by law. But for the most part, the lower river is fishable from a boat. In fact, fly fishing from a boat is often excellent. Most fly anglers use long and heavy sinking-head lines and large baitfish imitations to reach the depths at which this river's very large and robust steelhead are found. The only safe way to do this is with an experienced guide with first-class equipment—a boat and large motor.

Believe it or not, walk and wade fishing is not only possible, it is in wide practice and very effective. It is however, somewhat demanding in terms of commitment, energy, and caution. But the rewards are significant. Steelhead begin to show in good numbers in October and the run builds through November. Good fly fishing can be had throughout the winter and into spring. The peak months for steelhead are November and June. King salmon from 15 to 30 pounds use the river heavily in September and October. Brown trout and lake trout are present through the fall and winter months.

Niagara steelhead are special. They represent an adaptation to the Niagara's incredible current; they are a blend of Ganaraska, Chambers Creek, and Salmon River strains from Lake Ontario. Fish in the 20-pound class are almost common. They are extremely vigorous. Combine sheer size with high energy and the heavy, fast current of this huge river and you get a sense of the battle these fish present on fly-fishing gear.

Long, two-handed rods are not a requirement for wading anglers, but they are a big help in reaching out to fish. Single-handed rods in 8- to 10-weight are also serviceable. Fast-sinking shooting heads are the standard fly lines. The fly line density and sink rate must be sufficient to get your fly down quickly and hold it at the proper depth throughout the swing or drift. A sink rate of 8 to 10 inches per second is not too fast. Floating lines are also used with nymphing techniques to drift egg and nymph patterns. This is most effective when fish are visible and near gravel during the spring.

The water level fluctuates each day due to power generation requirements. Hydroelectric plants on both sides of the river below Devil's Hole take in and discharge water on a regular basis, and the discharge raises the river's level dramatically. One of the keys to safe, successful fly fishing on the Niagara is timing. If the water is too low and clear, steelhead take up positions too far from the bank to be reached. If the water is too high, the fish will be in closer but wading may not be safe.

Fly anglers have access to the Niagara at several locations on both the Canadian and United States sides of the river. On the New York side, the best access points are at Whirlpool Park, Devil's Hole, and near the Art Park Performing Arts Center. Best access points on the Ontario side are at Niagara-on-the-Lake and Queenston. Good steelhead water is easy to reach from these locations, but these areas can become crowded during peak periods. Also on the Ontario side of the river, the Glen and Whirlpool access points require lengthy, difficult hikes but afford excellent conditions and water for fly anglers. The Glen has long, deep pools interspersed with productive runs and boulder-studded back eddies that attract and hold steelhead for long periods. This area resembles some of the larger steelhead rivers of British Columbia.

The Whirlpool is a large elbow pool several hundred yards wide and over 200 feet deep in the center. At the bottom of the Whirlpool trail, the

---

NIAGARA RIVER

Location: Niagara Falls, Ontario and New York; east of Buffalo, west of Toronto.

Airport: Forty-five minutes from Toronto or Buffalo.

Lodging: Numerous chains.

Fly shops and Guides: Grindstone Angling, www.grindstoneangling .com, 905-689-0880; Wilson's, www.wilsonstoronto.com, 416-869-3474; Buffalo Outfitters Fly Shop, www.cattaraugusflyshop .com, 716-631-5131; Oak Orchard Fly Shop, www.oakorchardflyshop .com, 716-626-1323.

Stonefly nymphs are a good choice for Niagara River steelhead.

surroundings open to a large gravel- and boulder-strewn beach area. This entire run of river, on the Canadian side, attracts hundreds of thousands of smelt and shiners in the spring. This, of course, attracts and holds hungry steelhead. The Whirlpool features glasslike runs that are near perfect for swinging Spey flies and baitfish patterns. When water temperatures warm and reach into the 50s F (10 to 15 degrees C) in May and June, these runs are ideal for skating large dry flies like Bombers and various waking patterns. The river just upstream from the Whirlpool is very difficult to fish and has areas that are completely treacherous and must be avoided.

Standard nymphs and egg patterns work well in the Niagara River. Many anglers use shooting lines and heavy pencil weight to sink their flies to depth, but the sinking-leader technique described in Chapter Three also works well and is a reasonable alternative to the addition of heavy sinkers to the leader. Joe's Canadian Stone in black or white is a top producer. The Spring Stone is another good choice. Sparrow Nymphs, Flashback Hare's Ears, and Woolly Buggers in black and olive complete a fair selection for this water. You will need a range of colors and sizes of egg patterns to match water clarity. Bright and large on cloudy days with high or slightly stained water, pale and small on bright-sky, clear water days is the standard rule.

The best streamer patterns are those that imitate dominant baitfish populations. Joe's Niagara Shiner and Joe's Smelt are two of the most productive streamers yet developed for this river. A mix of white and light olive Clousers and Deceivers will also catch these steelhead. Patterns that mimic baby rainbow and brown trout can be very productive at times. Classic and marabou Spey flies in purple, purple and red, chartreuse, gold, gold and brown, black, and black and purple or red are favored here. Dry flies need to be buoyant and large. Clipped deerhair bodies enhance floatability and present the necessary bulky profile to induce strikes. Large Bomber and Wulff patterns on No. 6 hooks in natural tan or gray, chartreuse, and black are best. White wings enhance visibility.

It is not possible to overemphasize the need for caution when fishing the Niagara. Water level fluctuations, heavy and deep current, and slippery rocks demand attention. Between April 1 and November 1, water levels begin to rise about 7 AM and start to level and recede about 9 AM. Proper wading boots are important. Felt soles with carbide or steel studs are required for safety. Bring a personal flotation vest, a wading staff, and a friend. Carry a small backpack with a camera, lunch, water, and extra flies.

The Niagara is an awesome, daunting river but its gifts are often extravagant. The sheer power of a chrome, rock-hard, 20-pound steelhead in heavy current is an adrenaline thrill beyond description. The river's rushing, curling majesty is inspiring. Its deep, foreboding gorge is a rugged and glistening beauty. And the knowledge that when you cast a fly here you are fishing the raw edge of life itself is its own special reward.

Oswego River

This is a mighty river. Excepting the thundering, massive Niagara, the Oswego River is the largest-volume tributary to Lake Ontario. Flowing north by northwest from Syracuse, the river parallels the course of NY 481 through Fulton, Minetto, and Lansing before hitting the lakeside town of Oswego and its mouth at Lake Ontario.

The water accessible to steelhead between the mouth and the upstream barrier at Varick Dam is short but because of the width and volume of the river, the actual habitat space for steelhead and other anadromous species approximates what is available on many longer but smaller rivers.

Like many other Lake Ontario rivers, the Oswego's steelhead runs dropped in volume in the late 1990s and into the first couple of years of the new century. A combination of overharvest, weather conditions, and severe predatation negatively impacted steelhead smolt numbers and subsequent returns of adult fish. Northern pike, smallmouth bass, lake trout, and ravenous brown trout hammered pen-raised smolts as soon as they reached the harbor. Perhaps the most devastating impact from predators came in the form of periodic cormorant infestations along the river, into the harbor, and out into the big lake.

Now, some really good news. The United States, in cooperation with the State of New York, has relaxed restrictions on cormorant control on New York waters, and this is showing an immediate positive result.

Another development with positive impact is the creative problem-solving approach to smolt survival undertaken in a cooperative effort by charter boat captains, river anglers, and guides. Fish pens are placed in the lower harbor. Thousands of steelhead smolts are placed in these sheltering pens for an acclimation period. During this time, smolts adapt to natural food forms flowing in the river's current and are fed supplementally by their guardians. This greatly speeds growth and survivability in the wilds of Lake Ontario. And through this period they are sheltered from predation. Once the smolts have adapted and grown to a certain size, the charter boat captains and other volunteers tow the fish pens approximately 5 miles out into the lake and release the baby steelhead. These fish pen smolts receive tiny tags of stainless steel in their noses that carry individual bar codes. The bar code tags allow careful, precise calculation of growth, survivability, and return against a like number of smolts released under the traditional method and timing directly into the river. So far, results show returns of steelhead sheltered in the pens are two orders of magnitude larger than those planted with standard release procedures. The results are so positive and significant that this method is now being used at Oak Orchard Creek and may well expand to every suitable New York tributary. It is reasonable to think that this process would produce similar results in other parts of the Great Lakes basin.

> ## OSWEGO RIVER
>
> ———————●———————
>
> **Location:** Oswego, New York, on NY 48, north of Syracuse.
>
> **Airport:** Forty minutes from Syracuse.
>
> **Lodging:** Smaller chains and local motels.
>
> **Fly shops and Guides:** Two Dogs Outfitters (John Dembeck), www.steelheadfishingoutfitters.com, 315-564-6366.

Runs improved greatly in the fall of 2004. There were more and bigger steelhead entering the Oswego beginning in September and continuing through the end of the year.

In addition to great steelhead fly fishing, the Oswego River has fantastic fly fishing for very large brown trout that spawn in the gravel and cobble below Varick Dam. A huge run of Pacific salmon, both kings and silvers, also use the river in the fall. Atlantic salmon and lake trout are also available to fly anglers, but are less frequently caught. Pacific salmon dominate angler attention in September and October. By October 15, most of the crazed salmon hoopla fades, and fly fishing for steelhead begins in earnest. Steelhead are available in the river from early October through April; the best fishing months for steelhead are November, December, February, and April. The best mixed-bag fly fishing occurs in October and November, with good chances for steelhead, lake-run brown trout, lake trout, and salmon.

All of these species grow to large size. You can expect silver salmon in the 8- to 12-pound range, king salmon between 10 and 40 pounds, brown trout up to about 15 pounds, and steelhead from 8 to 20 pounds. The odd gift of an Atlantic salmon will weigh anywhere from 8 to 20 pounds.

The size of the steelhead and the power of the river dictate strong tackle. You will be undergunned with any fly rod lighter than a 7-weight, and an 8-weight is a better all-around choice. John Dembeck, a marine biologist and fly-fishing guide since 1983, recommends a sink-tip line as a better choice for this river than a floating line, with added split shot for weight. He suggests using a high-density sinking tip about 10 feet in length in combination with a short leader of about 4 feet. His favored method is to cast quartering upstream from the target zone and to throw a large mend to sink the fly to the proper depth.

I suggest using the best reel you have or can afford to buy. It *must* have a very smooth disk drag with low start-up inertia and large backing capacity. Extra spools with lines of varying sink rates are helpful. A few years ago I managed to lose a very large steelhead that decided to visit the Canadian shore after being hooked close below the dam. My reel on that day was a Hardy Zenith that I thought would be more than adequate. I was wrong. As the backing melted away, the reel's sound went from that pleasing, chirping song to a large pop. The reel literally exploded. The spool flew off, several screws from the click-and-pawl drag went flying, and the great fish was lost. I take good care of my reels. This was not an issue of negligence; it was an issue of power and speed mismatched to an inadequate drag.

John Dembeck suggests standard Glo Bug egg flies and nymphs for steelhead in the upper part of the river. As the river slows and deepens near the harbor, he switches to Spey and streamer techniques and patterns. Streamers that copy alewives and herring are very effective here. Alewife patterns should be 6 to 7 inches long. Herring flies are most productive in the 4-inch range. Another pattern of choice is the Oswego Smelt. John developed this fly for brown trout, but it works equally well with steelhead. Additionally, Clousers and Deceivers produce hits in the lower river. Technique is critical when fishing streamers, and it is important to change retrieves and speed to find what fish prefer on any given day.

The bottom structure on this river is varied, with ledgerock, gravel, sand, rocks, and cobble. Look for a mixed bottom structure with ledges, pockets, and shade. These areas are much more attractive to steelhead than smooth, even areas of ledgerock, clay, and sand.

Rabbit-strip, marabou, and more traditional Spey flies also catch a lot of steelhead on the Oswego. Because the current often carries at least some stain, dark colors are more visible. Black and red is one of the best

Spey flies account for large numbers of brown trout and Pacific salmon, as well as steelhead, in New York's Oswego River.

combinations for Spey patterns here. Dembeck's Loch Seven fly is superb. It has a yellow rabbit-strip tail, a red rabbit wing, a black marabou collar, and a silver tinsel body. The Popsicle series of marabou Spey patterns are also effective on this river. Purple and black, black and red, and purple and red are good combinations. You can see some of John's fly patterns at his Web site.

The Oswego is only a few hours from Boston, New York City, Toronto, Philadelphia, Pittsburgh, and Detroit. It is a short drive from Buffalo, Syracuse, and Rochester. Still, with the exception of the salmon run's peak in October, it is not crowded with anglers. The scope of the river, both at Varick Dam and at the harbor, can be daunting to new-comers but wading is safe enough in the upper river for people with any measure of common sense. A boat—most wisely a boat and a guide—is the only productive and safe means to exploit the excellent potential of the lower river.

"Fish the close-in water first on this river. Most newcomers wade out too far and start with very long casts. Most often there will be steelhead very close to shore, and people spook them when first entering the river. Fish close first, then gradually lengthen your casts before wading farther out into the river," John said.

Oswego is a very friendly, working-class town with all the needs and amenities a visiting angler requires. It has the only doughnut shop I have ever seen that is completely decorated with mounted trophy steelhead, brown trout, and salmon.

Salmon River

Steelhead sport angling in the Salmon River has changed dramatically in the last 20 years. Some say it has greatly diminished; others feel it has significantly improved. The opinion held is obviously a matter of interpretation measured against personal values. Through the 1980s and into the early 1990s, steelhead runs in the Salmon River were massive. Some estimates say that up to 40,000 steelhead made the migration each year. Most agree that the number exceeded 30,000. Combine either of these incredible numbers with large spawning runs of king salmon and brown trout packed into approximately 18 miles of accessible water on a medium-size river, and it is hard to imagine a small spot in the stream without a shadow or direct view of a large salmonid.

Huge numbers of trophy-size trout and salmon attracted lots of people, and the result was not always pleasing. The river became too crowded during peak run activity, particularly in the fall of the year. Not all the people present were sport anglers. Snagging of salmon was legal for a period. It is not hard to picture a range of serious problems and poor behavior under these circumstances. It became obvious that some changes would be necessary to improve the quality of the Salmon River fishing experience.

Beginning in 1989, New York State officials began to reduce and limit areas of the river open to snagging of Pacific salmon. Also in 1989, the first fly-fishing, catch-and-release area opened below the hatchery. The Douglaston Salmon Run, a private, 2-mile stretch on the lower river, provided a high-quality fishing experience and controlled access for a nominal daily fee. A side benefit to increased quality of angling in the controlled area is that reduced fishing pressure allows more fish to reach upstream portions of the river.

In 1992, a second fly-fishing area opened above the hatchery. The two fly-fishing-only reaches have become very popular and afford some of the highest-quality angling on the Salmon River. Public fishing sites expanded when 12 miles of river access opened through conservation easements obtained from Niagara Mohawk Power Company in 1994. These easements include water below the hydro station, the Salmon River Falls reach between the reservoirs, and along the north shore of the upper reservoir. In

1995, all legal snagging ceased on the Salmon River. This event produced a much greater opportunity for true sporting anglers to fully enjoy the river.

The Federal Energy Regulatory Commission (FERC) relicensed Niagara Mohawk in 1996, subject to "base flow" limits that protect salmonid populations. From May 1 to August 31, the minimum flow must be 185 cfs. This provides sufficient water for juvenile salmonids as well as habitat requirements for summer-run fish including Skamania steelhead, brown trout, and resurging Atlantic salmon. From September 1 to December 31, minimal flows of 350 cfs protect habitat needs for migrating Pacific salmon, Atlantic salmon, brown trout, and the terrific fall run of steelhead. Between January 1 and April 30, a flow of 285 cfs serves the requirements of winter-run steelhead and the need for adequate flows to ensure natural egg incubation in the streambed.

These base flows have resulted in a dramatic increase in natural reproduction among Pacific salmon, steelhead, brown trout, and Atlantic salmon. Wild king salmon smolts now number close to one million per year! Wild steelhead smolt numbers have also increased dramatically, and the rehabilitation of Atlantic salmon is underway. Small but growing and fishable returns of Atlantic salmon have been occurring since 1998.

Steelhead runs are less prolific than in the 1980s. The proliferation of exotic species in the eastern basin of Lake Ontario is probably one factor. Illegal snagging also has been a factor in the main river and in some smaller tributaries. In 2002, new, tougher regulations gave law enforcement officers the ability to stop some of the more subtle methods employed by snaggers and poachers. In 2004, new regulations reduced the kill limit to one steelhead per day, not only for the Salmon River but for all New York tributaries to Lake Ontario. An angler survey indicated widespread acceptance of this harvest reduction: 77 percent of respondents wanted a zero or one steelhead limit, 22 percent preferred a two-fish limit, and only 1 percent wanted the limit to be three or more. Ongoing discussions with the boat angling and charter community are attempting to work out an acceptable reduction in lake harvest of steelhead. If an agreement is reached, it will have additional positive impact on steelhead numbers in the Salmon River.

Current estimates of the numbers of steelhead returning to the river range from 7,000 to 8,000 fish per year. This is a serious reduction from the extravagant numbers in the 1980s, but still provides more than enough fish for high-quality angling. Remember, this is not a large river

Jerry Kustich chases a fast-running Salmon River steelhead.

PHOTO BY RICK KUSTICH

and the accessible water stretches only about 18 miles. Angling pressure has lessened in recent years, and catch-and-release has become common practice. Eight thousand fish is still a big number.

Steelhead begin to show in large numbers during early October and build through November. This period has typically been the best for fly-fishing techniques. There is little pressure on the fish from mid-December through February, yet angling remains very good. The spring run usually peaks in late March and holds through mid-April. The spring run also produces excellent fishing but is susceptible to wide variation due to rains and snowmelt, which can cloud the river quickly.

The Chambers Creek strain is the base genetic pool for Salmon River steelhead. It has been very successful in this river system. Years of adaptation and continual stocking of smolts reared at the Salmon River hatchery have heightened awareness of this strain and slowly changed its popular name. Many people now refer to these steelhead as the Salmon River strain. Regardless of name, this is a handsome, vibrant fish that eats flies readily, fights with reckless abandon, and grows very large. The average steelhead is in the 7-pound range, but 20-pound fish are caught with fair regularity each season.

Public access to the steelhead water is very good from the lower reservoir through the town of Pulaski. The upper fly-fishing-only stretch is off NY 22 upstream from the village of Altmar, and another such reach is just upstream from the fish hatchery. Several access points downstream from Altmar are right off NY 13. These include Ellis Cove, the Trestle Pool, Sportsman's Pool, and the County Road 2A access. The Douglaston Salmon Run access is a short distance downstream from the intersection of NY 11 and NY 13 off NY 2.

Although the river is not large in terms of flow volume it is fairly wide in most areas, with plenty of room to cast. Widths run from about 70 to more than 100 feet. Depth varies widely according to current speed and bottom configurations, but generally affords easy enough wading in the best fishing stretches.

The river rises in the Tug Hill Plateau, the most densely forested region of New York outside the Adirondack and Catskill preserves. The Tug Hill region receives the highest annual snowfall east of the Rocky Mountains, with about 300 inches per year. The deep, sheltering forests and high level of precipitation produce the highest possible water quality for trout and salmon. This pure water and the abundant spawning gravel of the main river and its feeder streams create a steelhead paradise. A riffle-pool configuration dominates the Salmon. Steelhead hold in deep pockets, in current seams, at the heads and tail-outs of pools, and in deeper corner holes.

SALMON RIVER AND NORTH AND SOUTH SANDY CREEKS

———————•———————

Location: Pulaski, New York, NY 3, west of I-81, north of Syracuse.

Airport: One hour from Syracuse, two hours from Rochester.

Lodging: Local motels. Check the Pulaski/Eastern Shore Chamber of Commerce Web site, www.pulaski nychamber.com/

Fly shops and Guides: Whitaker's Sports Store, 315-298-6162; Dave Barber, www.strikesilver.com, 1-866-GUIDING (484-3464); Peter Basta, www.flyfishingguide.com, 802-867-4103; Greg Liu, 201-788-8758.

Standard nymphing techniques are the popular choice here, but many fly anglers are expanding their knowledge and approach to the game. People are beginning to swing flies—both Spey and streamer patterns—on a more regular basis, particularly during the fall season. This is a great river for swinging flies on the longer rods, and this method seems most effective when flows are at or below 750 cfs. When the salmon run concludes in late October, a dedicated core of steelhead fly anglers reappears on the water. Many of these anglers experience excellent results with swinging-fly methods and all seem to exhibit high sporting ethics and respect for their quarry.

Stonefly patterns are important on this river. Hare's Ears, Pheasant Tails, and caddis larvae also produce fish with consistency. Standard egg patterns in chartreuse, orange, and Oregon cheese with a spot of contrasting color are best. Be sure to carry a few egg flies tied with Estaz or other light-reflecting material to enhance visibility when the water is high and stained.

Streamers that represent forage fish such as sculpins, smelt, and juvenile trout are effective throughout the year but produce best during the late fall. Spey patterns that feature purple, black, or pink as the dominant color work well. A marabou Spey called the Black & Tan is one of the best of this type of steelhead fly. Classic Pacific patterns also produce fish. The Polar Shrimp and Skunk are the most popular.

The Salmon is a great steelhead river. Despite a drop in numbers of fish using the system, it is safe to say that the actual quality of the angling experience has improved. Illegal snagging and poaching have been greatly reduced. Overall fishing pressure is down. Courtesy between anglers and respect for the fish have made a great leap forward. Catch-and-release is common practice. An evolution in techniques and equipment is in process that incorporates the best of the traditional Pacific Coast steelhead methods, classic Atlantic salmon tactics, and our own Great Lakes nymphing techiniques. This provides new opportunities for success when conditions are not ideal or even suitable for a particular method.

In addition to the great fly fishing for Chambers Creek/Salmon River strain steelhead during fall, winter, and spring, opportunities for Ska-mania-strain steelhead and landlocked Atlantic salmon expand the season through the summer months. Pacific salmon and huge brown trout add variety during the fall run.

There is more good news. In 2005 New York State acquired 2,500 acres of land to complement an earlier purchase of 4,000 acres along the Salmon River. This acquisition expands shoreline easements and public access, buffer zones for shoreline protection, and greatly expands the "greenway" zone from Pulaski to the reservoir, permanently protecting the river's corridor.

North and South Sandy Creeks

Two smaller steelhead streams just a few miles north of Pulaski host siz-able runs from late September through April. They both present an al-ternative to the Salmon River if a smaller, more intimate stream is of interest, or if the Salmon is running too high or dirty for good fly fishing. Either NY 3 or I-81 northbound takes you to these streams in about 15 minutes.

Both North and South Sandy are spate rivers with extreme fluctua-tions in volume but often clear more quickly than the Salmon River after a precipitation event. Weather along this end of Lake Ontario often moves in relatively narrow bands, and just a few miles can make a big dif-ference in rainfall and its effect on water clarity.

The steelhead in these two streams are from the same gene pool as fish entering the Salmon River. Despite their small confines they attract very large steelhead. The runs are particularly heavy in the spring. Steel-head start to feel the big urge in March and move into the current in growing numbers through April. A high percentage of these steelhead are wild and extremely volatile when hooked. Four-year-old, repeat spawners are usually in the 12- to14-pound class, and a five-year-old fish could be in the high teens, or even more. Expect an average size close to 8 pounds. Some precocious males in the 2- to 3-pound range and first-time hens in the 4-pound range will also be present.

A pleasant surprise. In late October, steelheaders on North and South Sandy Creeks might also catch big lake-run brown trout.

The streams average between 30 and 50 feet wide in most places. The bottom structure is typical of spate rivers in the area, with mixed reaches of gravel, sand, and bedrock. Large rocks in chutes and riffles are favored resting and holding lies. Any deep, dark water will likely hold a few steelhead. If the shaded, protected water is anywhere near gravel or cobble, so much the better.

South Sandy has a waterfall, but steelhead can pass it easily and continue upstream all the way to the village of Adams on NY 11 just east of I-81. Access to both streams is varied and spread out. Be sure to watch for and respect posted property.

Use the same tackle and flies on North and South Sandy Creeks as listed for the Salmon River. Because of the more narrow river channels, you will often find trees and shrubs close enough behind you to limit traditional backcasts. Roll-casting skills are quite helpful and in some locations a chuck-and-duck delivery is more effective. Sometimes we forget the reason behind the evolution of long Spey rods and Spey-casting techniques. They were specifically developed to overcome the obstacles to backcasting—trees, high banks, and other vegetation—common along the River Spey in Scotland. A Spey cast with a long rod delivers accuracy and distance in tight quarters and allows precise mending in complicated currents. This is the ideal solution to the problem of tight quarters on a small river.

Both North and South Sandy Creeks are beautiful, classic eastern steelhead streams. They feature lovely riffles, smooth pools, deep corner bends, and productive pocket water. The water is food-rich, well oxygenated, clean, and cold. Ideal spawning gravel and coarse cobble reaches attract wild steelhead and provide superb nursery conditions that enhance the survivability of eggs, fry, and smolts. Catch-and-release and careful wading around spawning areas are important to the future of these little rivers and their mostly wild steelhead populations.

Ganaraska River

The town of Port Hope nestles on Lake Ontario's north shore about an hour's drive on Highway 401 east of downtown Toronto, roughly at the midpoint of the lake. The Ganaraska River is fed by vital groundwater discharges in its coldwater tributaries. These tributaries and the upper river are sheltered by a healthy riparian corridor of mixed forests, woodlots, and agricultural lands. Urban sprawl pushing eastward from Toronto's suburbs has been relatively slow in this area. The upper main river and tributary network provide excellent spawning and nursery habitat for steelhead as well as brown trout, brook trout, and Pacific salmon.

Additionally, Atlantic salmon restoration efforts are underway. The Ganaraska once hosted one of the most prolific Atlantic salmon runs in this part of the world, but habitat destruction, overharvesting, and migration barriers devastated the population over time. The current Atlantic salmon program involves stocking of smolts that imprint on the river and return years later to spawn. Some positive results are beginning to show. A few adults are returning to the Ganaraska system each year.

As in the Salmon River on the New York side of Lake Ontario, steelhead runs in the Ganaraska have declined in number from historically high figures in the 1980s and 1990s. A combination of natural and human factors have contributed to the current situation. The big lake's supportive ecosystem is changing, in part due to invasive exotic species. Weather patterns in recent years have undermined successful spawning and survival of steelhead eggs and fry. Overharvest by both river and lake anglers has negatively impacted adult, repeat-spawning steelhead.

A 1999 survey is interesting. From April 24 through May 31, river anglers caught 10,693 fish in 24,400 hours of angling effort; 1,707 of these fish were harvested. From April 1 through September 30 of the same year, boat anglers caught 38,106 fish and harvested 28,286. These are big numbers. The "exploitation rate" (mortality from fishing) for Ganaraska steelhead is estimated to be as high as 48 to 50 percent. Most of the fish harvested are the larger, repeat spawners.

Still, the Ganaraska River is an excellent, productive steelhead river for the fly angler. The Ganaraska strain is a hardy, spring-spawning fish that has become one of the most successful and dominant strains within the Great Lakes basin. The current strain is maintained with brood stock for hatchery contribution to wild stocks. Interbreeding of naturally reproducing fish forms the bulk of the steelhead population. Ontario's contribution to the overall steelhead population in Lake Ontario is approximately two-thirds wild fish and one-third hatchery-produced fish. In the year 2000, approximately 4,000 steelhead were counted at the fishway on the Ganaraska River. Of these, roughly 40 percent were repeat spawners. With lower angler harvest rates, the number of repeat spawners should climb. Catch-and-release and extremely careful handling of steelhead are critically important here.

Much of the riparian zone surrounding nursery tributaries and portions of the upper main river is private property, and access is limited. Fortunately, there is public access to good fishing stretches of the river within the town of Port Hope and the surrounding area. There is extensive public access on the lower river right through town to the mouth at Lake Ontario. And the Sylvan Glen Conservation Areas provide excellent access to good water for several miles between Port Hope and the village of Kendal. There are 22 access sites between the Canadian National Parkway bridge near Jocelyn Street in Port Hope and the CR 18 access near Kendal.

The lower river through Port Hope has several long stretches of smooth flow over bedrock. Steelhead tend to duck into shelter where ledges create depth changes and in the deeper cuts in the bottom. In this

---

GANARASKA RIVER

Location: Port Hope, Ontario, QEW 401, east of Toronto.

Airport: One hour from Toronto.

Lodging: Numerous chains and local motels.

Fly shops and Guides: Wilson's, www.wilsontoronto.com, 416-869-3474. There is also limited fly-fishing tackle in local sporting goods stores. For more information, check the Web site www.the fishingguide.com.

area, a drag-free drift is critical to success. Small, single-egg patterns in natural colors and dark Woolly Buggers are the best flies in this part of the river. Oregon cheese or pale orange blended with cream or yellow are good colors for egg flies. Black, purple, dark brown, and dark blood-red, or maroon, are good choices for the 'Buggers. Egg-Sucking Leeches also produce fish in this stretch when drifted drag-free. A black body, hackle, and tail behind a pale orange egg are best. Leaders need to be long and fine. A strike indicator is very helpful in detecting subtle takes.

The upper river is a world apart. The channel width varies from 50 to 70 feet. The flow is more typical of Lake Ontario tributaries, with a natural, predictable progression of pools and riffles. The bottom structure is diverse and includes reaches of spawning gravel, bedrock, rock, and cobble. Woody debris is common throughout the upper river, and steelhead often hold in close proximity to its natural shade and shelter. This is ideal habitat for spawning salmonids and for a variety of important food forms. Aquatic insects are prolific throughout the upper river. Stonefly, mayfly, and caddis species dominate. Forage fish like sculpins are abundant, and juvenile trout and steelhead are also present in large numbers.

The upper river through the Sylvan Glen Conservation Area upstream to Kendal often runs quite clear, and the steelhead can be demanding. Natural-looking nymph patterns in the *appropriate* size to the time of year are often required to fool fish under these conditions. Remember that aquatic insects, for the most part, are smaller earlier in the year than they are just prior to emergence. Similarly, egg patterns should be of the "micro" variety, about 5mm in diameter, and tied only one or two to a hook when the upper "Ganny" is low and clear.

With moderate flows showing some color, bulkier fly patterns work very well on the upper river, but natural shape and coloration remain important. Under these conditions, Woolly Buggers, rabbit-strip leeches, meatier stoneflies, and larger egg patterns are productive choices. Dead-drift nymphing techniques are by far the most effective on this river, regardless of water level or clarity. Remember to use small stonefly, caddis, Hare's Ear, and Pheasant Tail flies when the water is low and larger patterns if the river is high or stained. Cover a run, riffle, or section of pool thoroughly. Before moving on or casting to a new target, pulse your fly with a light line strip or by twitching your rod tip. This often triggers a response.

Ten-pound fish are quite common throughout the river. Some four- and five-year-old fish are considerably larger. A medium-fast-action rod

Because of their exceptional steelhead fly fishing, Lake Ontario streams are attractive destinations. If possible, fish during the week to avoid the crowds.

of 9 to 10 feet with a powerful lower section and a sensitive tip is the best choice for this river. The strong lower portion of the rod provides enough strength to fight, subdue, and release a large steelhead quickly enough to safeguard its survival, and the sensitive tip is a boon in detecting strikes as well as setting the hook without breaking fine tippets.

Biologists with the Lake Ontario Management Unit have noted increased natural reproduction of steelhead, king salmon, silver salmon, lake trout, and lake sturgeon in the last couple of years, and this bodes well for the future of the Ganaraska fishery. The emphasis in managing steelhead populations in Lake Ontario is on the wild fish. Currently, the lake's population is about 40 percent wild.

If fly anglers can set an example with restraint, catch-and-release, and careful revival and handling of our trophies, the more successful, repeat-spawning adults will continue to safeguard the future. No river along the north shore of Lake Ontario is more vital to this future than the Ganaraska.

Appendix A

Suggested Reading

Combs, Trey. *Steelhead Fly Fishing*. Guilford, CT: The Lyons Press, 1991.

Fuller, Tom. *Underwater Flies for Trout*. Woodstock, VT: The Countryman Press, 2003.

Klausmeyer, David. *Tying Classic Freshwater Streamers*. Woodstock, VT: The Countryman Press, 2004.

Kustich, Rick. *Fly Fishing the Great Lakes Tributaries*. Grand Island, NY: West River Publishing Company, 1992.

Kustich, Rick. *River Journal: Salmon River*. Portland, OR: Frank Amato Publications, 1995

Kustich, Rick and Jerry. *Fly Fishing for Great Lakes Steelhead*, Grand Island, NY: West River Publishing Company, 1999.

Linsenman, Bob and Steve Nevala. *Great Lakes Steelhead: A Guided Tour for Fly Anglers*. Woodstock, VT: The Countryman Press, 1995.

Linsenman, Bob. *Michigan Blue-Ribbon Fly-Fishing Guide*. Portland, OR: Frank Amato Publications, 2002.

Linsenman, Bob, and Kelly Galloup. *Modern Streamers for Trophy Trout*. Woodstock, VT: The Countryman Press, 1999.

Linsenman, Bob. *River Journal: Au Sable River*. Portland, OR: Frank Amato Publications, 1998.

Linsenman, Bob, and Steve Nevala. *Trout Streams of Michigan: A Fly Angler's Guide*, 2nd Edition. Woodstock, VT: The Countryman Press, 2001.

Smith, Scott E. *Ontario Blue-Ribbon Fly-Fishing Guide*. Portland, OR: Frank Amato Publications, 1999.

Supinski, Matthew A. *River Journal: Pere Marquette*. Portland, OR: Frank Amato Publications, 1994.

Supinski, Matt. *Steelhead Dreams*. Portland, OR: Frank Amato Publications, 2001.

Appendix B

Information Sources

Cleveland–Lake Metroparks
11211 Spear Road
Concord Township, OH 44077
440-639-7275
www.lakemetroparks.com

Indiana Department of Natural
  Resources
608 State Office Building
Indianapolis, IN 46204
317-232-4020
www.in.gov/dnr/

Michigan Department of
  Natural Resources
PO Box 30028
Lansing, MI 48909
517-373-1280
www.michigan.gov/dnr

Minnesota Department of
  Natural Resources
Box 12, DNR Building
500 Lafayette Road
St. Paul, MN 55155
651-296-3325
www.dnr.state.mn.us

New York Department of
  Environmental Conservation
Region 9
Fisheries Office
182 E. Union St., Suite 3
Allegheny, NY 14706
716-372-0645
www.dec.state.ny.us

Ohio Department of Natural
  Resources
Fountain Square
Columbus, OH 43224
1-800-WILDLIFE
www.ohiodnr.com

Ohio Central Basin Steelheaders
PO Box 29577
Parma, OH 44129
www.ohiosteelheaders.com

Ontario Ministry of Natural
  Resources–Queenspark,
Fisheries Branch
Toronto M7A 1W3
416-965-4251
www.fishontario.com

Pennsylvania State Game
  Commission Box 1567
Harrisburg, PA 17120
717-787-3633
www.fish.state.pa.us
online maps at: www.fisheries.com

Wisconsin Department of Natural
  Resources
Box 7921
Madison, WI 53707
608-266-2621
www.dnr.wi.gov

Fish USA
www.fishusa.com

The Fishing Guide
www.thefishingguide.com

Index

(continued on next page)

(continued on next page)